AF600659

The Subject of Ecclesiastical Law According to Canon 12

THE CATHOLIC UNIVERSITY OF AMERICA
CANON LAW STUDIES
NO. 165

THE SUBJECT OF ECCLESIASTICAL LAW ACCORDING TO CANON 12

AN HISTORICAL SYNOPSIS AND COMMENTARY

By

REV. JOSEPH ALOYSIUS McCLOSKEY, A.B., J.C.L.
PRIEST OF THE ARCHDIOCESE OF PHILADELPHIA

A DISSERTATION

Submitted to the Faculty of the School of Canon Law of the Catholic University of America in Partial Fulfillment of the Requirements for the Degree of

DOCTOR OF CANON LAW

WASHINGTON, D. C.
1943

Nihil Obstat:

Eduardus G. Roelker, S.T.D., J.C.D.,
Censor Deputatus

Washingtonii, D. C., die XX Maii, 1942.

Imprimatur:

✠ D. Card. Dougherty,
Archiepiscopus Philadelphiensis

Philadelphiae, die XXVI Maii, 1942.

The Wickersham Printing Company
Lancaster, Pennsylvania

To

My Father

and

Mother

TABLE OF CONTENTS

FOREWORD

In the Code of Canon Law the treatment of the subject of Ecclesiastical Laws is contained in canons 12, 13, and 14. Canon 12 is concerned explicitly with those who are not subject to purely ecclesiastical laws. Implicitly it treats of those who are subject to purely ecclesiastical laws.

After a preliminary discussion of some general notions connected with the subject of Law the first part of this dissertation traces the historical outlines of the principles contained in canon 12 and shows in some way how these principles have been applied throughout the years in the Church's legislation. It takes into consideration only those human beings who are excused from purely ecclesiastical laws either by the divine positive law, the natural law, or the ecclesiastical law. Other historical notes, however, are included in the subsequent Commentary on this Canon.

Following this historical part is the commentary on canon 12. This has fundamentally the same division as the historical part because the Canon logically divides into three parts, even though no definite numerical divisions are present. In this commentary the canon is considered first in the negative manner in which it is set down in the Code. An attempt is made to show just why those who are mentioned in the canon are not subject to purely ecclesiastical laws. In the course of this treatment the general categories of those who are mentioned in the canon are made more specific.

Then, after it has been shown that canon 12 may be taken also in its positive sense, consideration is given to the various classes of baptized persons who are bound by purely ecclesiastical laws. It need not be noted that those who are certainly and actually bound by these laws are not treated explicitly. Those who are doubtfully baptized and, therefore, doubtfully subject to ecclesiastical laws, are treated. General rules for determining their subjection or non-subjection to the Church's legislation are recorded.

Throughout the commentary practical applications are made of the principles stated in Canon 12. Wherever diversity of opinion exists in regard to these principles, the opinions are weighed and the opinion that appears to be the best is selected and applied. Practical questions are discussed.

* * * * *

The writer takes this occasion to offer his sincere thanks to His Eminence, Dennis Cardinal Dougherty, for the opportunity of advanced study in Canon Law; to the members of the Faculty of the School of Canon Law for their help and kindness during the preparation of this work; and to any others whose assistance and generosity aided in bringing this dissertation to completion.

PRELIMINARY DISCUSSION

ARTICLE I.—MEMBERSHIP IN A SOCIETY

In any consideration of those who are obliged to obey laws there must be a treatment of the concept of membership in a society. That is to say that there must be an explanation of the legal status of those who can be bound by laws.

One may become a member of any society by means of some external sign which indicates the admission of that person into that society and his union with it. Through this union he is made subject to the authority of its head. This outward sign and union naturally vary with the nature of the group. Usually one becomes a citizen of civil society by being born of citizens of that organization. There are also some extraordinary ways of effecting this: by naturalization, by marriage, by actual grant of the ruler, etc.[1]

None of these ways, however, would give a person membership in the Church. The Church and the State are both perfect societies established for obtaining separate and distinct but not absolutely independent ends.[2] The State is concerned with man's temporal well-being; to the Church is entrusted his spiritual welfare. Hence admission into the Church is effected by a spiritual means—the Sacrament of Baptism—which sets up a spiritual bond of union.[3]

Entrance into civil society and the obtaining of membership therein of themselves give one the legal capacity to

1 Wernz-Vidal, *Ius Canonicum* (7 tom. in 8 vols., Vol. I, Romae: apud Aedes Universitatis Gregorianae, 1938), I, n. 147, footnote 99; Ottaviani, *Institutiones Iuris Publici Ecclesiastici* (2. ed., 2 vols., Vol. I, Civitate Vaticana: Typis Polyglottis Vaticanis, 1935), I, 35, 37.

2 Ottaviani, *Institutiones Iuris Publici Ecclesiastici*, I, 160.

3 Wernz, *Ius Decretalium* (6 tom. in 8 vols., Tom. I, 3. ed., Prati, 1913), I, n. 103, footnote 78; Wernz-Vidal, *Ius Canonicum*, I, n. 147, footnote 99.

enjoy the privileges of the law of that society and to be bound by the mandates of that law. In fact, it might even be said that such membership gives one the legal capacity to break the law, since no one can run counter to a law which he is not bound to keep. This is known as delictual capacity or the capacity to incur a liability for unlawful acts.[4]

By becoming a member of the Church similar results are obtained — one receives the privileges and obligations of its law.

ARTICLE II.—JURISDICTION

Closely associated with the concept of membership in a society and the consequent subjection to its laws is the concept of jurisdiction. This is so because, generally considered, no one can be bound by a law which is enacted by someone who has no authority over that person from some title or another. And no one can make laws that are binding on the individuals of a community unless he has the power granted by jurisdiction to enact such laws and to bind such persons. For the obligations of a law arise through the relationship which is constituted by jurisdiction on the one hand and dependence on the other. Jurisdiction, therefore, simply denotes the established authority and efficacious power of the ruler to direct his subjects and to care for their well-being.[5] Jurisdiction is exercised through a threefold source, that of making laws, of enforcing them, and of judicially applying them to historical situations. Hence, it is of the very nature of a law that it be passed by the actual legislator or his predecessor,[6] and a

[4] Sohm, *The Institutes* (Ledlie translation, 3. ed., Oxford: Clarendon Press, 1926), p. 219.

[5] Santi, *Praelectiones Juris Canonici* (2 vols., Ratisbonae, 1886), I, 21.

[6] Ottaviani, *Institutiones Iuris Publici Ecclesiastici*, I, 94; Santi, *loc. cit.;* St. Thomas Aquinas, *Summa Theologica*, $1^{a}2^{ae}$, p. 90, a. 4c.

law does not bind those who are not under the care of the legislator, i.e., those who are not his subjects.[7]

A law also does not oblige those subjects who do not have a sufficient use of reason for a law of its very nature is a regulation in accordance with reason inasmuch as it is promulgated by the head of the community for the sake of the common good.[8] It is a rule and a measure which directs human actions to the definite end of the community; and only those who are endowed with the use of reason can be directed by laws in a human manner.[9]

In an exceptional case a law may not bind one who is a subject of the lawgiver, inasmuch as the subject has been expressly exempted from the law by the lawgiver. This is the case in the exemption of those who actually have the use of reason but who have not yet reached the age of seven years.[10] This is based on a presumption of fact.[11]

In consideration of these essential points of the general concept of jurisdiction, ecclesiastical jurisdiction may be defined as the power, derived either directly from Christ Himself, or indirectly from the Church by canonical deputation, of publicly ruling baptized persons and of directing them toward a supernatural end, namely, their eternal salvation.[12]

[7] Santi, *loc. cit.*

[8] St. Thomas Aquinas, *loc. cit.*

[9] Bargilliat, *Praelectiones Juris Canonici* (37. ed., 2 vols., Parisiis: apud Baston, Berche, et Pagis, 1923), I, 62.

[10] Canon 12.

[11] Toso, *Ad Codicem Iuris Canonici Commentaria Minora* (2. ed., 5 vols., Vol. I, Romae: apud Petrum Marietti, 1921), I, 37, 38; Cicognani, *Commentarium ad Librum I. Codicis* (Romae: ex Schola Typographica "Pio X," 1925), p. 94.

[12] Canon 109; Maroto, *Institutiones Iuris Canonici* (2 vols., Matriti, 1919), I, 66; Vermeersch-Creusen, *Epitome Iuris Canonici* (2. ed., Mechliniae: H. Dessain, 1924), I, p. 177, n. 275. (Hereafter quoted as *Epitome*).

From this definition it is evident that only the baptized are subject to Church laws. This is true because God, by the strength of the character imprinted on the human soul by Baptism, has subjected all and only the baptized to the jurisdiction of the Church. And the Church itself has no power to bring under its spiritual jurisdiction those whom Christ has not subjected to it by Baptism.[13]

ARTICLE III.—THE ACTIVE AND PASSIVE SUBJECT OF ECCLESIASTICAL LAW

The subject of the ecclesiastical legislative power, which is inherent in the power of jurisdiction, may be either *active* or *passive*.

The *active* subject is the legislator himself, whether he acts individually or in a duly constituted group. Under the present discipline the following may make laws binding the universal Church:

The Pope, as the successor of Saint Peter, has the legislative power directly from Christ. And because of the singular manner in which he has this power, he may make laws for the universal Church independently of anyone.[14] All other legislators in the Church exercise their law-making power dependently on the Pope. Hence an Ecumenical Council which also can make general laws for the Church must be legitimately convened, celebrated and confirmed by the reigning Pope.[15]

It is generally held that the Supreme Pontiff and Ecumenical Councils are now the only sources of general ecclesiastical laws. The various Sacred Roman Congregations do not possess this absolute, universal legislative power. And their decisions and regulations cannot have the force

[13] Wernz, *Ius Decretalium*, I, n. 103; Wernz-Vidal, *Ius Canonicum*, I, n. 147.

[14] Canon 218.

[15] Canon 222.

of universal law unless they are approved by the Pope. Hence, as to legislation, their work seems to be merely preparatory.[16]

Particular laws are made by provincial councils for their own ecclesiastical provinces; by residential Bishops for their own dioceses; and by major Superiors of clerical exempt religious for their own institutes. In the same category as residential Bishops are Prelates *nullius*, Vicars and Prefects Apostolic and permanently constituted Apostolic Administrators. They may make laws for their own territories.[17]

The members of the Church for whose rule and guidance the laws, either general or particular, are made are considered as the *passive* subjects of the legislative power of the Church.[18]

In summary it may be stated that by divine positive law the unbaptized are exempt from strictly ecclesiastical laws; by natural law those baptized persons who have not a sufficient use of reason, such as infants and the habitually insane; and by positive ecclesiastical law, also those baptized persons who have not yet completed their seventh year of age even though they may actually have the use of reason.[19]

[16] Canon 244; Benedict XV, motu. propr. *Cum Iuris Canonici*, 15 sept. 1917—*AAS*, IX (1917), 483-484; Pius X, const. *Sapienti consilio*, 29 iun. 1908 —*Codicis Iuris Canonici Fontes cura Emi. Petri Card. Gasparri Editi* (9 vols., Romae (postea Civitate Vaticana): Typis Polyglottis Vaticanis, 1923-1929 [Vols. VII, VIII, et IX ed. cura et studio Emi. Iustiniani Card. Seredi.]), n. 682; (in future this set will be cited as *Fontes*); Wernz-Vidal, *Ius Canonicum*, I, n. 123, 124.

[17] Canons 290; 294; 315; 323; 335; 501, § 1; Maroto, *Institutiones Iuris Canonici* (3. ed., 1 vol., Romae: apud Commentarium pro Religiosis, 1921), I, 191, 192; (in future this edition will be cited); Coronata, *Institutiones Iuris Canonici* (5 vols., Vol. I, Taurini: Marietti, 1928), I, 12, 13.

[18] Canons 87; 201, § 1; Wernz, *Ius Decretalium*, I, n. 103; Wernz-Vidal, *Ius Canonicum*, I, n. 147; Maroto, *op. cit.*, I, 201; Coronata, *op. cit.*, I, 14, 15.

[19] Canon 12; Cicognani, *Commentarium ad Librum I. Codicis*, pp. 92, 93, 94.

PART I

DEVELOPMENT OF THE ECCLESIASTICAL LAW

CHAPTER I

The Unbaptized Not Bound by Strictly Ecclesiastical Laws

ARTICLE A.—INTRODUCTORY REMARKS

Christ Himself commissioned the Apostles to make all men members of His Church by baptizing them after teaching them His doctrine and showing them the necessity of believing in Him.[1] Thus He showed that Baptism is required for membership in the visible Church and also for eternal glory. Christ repeated this provision emphatically to Nicodemus: "... Unless a man be born again of water and the Spirit, he cannot enter into the kingdom of God."[2]

The Apostles carried out this command and various citations from the Bible show that Baptism was the means by which converts were made members of the Church: "Now they who received his word *were baptized,* and there were added that day about three thousand souls."[3]

Saint Paul also speaks of entrance into the Church by Baptism: "For in one Spirit *we were all baptized into one body. . . .*"[4]

Since Christ required Baptism as the only means for entering the spiritual society called the Church and for consequently becoming subject to its jurisdiction, by divine law those who are not baptized are not members of the Church and are not subject to strictly ecclesiastical laws.

1 Mark XVI: 15, 16: "And He said to them, 'Go into the whole world and preach the gospel to every creature. He who believes and is baptized shall be saved, but he who does not believe shall be condemned.'"

2 John III: 5.

3 Acts II: 41.

4 I Cor. XII: 13.

This principle was formulated by Saint Paul in these words: "For what have I to do with judging those outside? . . . For those outside God will judge."[5] The principal part of this quotation is verse 12. It was reiterated by the Council of Trent[6] when it pointed out one of the differences between the sacraments of Penance and of Baptism. H. J. Schroeder (*Canons and Decrees of the Council of Trent* [St. Louis: Herder, 1941], pp. 89-90) translates the canon of the Council thus: ". . . it is beyond question that the minister of baptism need not be a judge, since the Church exercises judgment on no one who has not entered it through the gate of baptism. *For what have I to do*, says St. Paul, *to judge them that are without?*"

In 1749 Pope Benedict XIV (1740-1758)[7] explained most clearly this principle expounded by Saint Paul when he noted that the sacred canons of the Church cannot be applied to those who have never been admitted into its bosom.

In the next three articles on Infidels, Jews and Catechumens, therefore, the endeavor will be to trace through the various periods up to the New Code of Canon Law the application of this principle.

Special mention is made of Jews because the extensive legislation enacted for them at times seemed to militate against the principle that infidels are exempt from Church Laws.

Catechumens are considered in an endeavor to ascertain whether their special position just at the door of the Church, as it were, ever was the cause of their being subject to the Church in a manner similar to that of the baptized.

[5] I Cor. V: 12, 13.

[6] Sess. XIV, *de poenitentia*, cap. 2.

[7] Ep. *Singulari*, 9 febr. 1749, ad 2—*Fontes*, n. 394.

ARTICLE B.—INFIDELS

a) *Pre-Gratian Period*

The early history of the Church and of its councils indicates that the first Popes and Bishops were occupied principally with the establishment of a basic government for the fast-growing membership and with the fight against heretics of all kinds. Their disciplinary legislation for the internal government of the Christian society, therefore, was of the most general kind and was enacted as emergencies presented themselves or as abuses became widespread.

For these reasons the first indication of legislation concerning the binding force of purely ecclesiastical laws upon the non-baptized is found only in 538 when the III Council of Arles[8] issued a canon relating to the impediment of affinity. It stated that recent converts who, even though related to each other by the bond of affinity, had been married while they were still infidels were not to be separated, but were to be advised that such marriages were forbidden to them in the future. The council thus indicated that infidels were not bound by the purely ecclesiastical impediment of affinity.

Then in 601 Saint Augustine of England had despatched a number of questions to Pope Gregory I (590-604). One of these concerned the custom that existed among the Angles that marriages were celebrated between parties related in degrees of consanguinity and affinity that would have constituted an impediment to Christian marriage. Saint Augustine wanted to know whether the parties to such marriages should be separated when they were converted. In answer the Pope wrote:[9]

[8] Canon 10—Mansi, *Sacrorum Conciliorum Nova et Amplissima Collectio* (53 vols. in 59, Vol. IX, Paris, 1901), IX, 14-15. (Hereafter quoted as Mansi).

[9] Ep. *Per dilectissimos filios meos*, iul. 601—*Monumenta Germaniae Historica, Epistolae*, II, pars II, *Gregorii I Registri Libri X-XIV* (ed. P. Ewald-L. M. Hartmann, Berolini, 1895), p. 335; (The *Monumenta* will be cited in

> Quia vero sunt multi in Anglorum gente, qui dum adhuc in infidelitate positi essent huic nefando conjugio dicuntur admixti ad fidem venientes admonendi sunt, ut se abstineant, et grave hoc esse peccatum agnoscant: tremendum Dei judicium timeant, ne per carnalem delectationem tormenta aeterni cruciatus incurrant. Non tamen pro hac re sacri corporis ac sanguinis Domini communione privati sunt, nec in eis illa ulcisci videamur, in quibus se per ignorantiam ante lavacrum baptismatis adstrinxerunt.... Omnes autem, qui ad fidem veniunt monendi sunt, ne tale aliquid audeant perpetrare. Si qui enim perpetraverint corporis et sanguinis Domini communione privandi sunt; quia in his, quae pro ignorantia fecerunt culpa aliquatenus tolleranda est. Ita in his fortiter insequenda, qui non metuunt sciendo praevaricari.[10]

The interpretation of this section of Saint Gregory's letter seems to be that those Angles who before conversion had contracted marriages which would have been invalid according to purely ecclesiastical legislation on consanguinity and affinity were not to be separated when they became Catholics. Their marriages were valid because as infidels they were not bound by purely ecclesiastical laws. This, of course, presupposes that there were no impediments of the divine law present at the time of the marriages and that there were no customs among the Angles forbidding such marriages. Also the married converts and those who were not yet wedded were to be admonished to refrain from such

future as *MGH*); Mansi, X, 418; Migne, *Patrologiae Cursus Completus, Series Latina* (221 vols., 1844-1864, Vol. LXXVII, Paris, 1849), LXXVII, p. 1190, n. 1155 (Migne's Latin Series will be quoted *MPL* hereafter); Jaffé, *Regesta Pontificum Romanorum ab Condita Ecclesia ad Annum post Christum Natum MCXCVIII* (Editionem secundam correctam et auctam auspiciis Gulielmi Wattenbach, curaverunt S. Loewenfeld, F. Kaltenbrunner, P. Ewald, 2 vols. in 1, Lipsiae, 1885-1888), n. 1843; (Hereafter Jaffé will be quoted JL, JK, JE, according to who edited the section from which the citation is taken, e. g., one edited by Ewald will read J E, n. 1843, etc.).

[10] Mansi, X, 418.

unions in the future. They must also be taught to realize the gravity of the sin that they would commit if they entered such marriages after they had been converted.

This interpretation presupposes that the Pope was acknowledging implicitly the basic principle mentioned in the preceding paragraph when he permitted the parties to live together. And the interpretation is based on a similar decision of a later Pope who actually gave this principle as his reason for permitting infidel marriages to stand after the conversion of the parties, even though those marriages had been contracted with what would have been a diriment impediment if the parties had been Catholics at the time of the ceremonies.[11]

The sentence in the foregoing answer of Saint Gregory that contains the words *se abstineant* evidently means that the converted Angles who were related to each other in degrees of consanguinity and affinity that constituted an ecclesiastical impediment were to be advised that they should not contract such marriages in the future because such unions were forbidden by the Church.

This letter of Pope Gregory, which appeared first in the *Historia Ecclesiastica Gentis Anglorum* of Venerable Bede [12] written around 732,[13] presents difficulties because, first of all there are various versions extant, and secondly its authenticity is questioned.

In one version [14] the Pope decides on two points: He says that those who contracted marriage while they were still infidels, even though they were under the bond of affinity

[11] Innocent III, const. *Gaudeamus*—c. 8, X, *de divortiis*, IV, 19; Potthast, *Regesta Pontificum Romanorum inde ab Anno post Christum Natum MCXCVIII ad Annum MCCCIV* (2 vols., Berolini, 1874-1875), n. 507; (hereafter this work will be cited as Potthast).

[12] Book I, Chapter 27.

[13] *MPL*, XCV, 21.

[14] Mansi, X, 404-414.

or consanguinity, are not to be separated. And he permits marriage after Baptism when the parties are bound by the ecclesiastical law regarding the impediment of consanguinity.

In the other version [15] he speaks only of the non-separation of those who had been married while they were still infidels with what would have been an impediment of the ecclesiastical law. It is this second rendering of Saint Gregory's answer that has been reproduced above.

Substantially the same as this second version is the one contained in the *Monumenta Germaniae Historica,*[16] except that here the concession to baptized Angles of marrying within forbidden degrees of consanguinity is also noted.

A footnote to this latter in the *Monumenta* [17] indicates its suspected authenticity and notes Theodore Mommsen's opinion for its genuineness.

Its authenticity is discussed also by Dr. Francis Wasner in an article entitled "De Authenticitate 'Libelli Responsionum' Beati Gregorii Magni Papae ad S. Augustinum Angliae Apostolum Animadversiones." [18]

15 Mansi, X, 415-423.

16 *MGH, Epistolae,* II, pars II, *Gregorii I Registri Libri X-XIV* (P. Ewald-L. M. Hartmann), p. 335.

17 *MGH, Epistolae,* II, pars II, *Gregorii I Registri Libri X-XIV* (P. Ewald-L. M. Hartmann), p. 331, footnote 1: "De hac epistula, an genuina sit, saepe disputatur.... Recte notat Mommsen (N. A. XVII, p. 390, 395): Bedam praefationem epistulae cognovisse quidem—nam Laurentium et Petrum in praefatione commemoratos ipse latores huius epistulae commemorat—sed non retulisse itaque mirum non esse, quod Bontifatii mandatarii epistulam nostram non reppererint. Sed verisimile est Bedae hanc cum ceteris epistulis Roma ex registro allatam esse. Eadem epistula eodem fere tempore vel paulo post in Italia edita esse videtur cum initio 'per dilectissimos, etc.': ex qua editione ceterae collectiones canonum hauserunt. Quae cum ita sint neque quicquam in hac epistula inveniatur, quod quin noster scripserit, fieri non possit, *non dubito, quin genuina sit* . . ."; *MPL,* LXXVII, 1183, footnote a; Wernz-Vidal, *Ius Canonicum,* V, 406, footnote 40.

18 *Ius Pontificium,* XVIII (1938), 174-185, esp. pp. 174-176; 293-299, esp. p. 297c: ". . . Dubia aliqua contra authenticitatem libelli jam pro-

In order to avoid any misunderstanding about this letter of Saint Gregory I it is well to point out that subsequent letters of ecclesiastical authorities concerning it refer to a section in one of the versions wherein permission is granted to converted Angles to contract marriage within the third and fourth degrees of consanguinity, evidently in the collateral line even though the text does not indicate this, in spite of the fact that the ecclesiastical law forbade marriage up to the seventh degree of the collateral line. The permission is worded as follows: "Unde necesse est, ut iam tertia vel quarta generatio fidelium licenter sibi iungi debeat. Nam secunda quam diximus, a se omnimodo debet abstinere. . . ."[19]

Rhabanus Maurus in 842[20] quoted Pope Gregory I's letter to Saint Augustine; and it was commemorated in the II Council of Douzy held in 874.[21]

It seems as if these two references to the letter under discussion might in some way serve as external proof of its authenticity. But a greater proof seems to derive from its use by Gratian,[22] for he employed it in discussing the de-

tulerunt editor Beati Gregorii Magni P. Gussanvillaeus et C. S. Berardi, ...Plerique canonistae authenticitatem negant cum R. von Scherer, et J. Freisen; alii hesitant, neque libelli authenticitatem defendentes, neque illam plene respuentes, ut J. Sägmuller, et A. Knecht, quibus se adiunxit etiam O. Bardenhewer. Inter Canonistas authenticitatem omnibus viribus defendere conatus est F. X. Wernz (*Ius Decretalium*, IV, 252). Pro authenticitate etiam stant non pauci historici, et quidem magni nominis. Ph. Jaffé responsa Gregorii a sua collectione regestorum pontificum Romanorum non exclusit; similiter fecit editor Registri Gregorii Papae (Ewald-Hartmann in *M. G., Epist.*, II, 331-343, XI, 56a). Fortiter in authenticitate insistit Th. Mommsen, item W. Peitz, dicens, *ne minimam quidem adesse rationem criticam ad authenticitatem negandam*..."

19 Mansi, X, 406-407; *MGM, Epistolae*, II, 335.

20 *Ep. ad Humbertum—MPL*, CX, 1085-D; *MGH, Epistolae Karolini Aevi* (5 vols. in 8, ed. E. Duemmler, K. Hampe, A. de Hirsch-Gereuth, E. Perels, E. Caspar, 1892-1928), III, 444-448; Mansi, XVI, 869-872.

21 *Ep. Synodica Concilii ad Episcopos Aquitaniae*—Mansi, XVII-A, 281.

22 C. 20, C. XXXV, q. 2 and 3.

grees of consanguinity. There is, however, no explanatory *dictum* concerning it.

In the proceedings of the Council of Rome [23] held under Pope Zachary in 743 there were mentioned certain abuses, and among them was indicated a custom then current in Germany, according to which Catholics were marrying within forbidden degrees of consanguinity. This practice was supposed to have resulted from a special permission granted to the Germans by Pope Gregory I but of which there was no record in the Roman archives. Certain Germans were supposed to have informed the Pope (Zachary) that, when divine Grace enlightened them to adopt the religion of Christianity, Saint Gregory had given them permission to marry in the fourth degree [presumably of consanguinity in the collateral line].

In one phrase of this chapter 15 of the Council of Rome, "*quod quidem Christianis licitum non est*", it was noted that marriage between persons related within the fourth degree of consanguinity in the collateral line was not permitted to Christians. This distinction between Christians and non-Christians in this matter gives some indication that marriages between persons related in these degrees of consanguinity were permitted to non-Christians.

On June 13, 879, Pope John VIII wrote Archbishop Airardus of Auch and his suffragans the following letter: [24]

> . . . Praeterea unum valde illicitum et execrabile malum contra venerabilia sanctorum patrum decreta eosdem vestros parochianos committere audimus: hoc est ut nulla propinquitatis parentela observata, unusquisque suam propinquam in quocumque fuerit gradu, accipiat uxorem, atque incesto et nefario se conjugio copulet. Quod licitum facere Christianis non est, dum usque se generatio cognoverit.

[23] Cap. 15—Mansi, XII, 384-a.

[24] *Epistola 198*—Mansi, XVII-A; J E, n. 3263.

Here again in making special note of the fact that such marriages were not permitted to Christians this Pope also makes an evident distinction between Christians and non-Christians in this matter. It naturally leads to the conclusion that non-Christians were not forbidden to contract such marriages and that, therefore, they were not bound at least by the purely ecclesiastical laws which prohibited marriages within certain degrees of consanguinity.

b) *Post-Gratian Period*

1. Decisions of Popes Clement III and Innocent III

During the course of this epoch there was an increase in the number of decisions involving the principle that infidels are exempted from strictly ecclesiastical laws. The cases were more explicit. The responses of the Popes and, after the Council of Trent, of the Sacred Congregations were more precise as though there had been at least a development of accurate terminology.

Three centuries has elapsed before the appearance of another decision involving the principle. Pope Clement III (1187-1191) in a decree [25] answering some questions sent to him by the Bishop of Angers said that Jews and Saracens who had been converted to the Christian religion could retain their unconverted wives if the latter consented to live with them, even though at the time of their marriage as infidels they were related within the second, third and fourth degrees of kindred. At the end of the letter he gave as a reason for his concession the fact that it made no difference whether they were related in the second or third degree when they contracted marriage while they were still outside of the faith, since in the old law there was but the

[25] Ep. *Interrogatum est*— J L, n. 16595; Mansi, XXII, 553; Gregory, *The Pauline Privilege,* The Catholic University of America Canon Law Studies, n. 68 (Washington, D. C.:. Catholic University of America, 1931), p. 30, footnote 89.

prohibition against uncovering the nakedness of one's sisters [that is, one's kindred within certain degrees of consanguinity and affinity indicated in the Book of Leviticus, XVIII: 1-30 e. g., (verse 9) "Thou shalt not uncover the nakedness of thy sister by father or by mother . . . ; " (verse 11) "Thou shalt not uncover the nakedness of thy father's wife's daughter, whom she bore to thy father, and who is thy sister; " (verse 16) "Thou shalt not uncover the nakedness of thy brother's wife . . ."].[26]

The phrase *veteri tantum lege* patently means the Old Testament and specifically refers to the prohibition of intermarriage within certain degrees of kindred,[27] because the Pope employs almost the same words as the Latin Vulgate Edition of the Old Testament.[28]

By citing the Old Law in this manner there can be no doubt that the Pope considered the Old Testament provisions as the only ones to which the persons in question were bound. Thus he implied that they were not bound by the Church laws in this matter. The very fact that he permitted the parties to remain together shows that he held their first marriage to be valid even though it was contracted between blood relations of the second, third or fourth degrees. The ecclesiastical law at that time[29] prohibited marriage between those who were related up to the seventh

26 Clement III, *ep. cit.*: "...nec refert, utrum in secundo, vel tertio gradu dum fuissent a fide alieni contraxerint, cum fuisset in veteri tantum lege prohibitum, ne sororum suarum turpitudine, revelarent."

27 *Leviticus*, XVIII: 6-18.

28 *Leviticus*, XVIII: 6: "Omnis homo ad proximum sanguinis sui non accedet, ut revelet turpitudinem eius . . ."—Hetzenauer, *Biblia Sacra Vulgati Editionis*, Sixti V Pont. Max. iussu recognita et Clementis VIII auctoritate edita (Ratisbonae, 1914), p. 96.

29 C. 1, C. XXXV, q. 2 and 3; Council of London (1125), c. 16—Mansi, XXI, 333; Wernz, *Ius Decretalium*, IV, n. 409 (This is quoted because it is a pre-Code work).

degree of consanguinity according to the present canonical method of computation.[30]

From Pope Innocent III (1198-1216) came what is probably one of the clearest expositions of the reasons for acknowledging the validity of certain acts performed by infidels, even when those acts would have been invalid if they had been performed by Catholics. The chief difference between his decisions and those already considered inheres in the more accurate language which he employed. The cases are almost similar.

In 1198 he ruled [31] that after their conversion infidels were not to be separated if during the time when they were still in their infidelity they had contracted marriage within the degrees of consanguinity which existed as impediments to intermarriage on the part of baptized persons. Although there is no mention of the degree of consanguinity involved in the case, the reply indicates that it was one which the Church recognized as establishing a prohibition against intermarriage. The Pope did not say so in so many words, but his statement was an indirect way of noting that non-baptized persons were not bound by ecclesiastical laws and that the particular law in question had no retroactive effect after the Baptism.

A similar decision was handed down by Pope Innocent III in 1201 to the Bishop of Ratisbon, in his Constitution *Gaudeamus*.[32] In this, however, he mentioned the second and third degrees of consanguinity. At the same time he decreed that a polygamist who became a member of the Church was to consider as his lawful wife the woman whom he had married first. Thus the Pope showed that infidels

[30] Cf. Wahl, *The Matrimonial Impediments of Consanguinity and Affinity*, The Catholic University of America Canon Law Studies, n. 90 (Washington, D. C.: The Catholic University of America, 1934), p. 18.

[31] C. 4, X, *de consanguinitate et affinitate*, IV, 14; Potthast, n. 507.

[32] C. 8, X, *de divortiis*, IV, 19—Potthast, n. 1325.

were not bound to observe the Church laws regarding the form of marriage, but were bound by the divine law regarding the indissolubility of valid marriage no matter where or how it was contracted by them.

The important point in this response is that the Pope repeated the rule that pagans were not bound by canonical constitutions and quoted the words of Saint Paul: "For what have I to do with judging those outside?"

On April 19, 1201, Pope Innocent III wrote to the Bishop of Livonia [now Riga] a letter[33] treating of the custom of the Livonian converts who married within degrees of consanguinity and affinity which constituted matrimonial impediments in the law of the Church, thereby ignoring the law. He took into consideration the antiquity of the custom and, realizing the hindrances to conversions that would be encountered if these people were forced to relinquish it suddenly, he gave a sanation for the marriages already contracted between a man and his deceased brother's widow when the purpose of such a marriage was to raise up children to his brother as provided in the old Mosaic Law.[34] He dispensed the converts from part of the law which forbade intermarriage between blood relations up to the seventh degree,[35] by permitting them to intermarry within the degrees that exceeded the fourth. This dispensation was to be in effect until they were more firmly grounded in the Faith.

Later in the letter the Pontiff seemed to anticipate a question that might be raised by converted infidels who, while still unbaptized, had intermarried within the second or third degree of consanguinity. He permitted them to remain married. His reason was based upon the exemption of the non-baptized from ecclesiastical laws. He stated the

[33] C. 9, X, *de divortiis*, IV, 19—Potthast, n. 1323.

[34] Deut. XXV: 5, 6; Ruth, IV: 5.

[35] Wernz-Vidal, *Ius Canonicum*, V, 409, 411.

principle and quoted the passage from Saint Paul's First Epistle to the Corinthians. In fact, the Pope used almost the exact words which he had employed earlier in his letter *Gaudeamus.*[36]

2. The Doctrine of the Decretalists

Toward the middle of the thirteenth century the works of the commentators on the Decretals of Gregory IX (1234) began to be published. Among these were the commentaries of Henricus de Segusio, Cardinal of the See of Ostia. He is commonly known as Hostiensis († 1271).

In his commentary on the letter *De infidelibus* of Pope Innocent III,[37] he upheld the principle that infidels are not bound directly by ecclesiastical laws. Explaining the phrase *non separandum* he stated that among infidels there existed a true marriage even if it was not a *matrimonium ratum,* for when the Jews asked Our Lord whether it was permitted to put away one's wife for every cause, He indicated [38] that there was true marriage among them by His answer: " What therefore God has joined together, let no man put asunder."

From this answer of Our Lord Hostiensis took the words *put asunder* and explained them [39] by saying that no man may separate those who have been legitimately married, since no man of his own power is authorized to do this. He enlarged on this by proposing a question and answering it: " Quid est ergo ut inter Christianos separantur coniuncti? "

He replied:

> Jesus Christus reliquit vicarium suum generalem Beatum Petrum et successores suos... Quibus reliquit plenitudinem potestatis... et ideo prohibitione facta per Papam ipse vere

[36] C. 8, X, *de divortiis,* IV, 19.

[37] C. 4, X, *de consanguinitate et affinitate,* IV, 14—Hostiensis, *Commentaria in Quinque Decretalium Libros* (5 vols. in 3, Venetiis, 1581), III, 28.

[38] Matt. XIX: 3, 6.

[39] Ad. c. 4, X, *de consanguinitate et affinitate,* IV, 14.

eam fecisse et sic inter Christianos non coniunguntur secundum Deum (immo contra Deum, qui vult ut suo vicario pareant) hi qui contra hanc prohibitionem coniunguntur et ideo sunt modis omnibus secundum Deum semper separandi; nec facit hoc homo, sed Deus, i. e., vicarius veri Dei, cui hanc potestatem dedit... alioquin sic coniuncti periculose vivunt: nec aliqua defenduntur longinquitate dierum, quod tamen periculum prohibitione revocata, evitant... Infideles attamen hac prohibitione non astringuntur, ut patet infra *de divortiis* "*Gaudeamus*," quia nihil ad nos de his, qui foris sunt, ut ibi dicit; ex quo secundum Deum coniuncti sunt, Papa ipsos separare non posset...

Hostiensis[40] in his commentary on Pope Innocent III's letter *Gaudeamus* affirmed that infidels do not come under the law of the Sacred Canons.[41] He also stated[42] in his commentary on the same letter that infidels cannot be subject to the sentence of excommunication because they are not under the Church's jurisdiction.

In the 15th century Nicolaus de Tudeschis (also known as Panormitanus, Abbas Modernus, and Abbas Siculus—1386-1453) lent the force of his authority to upholding the principle under discussion. He did this in his commentaries on the two letters of Pope Innocent III just noted above:

[40] *Commentaria in Quinque Decretalium Libros*, III, 46.

[41] Ad. c. 8, X, *de divortiis*, IV, 19, ad v. *non arctantur*: "...Patet ex praedicta quod infideles subjacent legibus imperialibus directe; sed directe non subjacent legi canonicae, nec in omnibus: quia nec in matrimonialibus, ut hic patet. Rationem diversitatis ostendit censura diversa, nam censura legis imperialis respicit corpore, et in facto consistit...qua arceri potest infidelis sicut et fidelis. Censura vero legis canonicae respicit animas, et in iure consistit—quia non potest arceri nisi fidelis et obediens Christianus ..."

[42] Ad. c. 8, X, *de divortiis*, IV, 19, ad v. *ad nos*: "...quoad excommunicationis sententiam in tales *infideles* proferendam, quod fieri non potest cum extra officium sint, et quoad fidem et quoad spirituale consortium,..."

De infidelibus [43] and *Gaudeamus.* In his comments on the latter one [44] he quoted the words from Saint Paul's First Epistle to the Corinthians already cited and he also explained the word *foris* as meaning outside of the Church or of the Catholic faith.

3. Doctrine of Barbosa on Some Letters of Pope Innocent III

After the Council of Trent (1545-1563) another commentator on the Decretals of Gregory IX, Augustine Barbosa (1589-1649), treated the letters that have just been cited. On the decretal *De infidelibus* he noted,[45] in almost the words used by Pope Innocent III, that: "Infideles coniuncti matrimonio in gradu prohibito ab Ecclesia, si convertantur non sunt separandi, quia quod Deus coniunxit homo non separet. . . ."

In his treatment of the letter *Gaudeamus* the same author commented [46] on the phrase *Qui constitutionibus canonicis*

[43] Ad. c. 4, X, *de consanguinitate et affinitate*, IV, 14, ad nn. 1, 2: "Judaeos non astringi a legibus canonicis circa Sacramentalia, et concernentia animam; unde licite contrahunt matrimonia in gradibus prohibitis humana lege tantum . . ."—Panormitanus, *Commentaria in Quinque Libros Decretalium* (5 vols. in 7, Venetiis, 1588), VII, p. 54, col. 4.

[44] Ad. c. 8, X, *de divortiis*, IV, 19, ad n. 1: ". . . unam regulam generalem, quia lex canonica in prohibitione matrimonii non extenditur ad infideles, et idem dicendum in aliis spiritualibus per illam auctoritatem Apostoli, 'quid ad nos de his, qui foris sunt iudicare?' dic. *foris*, i. e., extra ecclesiam vel fidem Catholicam."—*Commentaria in Quinque Libros Decretalium*, VII, p. 82, col. 2.

[45] Ad. c. 4, X, *de consanguinitate et affinitate*, IV, 14—Barbosa, *Collectanea Doctorum tam Veterum quam Recentiorum in Jus Pontificium Universum* (5 vols. in 4, Lugduni, 1656), II, 604.

[46] Ad. c. 8, X, *de divortiis*, IV, 19: "Notatur ad hoc, quod per canonicas constitutiones vetitis in matrimoniis contrahendis, non vendicant sibi locum in matrimoniis inter Judaeos, seu infideles, sed ipsi licite contrahunt in gradibus per Canones prohibitis . . . ex ea ratione, quia Judaei et infideles non ligantur constitutionibus, quae ab Ecclesia feruntur, ad dirigendum regimen spirituale . . . tum quia Ecclesia non potest infidelibus impedimenta matrimonium dirimentia statuere . . . Unde matrimonia contracta per Judaeos et infideles in gradibus humana lege prohibitis post conversionem ad fidem non separari . . ."

non arctantur, and upheld the principle of exemption for infidels from strictly Church laws. He specifically mentioned that Jews and infidels were not bound by laws which were made by the Church for the regulation of spiritual matters. He said that the Church [by its own authority] could not determine diriment matrimonial impediments for infidels.

Barbosa in commenting on another letter of Pope Innocent III—*Deus qui ecclesiam suam*[47]—noted that even if infidels, prior to their conversion to the true Faith, contracted marriages that were forbidden by Church law those marriages could not be declared invalid after the Baptism of the infidel parties. He corroborated this statement with the reason given by Pope Innocent III in his letter *Gaudeamus,* namely, that Jews and infidels were not subject to ecclesiastical laws before they were converted to the true Faith.[48]

4. The Council of Trent

One of the most important texts on the principle under discussion comes from the Council of Trent (1545-1563).[49]

This has been noted already in the discussion preliminary to the present study. The Tridentine decree was issued on November 25, 1551. It reads as follows:

[47] C. 9, X, *de divortiis,* IV, 19; Potthast, n. 1323.

[48] Ad. c. 9, X, *de divortiis,* IV, 19, ad v. *ut matrimoniis contractis cum relictis fratrum utantur*: "Primo quia si ante conversionem contraheret, nulla Pontificis concessione opus esset, matrimonium enim contra leges Canonicas ab infidelibus contractum valet, et post Baptismum dirimi non potest, ex cap. *Gaudeamus,* supra hoc tit..."—Barbosa, *Collectanea Doctorum tam Veterum quam Recentiorum in Jus Pontificium Universum,* II, 606.

[49] Conc. Trident., sess. XIV, *de poenitentia,* c. 2.—Pelella, *Canones et Decreta Concilii Tridentini ex Editione Roma A. MDCCCXXXIV Repetiti* (Neapoli, 1859), p. 76.

> Ceterum hoc Sacramentum multis rationibus a Baptismo differre dignoscitur. Nam praeterquam quod materia, et forma, quibus Sacramenti essentia perficitur, longissime dissidet; constat certe, Baptismi ministrum iudicem esse non oportere, cum Ecclesia in neminem iudicium exerceat, qui non prius in ipsam per Baptismi ianuam fuerit ingressus. "*Quid enim mihi,* inquit Apostolus, *de iis, qui foris sunt, iudicare?*" . . .

Here the Council was comparing the Sacrament of Baptism and the Sacrament of Penance and indicating their differences. In doing this it explicitly stated that the Church cannot exercise judgment over anyone who has not first entered the Church through the gate of Baptism. Then it quotes the important phrase from the First Epistle to the Corinthians.[50]

5. Post-Tridentine Decisions

The exemption of infidels from ecclesiastical laws was clearly emphasized by the canonist-Pope, Benedict XIV (1740-1758). This Pope in an encyclical letter [51] of the second of February, 1744, stated that the unbaptized are not bound by the precepts of the Church: ". . . Ecclesiae praecepta ad eos, qui foris sunt, minime pertinent."

Five years later the same Pontiff [52] stated the same principle in different language and repeated the passage from Saint Paul's Epistle.

[50] The very fact that this section from the Council of Trent is cited in the footnote to canon 12 in the Gasparri Edition of the Code of Canon Law indicates that it was one of the chief sources for the present regulation about infidels.

[51] *Inter omnigenas,* 2 febr. 1744, § 16—*Fontes,* n. 339.

[52] Ep. *Singulari,* 9 febr. 1749, § 2: "Initium igitur a Viro sumimus, ac breviter indicamus quidquid hac in re tum Hebraica lege sancitum, tum Principum decretis constitutum sit; omissis Sacris Ecclesiae Canonibus, cum nullo modo possint iis accommodari, qui numquam in eius sinum admissi sunt. 'Quid enim mihi de iis, qui foris sunt, iudicare?' . . ."—*Fontes,* n. 394.

Because of the importance of the distinction between the impediment of affinity, which cannot be contracted by infidels while they are still in infidelity, and physical affinity, which can be contracted by them, consideration must be given to the following case and response of the Sacred Congregation of the Holy Office: [53]

The Archbishop of Quebec sent in the following case: Paul, a Christian widower had married Balbina, an infidel, who now desires to become a Christian, in order that she may contract marriage with Paul in the Christian manner. Meanwhile, Demetrius, the son of Paul by his former wife, declares that he had illicit intercourse with Balbina. The question was asked, whether from such intercourse with an infidel woman there arises the impediment of affinity in the first degree? [54]

The answer of the Holy Office in effect stated that Balbina while she was still an infidel was not affected by the ecclesiastical impediment of affinity through her carnal intercourse with Demetrius. Nevertheless, she had contracted a physical affinity by this illicit act, for a man and woman are made one flesh by the very act of copulation. In view of this, the only way Balbina could contract the ecclesiastical impediment would be by subsequent Baptism when the physical affinity which she had contracted in infidelity would cause her to be bound by the ecclesiastical impediment which affects only those who are subject to the Church's laws.

About the middle of the nineteenth century the Sacred Congregation of the Holy Office in a response [55] again up-

[53] Instr. (*ad Archiep. Quebecen.*), 16 sept. 1824, ad 2—*Fontes*, n. 866.

[54] It must be noted here that in the pre-Code legislation the impediment of affinity could arise from illicit carnal intercourse. Cf. Wernz, *Ius Decretalium*, IV, n. 430; Ayrinhac-Lydon, *Marriage Legislation in the New Code of Canon Law* (revised ed., New York: Benziger Brothers, 1936), p. 176.

[55] S. C. S. Off., (*ad Vic. Apos. Pondicher.*), 17 apr. 1839—*Collect. S. C. Prop. de Fide*, n. 884.

held the principle that is being considered: The case concerned two infidels—an uncle and his niece—who were married according to their own infidel rite when the boy was about twelve years of age and the girl about five or six. They never lived together. When the girl was ten years old both the parties were baptized. The question was asked whether, after the spouses had reached the age required by the Church for valid marriage, they should renew their consent and obtain a dispensation from the impediment of consanguinity of the collateral line in the second degree touching the first; or whether their former marriage was raised to the dignity of a sacrament by the subsequent Baptism?

In answer, the Congregation requested the Vicar Apostolic not only to have the parties renew their consent *ad cautelam* but also to obtain *ad cautelam* a dispensation from the impediment of consanguinity.

The reason for the renewal of consent *ad cautelam* is clear for true marital consent may or may not have been present originally. Almost all the circumstances indicated that it was absent on the part of both children, but especially in the case of the girl. And since this consent is required by Natural Law and can be supplied by no other human agency but the parties,[56] the Congregation took all precautions to safeguard the validity of the marriage.

The dispensation from the impediment of consanguinity was required by the Congregation *ad cautelam* for these reasons: if the original consent was a true marital consent, then the first marriage was valid. The bond of consanguinity between the parties had no effect upon the marriage, for it could give rise only to an impediment of the ecclesi-

[56] Canon 1081; Payen, *De Matrimonio in Missionibus ac Potissimum in Sinis Tractatus Practicus et Casus* (2. ed., 3 vols., Vol. II, Zi-ka-wei: in typographis T'ou-sè-wè, 1936), II, p. 3, n. 1593.

astical law; [57] and thus the dispensation was not needed now after their conversion. But, if the original consent was not a true marital consent, then the original marriage was invalid and true marital consent would be given only now when they are Catholics. Thus the dispensation from consanguinity would be needed because the bond of consanguinity would perdure and they would now be bound by ecclesiastical laws. Hence it can be seen why the Congregation required the dispensation *ad cautelam.* And in consideration of the possibility of the first hypothesis that the true marital consent was present originally, it can be seen that the Congregation, by requiring the dispensation only *ad cautelam,* upheld the principle that infidels are not bound by purely ecclesiastical laws while they are still infidels.

Another provision by which infidels are not bound, inasmuch as it arises from purely ecclesiastical law, is that which governs the impediment of public propriety. Technically it is designated as *publica honestas.*

Prior to the promulgation of the Code of Canon Law the impediment of public propriety arose from valid espousals which were absolute and certain and it made marriage invalid between each of the engaged parties and the blood relations of the other to the first degree of both the direct and collateral lines. The impediment came also from a ratified but non-consummated marriage whether it was valid or not, provided the contract was not invalid because of a lack of natural consent or defect of the form prescribed by the *Tametsi* decree or the decree *Ne temere.* The contract had to have at least the appearance of marriage. The impediment extended to the fourth degree of both the direct and collateral lines of consanguinity.[58]

[57] De Smet, *Tractatus Theologico-Canonicus de Sponsalibus et Matrimonio* (4. ed., Brugis: Car. Beyaert, 1927), p. 530, n. 607.

[58] Ayrinhac-Lydon, *Marriage Legislation in the New Code of Canon Law,* pp. 180-181.

On the 19th of April, 1837 the Sacred Congregation of the Holy Office [59] rendered a decision concerning the impediment of public propriety. It permitted a marriage to be contracted without a dispensation in the case of a pagan who had never consummated his earlier marriage, and then, after his first wife's decease and his conversion, wanted to marry his sister-in-law who had also been converted. The Congregation permitted this marriage without a dispensation because the impediment of public propriety at that time, unlike the impediment of affinity, did not rest on a physical basis which upon the baptism of the parties acquires the attached status of an ecclesiastical impediment. The Congregation's decision is strictly in accord with the principle that infidels are not bound by purely ecclesiastical laws prior to their conversion, and since there was no basis upon which the impediment might rise after the parties were converted the impediment was not present when they desired to marry.

In 1852 the Sacred Congregation for the Propagation of the Faith indicated in a decision [60] that infidels upon conversion were not bound by the impediment of *crimen* that would arise from adultery and the killing of the guilty woman's husband if both of these acts preceded the conversion of the parties.

On the same day this Congregation considered this question: A Catholic man, prior to his conversion, had illicit carnal relations with a certain Catholic or infidel woman. He now desires to marry a Catholic blood relative of the aforementioned woman. The relative whom he desires to marry may have been baptized before or after the aforementioned carnal intercourse. May this marriage take place validly and licitly? The Congregation answered in

[59] S. C. S. Off. (*Tunkin. Occident.*), 19 apr. 1837—*Collect. S. C. de Prop. Fide*, n. 857; *Fontes*, n. 875.

[60] S. C. de Prop. Fide (*C. P.—Iaffnae*), 23 aug. 1852, ad 5—*Collect. S. C. de Prop. Fide.*, n. 1079; *Fontes*, n. 4835.

the negative. The decision was based on the fact that the two parties who desired to marry now were hindered by the impediment of affinity.

There are various angles to this case. When the illicit intercourse occurred:

1. either all the parties involved were infidels and then from the illicit intercourse there arose only the bond of affinity between the man and the blood relative of his consort. This would form the basis for the impediment of affinity after the man and the blood relative were baptized.

2. or the man was an infidel, the woman was baptized and the relative was baptized at the time of the illicit intercourse. Then the bond of affinity and the impediment of affinity were present between the man and the relative if they desired to contract marriage at that time, since the relative was a Catholic. The infidel man, however, would have been bound by this impediment only indirectly by reason of his association with the Catholic relative.

3. or the man was an infidel, the woman was baptized and the relative was not baptized. Then only the bond of affinity existed between the man and the relative for both were infidels. After their conversion this bond of affinity was the basis for the impediment of affinity that arose when they desired to marry. Prior to their Baptism this impediment did not exist between them because they then were not subject to the purely ecclesiastical law governing affinity.

The Sacred Congregation of the Holy Office rendered the decision[61] that a dispensation from the impediment of affinity in the first degree of the collateral line was necessary in the case where a man had married his deceased brother's wife. Both parties were infidels at the time of this marriage. Later the man became a Catholic. But

[61] S. C. S. Off. (*Yunnan*), 20 sept. 1854—*Collect. S. C. de Prop. Fide*, n. 1104; *Fontes*, n. 928; *ASS*, XXV (1892-1893), p. 586.

because the first marriage had been invalid in the eyes of the civil law which forbade such marriages even under pain of death the parties desired to be married by the priest. From the decision it can be deduced that the bond of affinity existed between the two parties even before the Baptism of the man and that after his Baptism and his subjection to ecclesiastical laws that bond of affinity formed the basis for the impediment of affinity as it exists in ecclesiastical law. Hence, when these two persons desired to be married according to the rite of the Church it was necessary to grant the man a dispensation from the impediment of affinity in the first degree of the collateral line.

This Congregation [62] indirectly excluded infidels from obligation to all laws constituting ecclesiastical impediments. It indicated indirectly that impediments of the divine positive or natural laws are the only ones that invalidate infidel marriages. In this manner it eliminated ecclesiastical impediments and indicated implicitly that infidels, when they marry as infidels, are not bound by strictly ecclesiastical impediments. The Congregation did not seem to take into consideration invalidating civil laws. Perhaps there were none in the place from which the question came.

In the same indirect manner this principle was expounded ten years later in a decision [63] concerning the impediment of age and its relation to infidel marriages.

[62] S. C. S. Off., 18 jun. 1856—*Fontes*, n. 936: "Cum matrimonium infidelium cui nullum obstet impedimentum iuris divini, aut naturalis, sit validum, ideo quotiescumque constet valide initum, nulla adest necessitas renovandi consensum (in casu conversionis unius coniugis) . . ."

[63] S. C. S. Off. (*ad Vic. Ap. Hu-nan*), 2 maii 1866—*Collect. S. C. de Prop. Fide*, n. 1289, ad 2: "Christianos impuberes, qui in infidelitate matrimonium contraxerunt, nisi in iisdem malitia, id est potentia, suppleat aetatem, separandos esse quoad torum et, si prudenter fieri poterit, a missionariis curandum ut etiam separentur quoad habitationem, iniuncto tamen onere vivendi maritaliter cum ad aetatem pubertatis pervenerint, dummodo huiusmodi matrimonia non probentur irrita ob aliquod impedimentum iuris naturalis vel divini, et praesertim ob defectum veri consensus."

It will be noted in this response that the Congregation took into consideration the phrase in the contemporary law —*nisi malitia suppleat aetatem* [64]—but it did so only insofar as the children were now Catholics and only in relation to the separation *quoad torum* which it had ordered until the children reached the age of puberty. This conclusion is drawn from the subsequent words of the response which advised that the children be reminded of their obligation of living a marital life together after they reached the age of puberty. Thus the congregation considered the infidel marriage valid even if the parties were not physically capable of the marital act and at the same time lacked the canonical age required for marriage. Then the Congregation indicated indirectly that infidel marriages were not affected by the ecclesiastical impediment of age. The interpretation just adopted is based on the following decision as well as on decisions respecting ecclesiastical impediments in general. Some of the latter have been noted already.

About the impediment of age there was another response in the latter part of the nineteenth century.[65] It showed again that marriages contracted by infidels are true marriages even if the parties were *impuberes* when they were united in matrimony. Hence they were not subject to the ecclesiastical impediment of age.

The exact age of the parties was not disclosed, but they were below the age of puberty as already noted. How young they were may be determined from a response of the next year [66] in answer to a question concerning this same

[64] Cf. c. un., C. XXX, q. 2; c. 9, X, *de desponsatione impuberum*, IV, 2; c. 14, X, *de desponsatione impuberum*, IV, 2, for the source of this expression.

[65] S. C. S. Off., 10 dec. 1885—*Collect. S. C. de Prop. Fide*, n. 1645: "Dummodo constet nullum fuisse impedimentum iuris naturalis vel divini, et praesertim contrahentes verum consensum praebuisse, non esse sponsalia sed vera matrimonia."

[66] S. C. S. Off. (*ad Vic. Ap. Myssur.*), 6 aug. 1886—*Collect. S. C. de Prop. Fide*, n. 1662; Wernz-Vidal, *Ius Canonicum*, V, 235, footnote 32.

impediment in which the age of the children was given at nine or ten years.

This second response may be used for the purpose of clarifying the first one because a reference to the response of 1885 was contained in the answer given in 1886, thus exhibiting evidence that the cases were almost parallel. Further this Congregation [67] in a response of 1891 gave probably the clearest exposition of the difference between the natural (physical) affinity contracted by affined infidels and the ecclesiastical impediment of affinity contracted by affined Christians; and indicated how the natural affinity causes an infidel, upon conversion, to be subject to the impediment of affinity:

> Affinitatem quae in infidelitate naturaliter contrahitur ex copula tum licita, tum illicita, non esse impedimentum pro matrimoniis quae in infidelitate ineuntur: evadere tamen impedimentum pro matrimoniis quae ineuntur post baptismum, quo suscepto, infideles fiunt subditi Ecclesiae, eiusque proinde legibus subjecti.

Near the turn of the last century the Sacred Congregation of the Holy Office [68] was also asked to solve an interesting case involving two Jews and a Catholic woman and concerning the impediment of affinity:

The Catholic women had illicit relations with two Jewish brothers, Samuel and Jacob. Later she lived in concubinage with Samuel and finally conceived a child. In order that the child might be legitimate they were married in the Catholic Church after Samuel's Baptism. The question arose as to the validity of the marriage which had been contracted without a dispensation from the impediment of affinity. The response reads: " Quatenus praevio

[67] S. C. S. Off., instr. (*ad Vic. Apos. Nankin*), 26 aug. 1891—*Collect. S. C. de Prop. Fide*, n. 1766; *Fontes*, n. 1145.

[68] June, 1895—*Analecta Ecclesiastica seu Romana Collectanea*, V (1897), 381; De Smet, *De Sponsalibus et Matrimonio*, p. 381, n. 438bis, footnote 2.

processu saltem summario, servata tamen in substantialibus Constitutione Benedicti XIV, '*Dei Miseratione*,' moraliter constet certo de contracta affinitate, deque dispensatione non concessa, matrimonium fuisse invalidum. Vide decretum S. Officii diei 26 august 1891."

At first this response does not seem to give any evidence that it upholds the principle that exempts unbaptized persons from purely ecclesiastical laws, but the reference to the decree of 1891 shows that it took into consideration the status of the Jew, because the 1891 decree concerns only infidels and the manner in which they are exempt from the impediment of affinity. The Jew in this case who wished to marry the Catholic woman was subject, prior to his Baptism, to the impediment of affinity indirectly by reason of his association with the Catholic woman.

A later case before this Congregation [69] involved a multiple bond of affinity. It followed the general principle of exemption of infidels from ecclesiastical laws. The case in summary is: Andrew, formerly an infidel, wished upon his conversion and Baptism to marry a catechumen who was about to be baptized. The woman previously had been the illegitimate wife of Andrew's father, paternal uncle and grandfather. A dispensation from the multiple impediment was requested because Andrew was already a Catholic.

The response was given as follows: ". . . Si ambo sponsi, in infidelitate affines, post susceptum baptisma matrimonio coniungi petant, supplicandum SSmo. pro dispensatione."

This does not state explicitly that these parties were exempt from the impediment of affinity while they were both infidels, but without a doubt the decision expressed in the Holy Office decree of 1891, already cited several times, could be applied here. Also the wording of the answer to

[69] S. C. S. Off., 16 dec. 1898—*Analecta Ecclesiastica*, VII (1899), 61, 62; Wernz-Vidal, *Ius Canonicum*, V, 442, footnote 49; De Smet, *De Sponsalibus et Matrimonio*, p. 381, n. 438bis, footnote 2.

the present case seems to indicate that the parties were exempt from the impediment while they both were infidels:

First, it does not explicitly state anything about the impediment but speaks of the parties as being *affines in infidelitate.* Then it enjoins that a dispensation be sought if they wish to be married *post susceptum baptisma.* In a footnote to this decree in the periodical just cited there is an explanation of the response. This substantiates what has just been noted about the response.[70] The author of this explanation gave as a basis for his interpretation a former decree which has been cited above.[71]

ARTICLE C.—JEWS

a) *Introduction*

In the preceding section it was shown by various citations that the Church has always adhered to the principle that those who are not subject to its authority through Baptism are not directly bound by its strictly human statutes. Since unbaptized Jews are infidels, those citations apply to them also.

From a consideration of those texts a transition must now be made to a consideration of the vast amount of special legislation passed by the Church for unbaptized Jews or enacted as at least affecting them; and of the various opinions on its lawfulness.

[70] *Analecta Ecclesiastica,* VII (1899), 61, 62, footnote 2: "In casu exposito triplex habetur ex copula illicita affinitas contracta in infidelitate. Illa autem per se non inducit impedimentum canonicum, quia affinitas ex copula illicita est iuris ecclesiastici tantum, quod non afficit infideles.... Quando ambo sponsi, affines in infidelitate, transeunt ad religionem Christianam ... naturaliter reperiuntur affines, quamvis hoc ligamen contractum fuerit in infidelitate; et ideo subiacent legibus Ecclesiae, quae agnoscunt in tali affinitate impedimentum dirimens matrimonium."

[71] S. C. de Prop. Fide (*C. P.-Jaffnae*), 23 aug. 1852, ad 3—*Collect. S. C. de Prop. Fide,* n. 1079.

It has been indicated already by various passages from Holy Scripture that the right and the duty of preaching the revealed doctrine to all people came to the Church from the divine law as expressed by Christ, Himself.[72] This instruction was to be given not only in Christian countries but especially in infidel nations. And this right and duty were truly juridic because Christ, who as God, had the plenitude of power in heaven and on earth [73] gave them to the juridic society which he founded. That His Church was established as a juridic society is proved by the fact that it possessed the characteristics of such a body: It was founded by One who had the power to institute it, and at the same time gave it the right of existing and operating in conformity with its proper end. As such the Church is established by divine law to which all men are subject.[74]

Under the same divine law, since God is the Lord of all things, all men even the non-baptized have the obligation of observing the divine natural and positive laws, according as they are declared by the Church. The obligations that non-baptized persons have of joining the Church and of observing divine law as declared by the Church cannot be enforced, however, by the jurisdictional power of the Church,[75] because such persons have not received Baptism and cannot be under such a juridic obligation in the strict sense. They have only an ethical obligation.[76]

From the very nature of things, nevertheless, the Church has the right of preventing infidels from doing injury to

[72] E. g., Matt. XXVIII: 18, 19; Mark XVI: 15.

[73] Matt. XXVIII: 18.

[74] Cavagnis, *Institutiones Iuris Publici Ecclesiastici* (4. ed., 3 vols., Romae, 1906), I, p. 114, n. 205.

[75] Van Hove, Commentarium Lovaniense in Codicem Iuris Canonici, II, *De Legibus Ecclesiasticis* (Mechliniae: H. Dessain, 1930), p. 195. (Hereafter quoted as Van Hove, *De Legibus Ecclesiasticis*.)

[76] Coronata, *Institutiones Iuris Canonici* (2. ed., Vols. I-II, Romae: Marietti, 1939), II, 242, n. 907; cf. Canon 1351.

Christians; of defending itself against those who impede the Church in carrying out its purpose and in regulating the manner in which Christians should act toward infidels.[77] This right is based on that principle of the natural law which gives to every human being and to every society the right of defending themselves against those who unjustly attack them and those who unjustly impede them in the attainment of their duly-appointed end.[78]

Because of this the Church can make laws which not only directly affect its own subjects but also indirectly touch those who are not its subjects. Besides, she can use coercion and pass judgments against infidels who attempt to disturb the order, security and peace of the ecclesiastical state or do harm to it in spiritual or temporal matters, or influence its subjects to disobedience or defection.[79]

Against the background of these principles the history of the Church's manner of acting with infidels, and especially with Jews, is explicable.

b) *From the Fourth to the Seventh Century*

As far back as the first Councils of the Church there was legislation that regulated the social and business contacts of Christians and Jews:

The Council of Elvira (305) [80] forbade Christians to have their fruits blessed by Jews and decreed that violators of this law should be removed from the Church. The Council also prohibited [81] Christians from marrying Jews. In 506

[77] Van Hove, *De Legibus Ecclesiasticis*, p. 195.

[78] Chelodi, *Ius de Personis Iuxta Codicem Iuris Canonici* (altera ed., a Ernesto Bertagnolli recognita et aucta, Tridenti: Libr. Edit. Tridentum, 1927), p. 67 (Quoted hereafter as Chelodi-Bertagnolli, *Ius de Personis*); St. Thomas Aquinas, *Summa Theologica*, II^{a}, II^{ae}, q. 64, a. 7; Cathrein, *Philosophia Moralis* (16. ed., Friburgi Brisgoviae: Herder & Co., 1932), p. 261, n. 371.

[79] Chelodi-Bertagnolli, *Ius de Personis*, p. 67.

[80] Canon 49—Mansi, II, 14.

[81] Canon 16—Mansi, II, 8.

the Council of Agde[82] prohibited Christians from eating with Jews and gave the reason.[83]

From the legislation that affected the Jewish population only indirectly, some councils of this period went a step farther and made laws that applied only to Jews. Such a statute[84] forbade the Jews, during the last days of Holy Week, to go among the Christians or mingle with them in any place or on any occasion.

This is recorded because the Jews seem to have taken some delight in mocking the Catholics and pelting them with missiles of various kinds during processions and other outdoor celebrations. Hence, it is obvious that there was very good reason for a regulation of this kind.

A law which in its enforcement reached into the very homes of the Jews was passed in 581 at the I Council of Mâcon.[85] The Council decreed that no Christian slave was to serve a Jew, and if there were any such Christian servants they were to be redeemed for twelve *solidi*,[86] which at most probably amounted to $25. Its conciliar canon applied even if a pagan slave of a Jew wished to become a Christian and was not permitted to do so by his master.

The Council of Narbonne (589)[87] forbade those Jews accompanying the body of a dead person to sing psalms.

[82] Canon 40—Mansi, VIII, 331-332.

[83] "...Quia cum apud Christianos cibis communibus non utantur, indignum est, atque sacrilegium, eorum cibos a Christianis sumi, cum ea quae Apostolo permittente nos sumimus, ab illis judicentur immunda . . ." —Mansi, VIII, 331-332.

[84] Council of Orleans (538), c. 30—Mansi, IX, 19.

[85] Canon 16—C. 1, X, *de Judaeis, Sarracenis, et eorum servis*, V, 6; Mansi, IX, 935.

[86] *Solidi*—Gold coins equal in value to a ducat which ranged in value from 83c to $2.28 (cf. Funk & Wagnalls, *Desk Standard Dictionary of the English Language* (New York: Funk & Wagnalls Co., 1930), *solidi; Shorter Oxford English Dictionary on Historical Principles* (Oxford: Clarendon Press, 1934), *solidus* and *denarius*).

[87] Canon 9—Mansi, IX, 1016.

Violators of this regulation were to pay a fine to the civil authorities.

Some of the most important regulations concerning the Jewish people were contained in the letters of Pope Gregory the Great (590-604). He is known for having been solicitous about preserving their religious liberty and rights.[88]

One of his letters (602) [89] on this topic appears in the Decree of Gratian. In it the Pope advised Pascasius, Bishop of Naples, that they who have a sincere intention of leading those who are outside the Christian religion into the true fold should do so by soft and not sharp words. He was referring particularly to certain harsh treatment that was given to the Jews.

The same Pope on another occasion, however,[90] showed that he was not unaware of the abuses that arose when the Jewish population was permitted to associate freely with the Christians. That was in 594, when he advised Venantius, Bishop of Lugo, that Jews were not permitted to retain Christian slaves. And he gave as his principal reason the danger that the unlearned slaves might be persuaded or forced to accept Jewish superstitions.

The reason given by Pope Gregory shows that, as head of the Church, he was exercising the right which has already been mentioned—that of restraining those who endangered the spiritual welfare of the faithful. To him the best way in this case was to take the slave out of the danger by having him or her freed.

On these two occasions the Pontiff indicated that, even though he was trying to overcome Jewish practices that were inimical to the spiritual welfare of his flock, neverthe-

[88] Van Hove, *De Legibus Ecclesiasticis*, p. 195: Chelodi-Bertagnolli, *Ius de Personis*, p. 67.

[89] C. 3, D. 45; J E, n. 1496.

[90] C. 2, X, *de Iudaeis, Sarracenis, et eorum servis*, V, 6; J E, n. 1293.

less, he did not want Christians to perpetrate injuries or injustices against the Jews.

In Spain perhaps the most severe restrictions were placed upon the Jewish population but it is difficult to determine accurately whether all these laws were for baptized or unbaptized Jews, because of the peculiar conditions that existed at that time.

The IV Provincial Council of Toledo (633) [91] prescribed concerning Jews that they were not to be forced to believe in the Christian religion, but once they had embraced Christianity, even if by force or necessity, they were to be compelled to practice it lest the Lord's name be blasphemed. This canon was enacted in criticism and denunciation of the practice of the Visigothic King Sisebut (612-621) who had compelled Jews to become Catholics or to be exiled.[92] Such compulsion has always been contrary to the mind of the Church.[93]

This same IV Provincial Council of Toledo also issued a number of laws regarding Jews but it made the distinction plain when it was referring to Jews who had been baptized and thereupon had fallen away.[94] Because of this it seems safe to hold that such other canons of the same Council which did not make this distinction referred to unbaptized Jews. It is necessary to note this difference because an-

91 Cap. 57—Mansi, X, 633.

92 Ziegler, *Church and State in Visigothic Spain* (Washington, D. C.: The Catholic University of America, 1930), p. 190.

93 Gregory I (590-604), Ep. *ad Virgilium Arelatensem et Theodorum Massiliensem*—*MGH, Epistolae*, I, pars I, *Gregorii I Registri Libri I-IV* (ed. P. Ewald, Berolini, 1887), p. 71; Mansi, IX, 1066; Clement III (1187-1191), Ep. *Sicut Judaei*—C. 9, X, *de Judaeis, Sarracenis et eorum servis*, V, 6.

94 Cap. 59—"Plerique qui ex Judaeis dudum ad Christianam fidem promoti sunt, nunc blasphemantes in Christum . . . ;" cap. 61—"Judaei baptizati . . ."—Mansi, X, 633, 634.

other of its statutes [95] made no such distinction and imposed on Jews the punishment of taking their children from them and of putting these children in monasteries or Christian homes.

This surely was a law about a spiritual matter, namely, the faith of the children. Hence, it appears as if the Church tried to coerce the Jews by ecclesiastical laws. How it was possible for the Church to enact such laws will be explained later. In connection with the law just mentioned, however, it must be noted that some manuscripts of this enactment contain the word *baptizatos.*[96] If those manuscripts contain the correct reading then it would seem that not only the children were baptized but it may be presumed that the parents were also. And it can be seen how the Church could make such an enactment.

Another canon of the same Council [97] also seems to be an ecclesiastical regulation for unbaptized persons because it ordered Bishops to advise unbaptized Jews, married to Christian women, that they must be baptized. If they refused they were to be separated from their wives. Their children were to follow the religion of the mother.

The XII Provincial Council of Toledo (681) [98] forbade the Jews to celebrate the Pasch or the Sabbath or other festivals according to their own rite. It even prohibited the practice of circumcision among them. Every Jew had to stop work on Sundays and Holy Days. They were not to distinguish between clean and unclean meats. Marriage with their own close blood relatives was interdicted; and they were not to read books which attacked the Christian religion.

[95] Cap. 60—Mansi, X, 634; cf. XVII Council of Toledo (694), cap. 8—Mansi, XII, 101.

[96] Hefele, *Histoire des Conciles,* translated by H. Leclercq (8 vols. in 16, Paris, 1907-1921), III, 274, note 1.

[97] Cap. 63—Mansi, X, 634.

[98] Cap. 9—Mansi, XI, 1035-1036.

These items touch upon some fundamental practices of the Jewish religion. They evidently were forbidden because the Christian religion had abolished them. They were contrary to Church regulations. Indeed, it would have seemed like a useless gesture to have made such laws if the Jews had had no obligation of obeying them. There is no unmistakable indication that the laws were enacted solely for converted Jews who had lapsed, although they give every indication of applying to baptized Jews since one of the great abuses in Spain at this time, as in later times, may have been the practice of Jews receiving Baptism and then still continuing the practice of Judaism or falling back entirely into their former religion.[99]

It is necessary to get the political background of the times in order to understand some of the legislation of the Church Councils held in this period of the Catholic Visigothic Kings in Spain (586-712). But because such information need not be exhaustive, it will be given by means of a synopsis of sections from another work.[100]

By a mass conversion like that of the Franks at the time of Clovis (466-511), the Arian Visigoths of Spain came into the Church together with their king, Recared (586-601) shortly after he began his reign.

At the III Provincial Council of Toledo (589) he united the Church and the State by making Catholicism the State religion. Because of this union and because they saw the need of educated and prudent men to dispense justice and to enforce laws, the succeeding Visigothic kings gave the Bishops jurisdiction in civil matters and supervision even over the civil magistrates.

99 Funk, *A Manual of Church History* (Translated by P. Perciballi; edited by W. H. Kent, O.S.C.), (London: Burns, Oates & Washbourne, Ltd., 1931), II, 39, 40.

100 Ziegler, *Church and State in Visigothic Spain*, pp. 33, 38, 43, 89-122, 143, 165, 189, 191-192, 197, 199.

The State also had some control over the Church in the right of the king to appoint Bishops and to convoke ecclesiastical councils which enacted both ecclesiastical and civil legislation. Under the direction of the king the Church councils passed civil legislation and proposed matters that were to be approved by the king for the welfare of the Church. Since there was such close collaboration between the king and the Bishops and since the king might very easily have secured the appointment of unscrupulous men as Bishops, it can be understood very easily how the laws about Jews as noted above could have come from the Spanish Councils of this period. It is well known that the actions of the Jews in Spain during many centuries were the cause of much internal strife. One of them has just been mentioned—the reecption of what might be called a *Baptism of convenience,* and then the non-rejection of the Jewish religious practices. And if the kings saw that legislation about spiritual matters would curb internal trouble it is almost certain they would have permitted it. Hence, Canon 14 of the Third Council of Toledo (589) [101] marks the inception of a new procedure by which the Jews were to be controlled by the united powers of Church and State. Primarily, most of the regulations that were enacted seem to have had the nature of police ordinances for public order.

Some explanation of this legislation for Jews and its sometimes evident disregard of the principle that the Church has no jurisdiction over the unbaptized in strictly ecclesiastical matters is noted in the following passage:

". . . The . . . program now promulgated (Fourth Council of Toledo—633) directly by the spiritual authorities reflects the position of the Church under the usurper Sisenand (631-636), who was quite willing to leave extensive powers

[101] Hardouin, *Acta Conciliorum et Epistolae Decretales ac Constitutiones Summorum Pontificum* (12 vols., Parisiis, 1714-1715), III, 481; Mansi, IX, 996.

with the bishops in return for the support they had given his throne."[102] That passage seems to indicate that the Church authorities were given much civil power and, since, as already noted, the actions of the Jews were causing internal strife, the Bishops could suppress it in any way that they saw fit. Some of the causes of the trouble touched on spiritual matters and therefore the laws against the trouble-makers necessarily had to touch on spiritual matters.

The most important point is that the Church in its concurrence with the kings in this matter was acting as a civil authority more or less dominated by the desires of the kings; or perhaps more accurately it proceeded as an ecclesiastico-civil power and for the greater part was using its right of self-defense, though its concept of the implications of that right were probably exaggerated. Thus the principle that the unbaptized are not bound by purely ecclesiastical laws remained intact for the laws were not purely ecclesiastical.

c) *From the Eleventh to the Thirteenth Century*

Another important point upon which the Church legislated for Jews was the paying of tithes.

In 1068 the Council of Gerona[103] ordered that tithes were to be paid to the Church by Jews who had purchased land from which tithes had been exacted. The reason given was that it was unjust for the Church to lose the income which it was accustomed to collect from the Christian owners of the land.

Later there was a pronouncement[104] of Pope Alexander III (1159-1181) on this matter in a letter to the Bishop of Marsi (Italy). The danger of defrauding the Church was his reason for requiring the payment of tithes by the Jews

[102] Ziegler, *op. cit.*, pp. 191, 192.

[103] Canon 14—Mansi, XIX, 1072.

[104] C. 16, X, *de decimis*, III, 30.

owning land from which tithes had been collected formerly. He told the Bishop to compel the Jews to pay these tithes or to give up the possession of the land.

Later Pope Innocent III at the IV General Council of the Lateran in 1215 made a regulation [105] regarding the payment of tithes by Jews. His sanction, however, affected the Jews only indirectly by forbidding Christians to have any dealings with them. This was the sanction attached to very much of the legislation concerning the Jews and, in most cases it was a legitimate way to correct abuses that were doing harm to the Church either temporally or spiritually.

In explaining the laws about tithes, Suarez stated [106] that Jews could not be obliged to pay the tithes if the law was considered as being ecclesiastical for ecclesiastical precepts obliged only the baptized. Then he noted the quotation from the fifth chapter of the First Epistle to the Corinthians already cited. He finally distinguished between personal and predial [pertaining to the land] tithes and decided that Jews in the instances just noted were not obliged to pay personal tithes, but they could be required to satisfy for the predial tithes as a kind of tax on the land. This seems to indicate that the Church was exercising in this legislation simply the rights of a territorial, civil ruler.

Pope Alexander III (1159-1181) [107] forbade the Jews to erect new synagogues—they were permitted to repair the old ones but they were not to enrich them beyond their original condition.

Some decrees, however, were more favorable and protected the Jews. Such were the constitutions *Sicut Judaei* [108]

[105] Canon 67—C. 18, X, *de usuris*, V, 19.

[106] *Opera omnia* (26 vols. et 2 indices, Parisiis, 1856-1866 et 1878), Vol. XIII, p. 144 (*De divino cultu ex praecepto necessario praesertim per oblationes, decimas, ac primitias*), lib. I, cap. XIV, nn. 4-5.

[107] C. 7, X, *de Iudaeis, Sarracenis et eorum servis*, V, 6; J L, n. 9331.

[108] C. 9, X, *de Judaeis, Sarracenis et eorum servis*, V, 6.

of Clement III (1187-1191) and *Licet perfidia Judaeorum* of Innocent III (1198-1216).[109]

This latter Pope in December 1200, issued his constitution *Post miserabilem* [110] which commanded the secular authorities to return to Christians the money that had been obtained from the latter by Jewish usurers.

At the IV General Council of the Lateran (1215) [111] Jews were ordered to wear special marks on their clothing to distinguish them from the Christians. They were not to appear in public in gala attire on Passion Sunday and on other special Christian days of sorrow. Violators were to be brought before the secular rulers.

Pope Innocent IV in his Constitution *Impia Judaeorum perfidia* (9 may, 1244) [112] ordered the Talmud to be burned by the civil authorities of France because of its blasphemies against God and the Blessed Virgin. But he protected the Jews against persecution when he wrote to the Archbishop of Vienne [113] protesting about Jews being despoiled of property and being incarcerated unjustly. He also received the Jews of that region under the protection of the Holy See.

On the 5th of September 1288, Pope Nicholas IV (1288-1292) sent to some of the members of the Inquisition his constitution *Turbato corde audivimus,*[114] which ordered them to mete out due punishment to the Jews who had induced Christians to embrace the Jewish religion.

109 Potthast, n. 834.

110 C. 12, X, *de usuris,* V, 19; Potthast, n. 1237.

111 Canon 68—Potthast, I, p. 438; c. 15, X, *de Iudaeis, Sarracenis, et eorum servis,* V, 6.

112 *Bullarum Diplomatum et Privilegiorum Sanctorum Romanorum Pontificum Taurinensis Editio* (25 vols., Vol. III, Augustae Taurinorum, 1859), III, 508, 509 (hereafter quoted as *Bullarum Taur.* an abbreviation of *Bullarum Taurinensis Editio.*); Potthast, n. 11376.

113 Berger, *Les Registres D'Innocent IV* (4 vols., Paris, 1884-1897), n. 2815.

114 *Bullarum Taur.,* IV, 88; Potthast, n. 22795.

It will be noted that many of the documents cited here have been from a title of the Decretals of Gregory IX: *de Judaeis, Sarracenis, et eorum servis,* and it may be asked, why these documents are there if such persons are not bound by ecclesiastical laws? One of the commentators on the Decretals [115] gives the answer by stating that these laws were enacted only for the Jews living in the temporal possessions of the Holy See, or of other ecclesiastical authorities, or of Christian princes, and that many of them affected the Jews only indirectly.

Some explanation of this activity on the part of the Roman pontiffs has been attempted by a study of their political thinking during the Thirteenth Century. Pope Innocent IV, according to some,[116] seemed to hold that the Pope as visible representative of Christ had juridical power even over infidels and Jews. But this view has been attributed to him falsely because of some of the writings that were published, during his time and later, on the controversy about the doctrine of the two swords (those of the spiritual and the temporal power).[117]

The opinion is only a deduction based on a false notion of the true doctrine which it is certain was held by Pope Innocent IV and other Popes who were involved in this matter. This true doctrine is that there are two distinct authorities—one having jurisdiction over temporal matters (the State) and the other having jurisdiction over spiritual matters (the Church). Each power is granted by God and each is supreme in its own designated sphere. Nevertheless, because the Church has a more exalted end the State is indirectly dependent on the Church. This means that the

[115] Reiffenstuel, *Ius Canonicum Universum complectens Tractatum de Regulis Iuris* (5 vols., in 7, Parisiis, 1864-1882), I, 163 (quoted in future as *Ius Canonicum Universum*).

[116] Cf. Van Hove, *De Legibus Ecclesiasticis,* pp. 195, 196; Carlyle, *A History of Mediaeval Political Theory in the West* (6 vols., New York: G. P. Putnam's Sons, 1903-1928), V, 323, footnote 2.

Church may not interfere in strictly temporal matters but only in temporal matters in which grave sin is involved.[118]

Even though many of the regulations concerning Jews affected them only indirectly and seem to have been made by the Church acting as a civil power, the Council of Oxford, 1222 [119] speaks of inflicting a canonical penalty on Jews who continued to keep Christian slaves. And they were to be compelled *per censuram ecclesiasticam* to wear some mark of identification on their clothing to distinguish them from the Christians.

The Council of Narbonne (1227) [120] and the Council of Beziers (1246) [121] went as far as to exact a kind of tributary offering of five or six *denarii* from each Jewish family on Easter Sunday. This, however, might be a civil tax.

One Council in 1231 [122] ordered that Jews who did anything or spoke anything in contempt of the Christian faith, or blasphemed the Saviour, were to be tried before an ecclesiastical court and, if convicted, were to be deprived of association with the faithful. This does not seem to refer to converted Jews, as will be noted from its wording, and because the preceding canon of this council makes a distinction between Jews and the faithful.

[117] Carlyle, *op. cit.*, V, 335.

[118] Ottaviani, *Institutiones Juris Publici Ecclesiastici*, I, 55, 56; Carlyle, *op. cit.*, V, 359; Maritain, *The Things That Are Not Caesar's*, Unicorn Series, n. 10 (London: Sheed & Ward, 1939), pp. 12, 13; 128-132; Boniface VIII, Bulla *Unam Sanctam*, 18 nov. 1302—Denzinger-Bannwart, *Enchiridion Symbolorum, Definitionum et Declarationum de Rebus Fidei et Morum* (16 & 17. ed., Friburgi Brisgoviae: Herder & Co., 1928), p. 206, n. 469; Leo XIII, ep. encycl., *Immortale Dei*, 1 nov. 1885—Denzinger-Bannwart, *Enchiridion*, n. 1866 (quoted as *Enchiridion* from now on); *Fontes*, n. 592. Cf. pp. 53, 54 and 55 for further discussion.

[119] CC. 11, 39—Mansi, XXIII, 22.

[120] C. 4—Mansi, XXIII, 22.

[121] Cap. 42—Mansi, XXIII, 702.

[122] Council of the Archdiocese of Tours, cap. 32—Mansi, XXIII, 239.

d) *From the Thirteenth to the Sixteenth Century*

On August 4, 1278 Pope Nicholas III (1277-1280) published his Bull, *Vineam* [123] in which he appointed preachers to bring the Catholic doctrine to the Jews. He advised that those Jews who in their obstinacy would not listen to the words of the preachers and especially those who would flee from the place, were to be reported to the Pope. He in turn was to decide what salutary remedies needed to be applied to the guilty ones.

Pope John XXII (1316-1334) in his Constitution *Dignum arbitrantes* of July 23, 1320 [124] protected the Jews and gave strict orders that those converted from Judaism should not be despoiled of their goods, but should be protected against injuries and harm.

Pope Martin V (1417-1431) on the 3rd of June 1425,[125] decreed a drastic punishment for Jews who bought and sold Christian slaves, especially if the slaves were sold to Saracens who were accustomed to compel Christian slaves to deny their faith. The punishment was: ". . . res et bona sua omnia in quibuscumque et ubicumque, ac quibusvis pondere, numero et mensura consistant, prorsus amittat . . ." And what was thus appropriated was to be used to redeem those sold into slavery or, if that was impossible, it was to be used for pious works. This was only a local decree.

The Constitution *Si ad reprimendos* [126] of Pope Calixtus III (1455-1458) issued on the 28th of May 1456, marked the beginning of a series of Papal documents that affected everyone living among Christians anywhere in the world. At first these documents contained only such regulations as could have been made by any civil ruler, and were addressed

[123] *Bullarum Taur.*, IV, p. 45, § 4; Potthast, nn. 21382, 21383.

[124] C. 2, *de Judaeis*, V, 2, in Extravag. com.

[125] *Bullarum Taur.*, IV, 719.

[126] *Bullarum Taur.*, V, 127-130.

not only to ecclesiastical dignitaries but also to the civil authorities who at that time supported the Church authorities. The document just cited enumerated prohibitions forbidding Christians to eat with the Jews and Saracens; to live with them; or to receive medical care from them. The Pope sent this to every patriarch, primate, archbishop, bishop and prince, baron, and noble. And he ordered them to observe it and see that Christians, Jews and Saracens observed it.

Saint Pius V (1566-1572) issued a decree—*Hebraeorum gens,* 26 febr. 1569,[127]—ordering the expulsion of the Jews of both sexes from all the possessions of the Holy Roman Church and of the lands subject to it. Those Jews in the cities of Rome and Ancona were excepted. He begins the decree by enumerating all the troubles and strife caused by the various abuses of the Jews against the Christians and gives these as some of the reasons for ordering the Jews to leave. The punishment for those who remained or returned to the forbidden places was confiscation of all their goods and reduction to slavery under the Roman Church forever.

This was evidently an enactment of the Pope as the purely civil ruler of the Papal States and is an order that any civil ruler might give (especially in that day and age) if a certain group was at the root of continual, serious disturbances even if they were not always the cause of them.

e) *Final Period—Up to the Present*

Some of the most important Papal letters concerning the Jewish question were issued by Pope Gregory XIII (1572-1585):

On July 1, 1581, he promulgated a decree against the Jews—*Antiqua Judaeorum.*[128] It was one of the most com-

127 *Bullarum Taur.,* VII, 740-742.

128 *Bullarum Taur.,* VIII, 378.

prehensive in its regulations and had universal force. The Pope even ordered the officials of the Inquisition to proceed against those Jews who did not obey his mandates. Ferraris [129] gives a summary of the offenses enumerated in this decree:

> Inquisitores libere contra hebraeos procedere possunt in sequentibus casibus: Si negaverint quae circa fidem communia sunt cum Christianis. Si daemones invocaverint. Si quem Christianum haec docuerint, vel ad ea perduxerint. Si haereticas blasphemias dixerint. Si Christianum de fide deviaverint. Si infideles ad fidem Christi transire impedierint. Si haereticum scienter receptaverint. Si libros haereticos vel thalmudicos, aut alios Judaicos quomodolibet damnatos tenuerint. Si hostiam salutarem aut crucem et similia vel Christianos deriserint.

The following punishments were to be meted out according to the nature of the offense: [130]

> . . . In quibus casibus universis et singulis, omnes praedictae pravitatis inquisitores omnium regnorum, provinciarum, etc., *universi orbis Christiani,* judices in suis quemque locis perpetuo delegamus ut super his contra Iudaeos atque infideles quoscumque, simul vel separatim, prout in causis fidei, iuxta sacrorum canonum formam necnon Officii Inquisitionis huiusmodi constitutiones, diligenter inquirunt et procedant, et repererint in eos pro culpae modo, ac etiam pro criminum numero vel multiplicatione aut consuetudine delinquendi, flagra, remigia, etiam perpetua, rerum quoque publicationes, exilia, aliaque atrociora decernant et alias de eis exempla edant, quae sceleratos illos deterreant ab huiusmodi flagitiis in posterum admittendis.

129 *Bibliotheca—Canonica, Juridica, Moralis, Theologica, necnon Ascetica, Polemica, Rubricistica, Historica* (9 vols., 1885-1899, Vol. IV, Romae, 1889), IV, s. v. "Hebraeus," n. 17. (In future this will be quoted as *Bibliotheca*).

130 Gregory XIII, Constitutio *Antiqua Judaeorum — Bullarum Taur.*, VIII, 378, § 12.

The words *Iudaeos atque infideles quoscumque* in the above quotation seem to indicate that these punishments were decreed for unbaptized Jews.

Pope Gregory XIII on the first of September 1584, promulgated another Constitution, *Sancta Mater Ecclesia*,[131] which surely was meant to apply to unbaptized Jews. He despatched this to all ecclesiastical authorities in whose territories Jewish synagogues had been erected. Then he commanded these authorities to assemble on Saturdays the Jews of both sexes over twelve years of age and to have competent teachers instruct them in the Holy Scriptures, especially in the Law and the Prophets. Those who refused to come were to be restrained from doing business with Christians, or were to be subjected to other indeterminate punishments acording to the discretion of the ecclesiastical superiors.

This constitution in a particular way gave evidence of being a purely ecclesiastical law affecting only a spiritual matter which was decreed for a class of non-baptized persons. It did not prescribe regulations for the preservation of public order or for the solemnities of acts, like wills. It was not decreed by the Church as a temporal power, since it treated of something connected with a spiritual matter—eternal life. It was, therefore, enacted by the Church acting as a spiritual power. Only in the sanction is the law imposed on the baptized rather than on the unbaptized. The Church as a spiritual power could enforce its regulation only by instructing its members not to buy from Jews, as had been done on previous occasions. To justify such a prescription one observes that the Pope was acting upon the authority given to the Church when Christ commissioned it to teach all nations and that the obligation of the non-baptized really arose from the divine law.

131 *Bullarum Taur.*, VIII, 487.

This decree of Pope Gregory XIII, although it should have been observed throughout the whole Christian world, actually was not received outside the City of Rome and soon fell into desuetude. Pope Pius IX (1846-1878) repealed it for the city of Rome in 1848.[132]

Even as late as the eighteenth and nineteenth centuries, Church councils were passing laws concerning Jews.[133]

f) *Opinions Giving Reasons for Legislation Concerning Jews*

It remains to be noted that the various enactments against the Jews were in many cases not fulfilled even by Christians and their ecclesiastical superiors as is evidenced by the constant repetition of the same prohibitions. They finally fell into desuetude and were abrogated by the New Code of Canon Law.[134]

There are various opinions on the reasons why the Church acted as it did toward the Jews. Some of these have been given already in the course of this treatment. Some others will be noted now.

Ojetti[135] thinks that the following opinions, some of which have been mentioned already, give a better explanation of the whole matter and resolve the various difficult cases more satisfactorily than other opinions:

132 Chelodi-Bertagnolli, *Ius de Personis*, p. 68.

133 Prov. Council of Avignon (1725)—*Acta et Decreta Sacrorum Conciliorum Recentiorum Collectio Lacensis* (7 vols., Friburgi Brisgoviae, 1870-1890), I, 487; (From now on quoted as *Collectio Lacensis*); National Synod of Hungary (1822)—*Collectio Lacensis*, V, 939-a; Council of Gran (Esztergom) in Hungary (1858)—*Collectio Lacensis*, V, 86-a; Prov. Council of Prague (1860)—*Collectio Lacensis*, V, 443-c; Prov. Synod of Utrecht (1865)—*Collectio Lacensis*, V, 801-c.

134 Van Hove, *De Legibus Ecclesiasticis*, p. 196.

135 *Commentarium in Codicem Iuris Canonici, I—Normae Generales* (4 vols., Vol. I, Romae: apud Aedes Universitatis Gregorianae, 1927), I, 106 (hereafter quoted as Ojetti, *Commentarium in Codicem Iuris Canonici*).

" Alii dicunt Ecclesiam in hoc usum esse iure defensionis; scilicet ob periculum nimiae diffusionis seu propagationis Hebraeorum ex una parte, et ex alia ob suspicionem, ne inimici christiani nominis paraturi essent insidias fidelibus, Ecclesia usa est hoc medio, ut eos ad fidem adduceret et de inimicis faceret filios. . . ."

" Alii dicunt, Ecclesiam non directe in Hebraeos potestate coactiva usam esse, sed dedisse legem suos fideles obligantem non communicandi cum Hebraeis, ex quo hi detrimentum caperent, nisi vellent audire concionem. . . ."

Unless the Church herself decides the matter, it seems that no definite decision can be made as to the lawfulness, in some cases, of the Church's manner of acting with the Jews throughout the years; or as to whether the various enactments, some of which were general laws, some local laws and others only regulations, were contrary to the principle that infidels cannot be bound by strictly ecclesiastical laws.

It may be gathered, however, from the material treated in this section that on occasions the Church was acting as an ecclesiastico-civil power because of a close union with the State as in Spain during the period of the Catholic Visigothic kings (586-712). On other occasions the Popes were legislating as the temporal rulers of the Papal States. On still others the Church was using its natural right of self-defense or carrying out its divine command to teach all nations.

There can be no denial that at times there were abuses in the manner in which the legislation was enforced, especially since the civil authorities were called upon often for assistance. And, as already noted, the laws were unpopular both with Jews and with some Catholics. A full explanation of the whole question is not within the scope of this work. Such an explanation would require a thorough investigation of the history of those times and an understanding of the ancient and the medieval mind. For the greater part of the time, and probably at all times even if she did not always appear to be doing so, the Church adhered to the principle that she has no direct spiritual jurisdiction over those who have never been validly baptized.

ARTICLE D. CATECHUMENS

In regard to catechumens there is available no special positive legislation showing their exemption from ecclesiastical laws. The point to be remembered, however, is that, because they are unbaptized, they are still infidels. They may have received the gift of Faith but they do not possess that bond of union with the Church which is acquired only through a valid Baptism of water. And because they are still classed as infidels, all that has been noted in the general section on infidels applied to them.

The following quotations will show just what status was given a catechumen in the early ages of Christianity when the catechumenate was an important institution in the Church. In fact, the elaborateness of the regulations for catechumens, the various stages of the catechumenate and the secrecy required by the *Disciplina Arcani* is evident proof of the Church's mind about catechumens.[136]

Some of the Fathers and writers of the early centuries of the Christian era gave to a catechumen the name *Christianus,* but they employed the word *Fidelis* to indicate a baptized person.

As early as the year 197 Tertullian[137] indicated the difference between a catechumen and one of the faithful. Speaking of some of the weaknesses of various heretical sects, he attacked especially their lack of regulation and

[136] Funk, *A Manual of Church History,* translated by P. Perciballi; edited by W. H. Kent, O.S.C. (2 vols., London: Burns, Oates & Washbourne, Ltd., 1931), I, 63, 65, 200, 201.

[137] *Liber De Praescriptionibus,* cap. XLI—*MPL,* II, 56.

discipline, saying: "In primis quis catechumenus, quis fidelis, incertum est."

Saint Augustine [138] also used the term *Christianus* for catechumens and gave the clear distinction between this term and the term *fidelis*. He noted that the catechumen has not yet received the Sacrament of Baptism.

A catechumen was considered as being in the same category as any other unbaptized person, i. e., outside of the congregation of the faithful.[139]

Saint Ambrose [140] warned Christians that they should not marry any unbaptized person. His words have been interpreted as though he included marriage with catechumens in this prohibition.[141]

Some of the early councils also made a distinction between catechumens and the faithful. The Council of Elvira (305) [142] stated that if a person had become a catechumen, even if he had not attended the church services for a long time, Baptism was not to be denied to him provided that some of the clergy or of the other members

138 *In Joannis Evangelium*, Tractatus XLIV, cap. IX, 2—*MPL*, XXXV, 1714: "Interroga hominem, Christianus es? Respondet tibi, Non sum, si Paganus est aut Judaeus. Si autem dixerit, Sum: adhuc quaeris ab eo, catechumenus, an fidelis? Si responderit, catechumenus; inunctus est, nondum lotus."

139 St. Joannis Chrysostomus, *Homilia XXV in Joannem*—Migne, *Patrologiae Cursus Completus, Series Graeca* (161 vols., Parisiis, 1856-1866), XIII, 151, n. 3: "Extraneus quippe est catechumenus fideli. Neque enim idem ipsum caput habet, non eamdem civitatem, ... sed omnia segregata." (Hereafter Migne, *Series Graeca*, will be quoted as *MPG*.)

140 C. 15, C. XVIII, q. 1: "Cave, Christiane, gentili aut iudaeo filiam tuam tradere. Cave, inquit [inquam], gentilem, aut iudaeam atque alienigenam, hoc est haereticam, et omnem alienam a fide tua uxorem accersas tibi. Prima coniugii fides gratia castitatis est. Si Christiana sit, non est satis, nisi ambo initiati sitis sacramento baptismatis ..."

141 Cf. S. C. C., *Brixien., Dubia baptismi et matrimonii*, § "Aliter"—*Thesaurus Resolutionum Sacrae Congregationis Concilii* (167 vols., Romae, 1718-1908), LXV (1796), 218.

142 Canon 45—*MPL*, LXXXIV, 306; Mansi, II, 13.

of the faithful knew that he was still a *Christian*. The same council [143] makes a clear distinction between the terms *fidelis* and *catechumena*.

The Council of Laodicaea (between 343 and 381) [144] forbade ordinations to be performed in the presence of catechumens. The I Council of Orange (441) [145] forbade catechumens to be admitted to the baptistry when others were being baptized and they were excluded from the blessings of the faithful.[146] About the same time (397) the III Council of Carthage [147] referred to some regulations of the Paschal season and made an evident distinction between catechumens and *fideles*.

The spurious *Capitula* attributed to Charlemagne (800-814) and Louis the Pius (co-regent with Charlemagne from 813-814; king from 814-840) [148] showed that distinction between baptized and unbaptized by not permitting the baptized to eat with the catechumens or to give them the "kiss of peace," or salute them with *ave*. This distinction became traditional.

Sanchez (1550-1610) [149] noted that the marriage of a baptized person with a catechumen would be invalid.

143 Canon 67—Mansi, II, 16.

144 Canon 4—Mansi, II, 585.

145 Canon 19—*MPL*, LXXXIV, 257; Hardouin, I, 1785-E; Mansi, VI, 439.

146 Canon 20—*MPL*, LXXXIV, 257; Hardouin, I, 1785-E; Mansi, VI, 439.

147 Canon 5—Mansi, III, 875.

148 *Liber Sextus*, cap. 93— Mansi, 17-B, 937; *MGH, Leges, Capitularia Spuria* (ed. G. H. Pertz, Hannoverae, 1837), II, pars II, 78. (As will be noted from this last citation, this *capitula* is listed under the spurious ones. It was among those which were received into the *Collection* of Benedictus Levita).

149 *Disputationum de Sancto Matrimonii Sacramento Libri Tres* (Antverpiae, 1626), tom. III, lib. VII, 236, n. 2: "Imo et inter personam baptisatam, et catechumenam est irritum matrimonium, eo quod catechumena baptismo, qui sacramentorum ianua est, careat, quamvis fidem teneat et in gratia constituta esse possit."

Suarez (1548-1617) [150] made a distinction between members of the Church and subjects of the Church. Because he held that faith made one a member of the Church, he considered both the faithful and the catechumens as members of the Church. He distinguished between them, however,[151] because he did not consider catechumens as subjects of the Church. He held that they became such only by baptism. He is evidently using the word *member* in the wide sense of one united to the rest of the faithful by the common bond of faith.

When the strict and minute rules of the catechumenate of the early ages of the Church were relaxed and the *Disciplina Arcani* was abandoned, these evidences of wide distinction between the catechumens and the faithful disappeared. The catechumenate or course of instruction for adult converts, of course, remained and still exists today. Also the fundamental distinction between the subjects of the Church and the unbaptized will always be present because, as has been noted already (p. xii), no one can be a member of a society in the true sense unless he has entered it by some formal procedure. The only means of becoming such a member of the Church is by Baptism.

The Sacred Congregation of the Council on August 27, 1796,[152] in speaking of the marriage of a baptized with an unbaptized person, even a catechumen, referred to the excerpt from Saint Ambrose already noted,[153] in which the Saint warned Christians that they should not marry any unbaptized person. The Congregation then quoted one of its own decrees issued September 26, 1623, in which are these words: " Sacra Congregatio censuit, matrimonium, ut

150 *Opera Omnia,* XII, p. 250, n. 18.

151 *Opera Omnia,* XX, p. 597, n. 9.

152 S.C.C., *Brixien., Dubia baptismi et matrimonii,* § "Aliter"—*Thesaurus Resolutionum Sacrae Congregationis Concilii,* LXV (1796), 218.

153 C. 15, C. XVIII, q. 1.

proponitur, cum infideli contractum nullum prorsus, atque irritum esse." Thus it showed that catechumens were still considered in the same class with infidels in regard to marriage with baptized persons and that no concessions were given to them because of the fact that they were under instruction to become Catholics.

In 1803 the Sacred Congregation for the Propagation of the Faith issued a decree [154] that a woman catechumen could not take advantage of the Pauline Privilege even though her infidel husband had repudiated her religion because the first marriage is not dissolved except by Baptism, i. e., there is no room for the dissolution of the marriage as long as Baptism has not been conferred.

These few citations, since they are typical, indicate that even though catechumens are united to the Church by the bond of faith, they are still treated as infidels, because they have not actually been admitted to the body of the Church by Baptism.

ARTICLE E. REFUTATION OF ADVERSE OPINION

It remains to be noted that aside from the laws affecting the Jews, there are some historical decrees that seem to indicate that the unbaptized were bound by purely ecclesiastical laws. And because of them some writers have held that all human beings are subject to these laws. Already a reference has been made to this opinion when an attempt was made to find some reason for the legislation concerning the Jews.

The first passage in the order of time is attributed to Pope Gelasius (492-496).[155] Found in a letter of his (February 1, 495) to the Bishops of Dardania (a region lying between

[154] S. C. de Prop. Fide (C. P. pro Sin. Pekini), 16 ian. 1803—*Fontes*, n. 4671; *Collect. S. C. de Prop. Fide* (2nd ed.), n. 665.

[155] C. 17, C. IX, q. 3; J K, n. 664: "Cuncta per mundum novit ecclesia, quod sacrosancta Romana ecclesia fas de omnibus habet iudicandi."

the provinces of Dalmatia and Thrace), it says in effect that the Holy Roman Church has the right of passing judgment in all matters.

The next one, found in canon 34 of the Council of Meaux (845),[156] seems to indicate that, without exception, the decrees of the canons were to be obeyed by all.

This idea was repeated in different words by Pope Gregory IX (1227-1241) in a letter to the Archpriest of Saint Mary Major in Rome (1227).[157]

Again in 1302 Pope Boniface VIII (1294-1303) inserted a similar passage in his Bull *Unam Sanctam.*[158]

Because of these passages the conclusion was drawn that even Jews and other infidels were subject to the ecclesiastical lawgiver and were obliged to obey ecclesiastical laws. This was based on the interpretation that the word *omnis* is general and excludes nothing.

Reiffenstuel[159] has given some kind of a refutation of this opinion. He said that, if the Pope exercised jurisdiction directly over all infidels, there would be no one outside the Church, and such a condition would be contradictory to the words of Saint Paul: "For what have I to do with judging those outside?" Reiffenstuel also denied this conclusion just stated above as being deducible from a consideration of the various texts, by stating that these texts refer exclusively to all those who are subject to the Church by Baptism, and not to all men alike whether or not they are baptized.

156 C. 1, X, *de constitutionibus*, I, 2: "Canonum statuta sine praeiudicio custodiantur ab omnibus..."

157 C. 13, X, *de constitutionibus*, I, 2.

158 C. 1, *de maioritate et obedientia*, I, 8, in Extrav. com.: Denzinger-Bannwart, *Enchiridion*, n. 468: "Porro subesse Romano Pontifici omni humanae creaturae declaramus, dicimus, definimus et pronuntiamus omnino esse de necessitate salutis."

159 *Ius Canonicum Universum*, lib. I, tit. II, nn. 283, 284.

If these texts are considered from the correct point of view it is evident that the first citation probably refers to Rome's primacy of jurisdicion over the whole Church. The second citation, which was addressed to the subjects of a particular district, could have been using the word *omnibus* in the sense of all those subject to the ecclesiastical authorities of that district by reason of their Baptism. Finally, the phrase from the Bull *Unam Sanctam* referred no doubt to the divine law obligation that all men have to embrace the Faith and thus to become subject to the Roman Pontiff, God's representative on earth. Finally, the Council of Trent stated definitely that the Church exercises judgment on no one who has not entered it through the gate of baptism.[160]

160 Sess. XIV, *de poenitentia*, cap. 2; Schroeder, *Canons and Decrees of the Council of Trent*, p. 90.

CHAPTER II

CHILDREN UNDER SEVEN YEARS OF AGE

As a result of investigation and research, it can be said safely that prior to the present Code of Canon Law the Church had enacted no legislation which specifically exempted baptized children under the age of seven from her strictly ecclesiastical laws. This statement is corroborated by Van Hove.[1]

Hence a treatment of the legislative provisions in this matter will have to proceed on analogies and general principles. A perusal of some of the legislative enactments touching on the legal liability of infants will show that many of the enactments were concerned with trying to define or set the age at which a child was able to reason enough to discern the difference between right and wrong.

In trying to determine this age theologians and canonists propounded divers opinions. Some set the age at seven years; others set it between ten and twelve years; still others set it approximately at eleven years.

Certain councils enacted canons in which such phrases as *the use of reason, the age of reason* or *the age of discretion* were employed, but, as far as can be determined, none of them gave even a precise definition of just what the phrase implied. It seems that most of these councils presupposed that this was generally known. A few examples of conciliar terminology and the views of selected writers will be cited in an endeavor to determine the age at which the use of reason usually was set. Through such a procedure one may perhaps discover the reason for the exemption, in the Code, of those under seven years of age.

[1] *De Legibus Ecclesiasticis*, p. 205.

An African Council held between the years 393 and 397 [2] prescribed the procedure to be followed when those who as infants had been baptized by the Donatists desired to enter the Church after they had reached the age of reason. It used the phrase: ". . . *posteaquam ad aetatem rationis capacem pervenerunt,*" but did not state at what age the capacity for reasoning was supposed to occur.

In the next century at a gathering of one hundred and fifty Bishops in Constantinople, called for the purpose of answering questions submitted by Bishops and clerics, a question was proposed [3] concerning the age at which God begins to judge a person guilty of sin. The response was that it depended on the knowledge and the prudence of each one—some were held guilty from the time they were ten years of age, but others only at a more advanced age.

In the same century Saint Augustine asserted [4] that the faculty of reason was indeed present in infants but that its operation remained dormant. He did not, however, indicate at which age this faculty reached the development necessary for its use by the person who possessed it.

One of the first express evidences of an assigned reason for the invalidity of acts performed by infants is found in the Council of London (1175),[5] which issued a prohibition against the custom by which very young children were espoused to each other. The reason given for the prohibi-

[2] Canon 24—Mansi, III, 763.

[3] Interrogatio XVIII—Mansi, III, 1254.

[4] Ep. XCVIII Bonifacio Episcopo [probably of Cataquas near the present location of Bona]: ". . . . ita potuit Omnipotens per infantis animam, non ubi ratio nulla est, sed ubi adhuc sopita erat . . ."—*MPL,* XXXIII, 361, n. 4. (Cf. also a passage from Pseudo-Augustine in c. 3, C. XV, q. 1: "Sacramentum fidei, quod est sanctum baptisma, quamdiu rationis aetas eorum capax esse non potest, sufficere ad salutem.")

[5] Canon 19: "Ubi non est consensus utriusque, non est conjugium. Ergo qui pueris dant puellas in cunabulis, nihil faciunt, nisi uterque puerorum, postquam venerit ad tempus discretionis, consentiat."—Mansi, XXI, 152.

tion was the lack of consent by the parties. This indicated that they were not capable of giving true consent to espousals before they reached the age of discretion, which the council indeed mentioned but did not define. The phrase *tempus discretionis* as it is used in the conciliar decree could point to that maturity of understanding which supposes more than just the use of reason. Canon 1081, § 2 would substantiate this latter observation.

About the same time Pope Alexander III (1159-1181) gave a response [6] to the Bishop of Hereford in England in answer to a question on the matter of espousals made by the parents of a girl who was still below the age of seven. He stated: ". . . desponsationes huiusmodi nullae sint, quae in cunabulis fiunt." The heading with which this decretal is introduced gives as a reason for the nullity the lack of consent on the part of the girl.

The same Pontiff sent a similar response [7] to the Archbishop of York in England.

These two answers stated that the espousals and marriages of persons below the age of seven were null because those under that age could not give true consent to them. The answers, however, do not indicate that children immediately after they have passed the age of seven would be considered as capable of giving true consent to espousals or marriage. The Pope simply pointed out that prior to the age of seven children could not give that consent. The manner in which he mentioned this age does not indicate that the Pope was setting seven as the age of discretion. Still he may have considered seven as the age at which children usually had the use of reason for he indicated that

[6] C. 4, X, *de desponsatione impuberum*, IV, 2.

[7] C. 5, X, *de desponsatione impuberum*, IV, 2: ". . . desponsationes et matrimonia ante septem annos fieri non possunt, praesertim si consensus postea non accedit . . ."

at sometime after this age children were presumed to be able to give true consent to espousals and marriage.

The question of just when the age of discretion or the age of reason occurred began to be discussed most profusely after the issuance, at the IV General Council of the Lateran (1215), of the canon *Omnis utriusque sexus* which legislated on annual confession and Communion.[8] One phrase in it—*postquam ad annos discretionis pervenerit*—was not definite enough and needed interpretation.

The gloss to the word *discretionis*[9] explained it as the age at which a child is *capax doli,* because then he is able to commit sin.

Many contemporary writers of that time interpreted the phrase *postquam ad annos discretionis pervenerit* as meaning when a child had reached the age of seven years,[10] because they considered a child of that age *capax doli,* i. e., capable of willing deliberately to violate the law.[11] They attributed to such a child the capacity to give consent, to enter valid espousals and to commit sin.

There were some at that time[12] who spoke of nine or ten as being the age at which a child was *capax doli,* but they admitted that the age varied according to the individual mental development of each child. This was the principal

[8] Canon 21: "Omnis utriusque sexus fidelis, *postquam ad annos discretionis pervenerit,* omnia sua solus peccata saltem semel in anno fideliter confiteatur proprio sacerdoti, et iniunctam sibi poenitentiam pro viribus studeat adimplere, suscipiens reverenter ad minus in Pascha Eucharistiae sacramentum..."—C. 12, X, *de poenitentiis et remissionibus,* V, 38; Denzinger-Bannwart, *Enchiridion,* n. 437.

[9] Glossa ad c. 12, X, *de poenitentiis et remissionibus,* V, 38, ad v. *discretionis*: "...id est, cum est doli capax: quia tunc potest peccare..."

[10] Cf. Gillmann, "Die '*anni discretionis*' im Kanon *Omnis utriusque sexus*"—*Archiv für katholisches Kirchenrecht,* CVIII (1928), 556-617, esp. pp. 560, 564, 570. (The *Archiv* hereafter will be cited in the abbreviated form *AKKR*.)

[11] Cf. Canon 2200, § 1, regarding the attitude of the present law on *dolus*.

[12] *AKKR, loc. cit.*

point in controversy because the variation in the mental development made it impossible to settle upon a definite age. All that could be settled was the time at which this *capacitas doli* usually obtained.

After its initial promulgation canon 21 of the IV General Council of the Lateran was repeatedly promulgated by many Bishops and particular synods,[13] if not in the same at least in a similar form.

The Council of Tarragona (1320) [14] quoted the *Omnis utriusque sexus* canon, but gave the years of discretion as fourteen for a boy and twelve for a girl. This was relatively a very high age but since there had been no official explanation of the phrase *annos discretionis* the various bishops probably interpreted it diversely in order to accommodate the law to the accepted usages and habits of their people.

The Council of Trent on November 25, 1551,[15] renewed this canon 21 of the IV General Council of the Lateran and retained the original phraseology regarding the years of discretion.

In 1866 the II Plenary Council of Baltimore [16] conformed to the Council of Trent in this matter.

Finally, the present Code of Canon Law [17] incorporated

[13] Council of Toulouse (1229), cap. 13—Mansi, XXIII, 197; Council of Sens (1269), c. 4—Mansi, XXIV, 5; Hardouin, VII, 650; Council of Saint Omer (1279), c. 5—Mansi, XXIV, 222; Hardouin, VII, 767; Council of Münster (1279), cap. 17—Mansi, XXIV, 318; Council of Beziers (1286), cap. 13—Mansi, XXIV, 632; Synodal Precepts of the Church of Constance (1300), n. 33—Mansi, XXV, 37; Council of Benevento (1331), cap. 66—Mansi, XXV, 971.

[14] Cap. 67: "... ad annos discretionis, masculus videlicet ad XIV, femina vero ad XII pervenerint..."—Mansi, XXV, 870.

[15] Sess. XIV, *de poenitentia*, can. 5.

[16] *Concilii Plenarii Baltimorensis II, Acta et Decreta* (Baltimore, 1868), n. 276.

[17] Canons 859, § 1; 906.

the decree *Omnis utriusque sexus* among its canons, but divided it into two canons. It also qualified the phrase *annos discretionis* with the phrase *idest ad rationis usum.*

Another matter that involved the question of the age of reason had to do with giving Holy Communion to children. There are several examples of canons that regulated this matter.

Canon 21 of the IV General Council of the Lateran (1215) [18] required those who had reached the years of discretion to go to Holy Communion at least at Easter. A particular council in 1235 [19] prohibited priests from giving the Sacred Host to children under seven years of age. The Synod of Bayeux (1300) [20] enacted the same prohibition.

There were other references to the age of discretion and to a certain mental debility in children under seven years of age.

In 1284 the Synod of Nîmes [21] issued a *Liber Synodalis.* In the chapter titled: *De Sponsalibus et Matrimonio,* it treated of the invalidity of espousals made when one or both parties were under seven years of age. This indicated that children were at least considered as not being able to give true consent to espousals before they reached the age of seven. The Council of Basel [22] issued in 1434 a decree ordering the ecclesiastical authorities to compel Jews and infidels to attend instructions on Christian doctrine. The authorities were to effect their purpose by forbidding the faithful to do business with those who refused to come.

[18] C. 12, X, *de poenitentiis et remissionibus,* V, 38; Densinger-Bannwart, *Enchiridion,* n. 437.

[19] Ancient Precepts of the Diocese of Rouen, cap. 19: "Prohibetur presbyteris ne hostias dent pueris ullo modo infra septennium constitutis."—Mansi, XXIII, 375.

[20] Cap. 16—Mansi, XXV, 63.

[21] Mansi, XXIV, 548.

[22] Sess. XIX, cap. 5—Hardouin, VIII, 1190; Mansi, XXIX, 98.

This provision applied to all Jews and infidels who had reached the age of discretion, but it did not note any specific age in years.

Pope Benedict XIV (1740-1758) [23] in speaking of the age required for the reception of First Tonsure, stated that only those who were endowed with the use of reason were to be initiated with it into the ranks of the clergy, and that such use of one's reason was presumed to be present in one's seventh year.

In his letter *Postremo mense* [24] issued February 28, 1747, the same Pope noted that the use of reason ordinarily is attained when a person has completed the first seven years of his life. He added, however, that sufficient use of reason could be present before the child reached seven years of age.

Schmalzgrueber (1663-1735) [25] wrote that children who do not possess the use of reason are not bound by ecclesiastical laws. He stated that the use of reason is usually present after a child has completed seven years of age and that this use of reason is the basis for obligation to ecclesiastical laws.

Some writers in the eighteenth century [26] held that children were obliged by ecclesiastical laws even before they reached the age of seven, provided that they had attained the use of reason. But Saint Alphonsus considered as probable the opinion which held that such children were not obliged by ecclesiastical laws. This latter opinion became the more common opinion in the nineteenth century. It received some confirmation from the response of the Sacred Penitentiary on March 15, 1837: [27] " Pueros post

[23] Instr. *Eo quamvis tempore*, 4 maii 1745, § 19—*Fontes*, n. 357.

[24] § 2—*Fontes*, n. 377; Ferraris, *Bibliotheca*, VI, s. v., " usus rationis," n. 1.

[25] *Jus Ecclesiasticum Universum* (5 vols. in 12, Romae, 1843-1845), lib. I, tit. II, n. 35.

[26] Cf. St. Alphonsus Liguori, *Theologia Moralis*, ed. M. Sanchez, 2 vols. in 1, Matriti, 1876), lib. I, n. 155.

[27] *Fontes*, n. 6424; Van Hove, *De Legibus Ecclesiasticis*, p. 206.

septennium [completum] teneri observare qualitatem ciborum ab Ecclesia praescriptorum." Since this response uses the words *post septennium* it evidently means seven years complete and thereby it implicitly indicates that children under the age of seven were not held to observe the quality of foods prescribed by the Church, even though they had reached the use of reason before they attained that age.

Finally, in 1910 the Sacred Congregation of the Sacraments [28] decided that the age of discretion relative to the reception of the sacraments of Penance and of Holy Communion came around the seventh year of age and that as soon as it was present the obligations of the yearly confession and of the reception of the Paschal Communion arose.[29]

The examples quoted above have been set down in order to show that the question of the use of reason as a basis of subjection to ecclesiastical laws had been variously considered by divers authorities. Most of them left it in the stage of vagueness and controversy possibly because they regarded it as something that depended upon the extreme variability of human mental development.

The IV General Council of the Lateran in 1215 intensified the uncertainty of the problem with its *Omnis utriusque sexus* canon, in which the age of discretion was mentioned. The majority of the writers who treated the question after the issuance of that canon held that the age of discretion occurred when the child was *capax doli,* or around the

[28] Decr. 8 aug. 1910—*AAS,* II (1910), 577-583; *Fontes,* n. 2103.

[29] In the decree *Quam singulari* of the Sacred Congregation of the Sacraments which has just been cited there are many historical points about the reception of Holy Communion by infants; about the regulations of various sections of the Church which required that First Holy Communion be postponed until a child was ten, twelve or fourteen years of age. But since the interpretation of the phrase *aetas discretionis* is the point under discussion here only the interpretation of this phrase as given in this decree has been cited.

seventh year of age, that is, at the age when the normal child began to reason.

It must be remembered, however, that the whole idea of exemption from law for those who do not enjoy the use of reason is based on the concept that human acts cannot be posited without the use of intellect and free will.[30] Consequently, a baptized person who does not have the use of reason cannot be actually bound by strictly ecclesiastical laws or to any law, for he cannot understand them nor can he carry them out properly.[31]

[30] Ballerini-Palmieri, *Opus Theologicum Morale* (3. ed., 7 vols., Prati, 1898-1901), I, 1.

[31] Ojetti, *Commentarium in Codicem Iuris Canonici*, I, 102.

CHAPTER III

Persons Lacking the Use of Reason

Much that has been noted in the foregoing article applies also in the present one, inasmuch as every human being must normally go through a period of mental and physical development before he can perform human acts. This period varies, but, as has been noted, it usually presupposes a duration of about seven years from the time of one's birth. No minimum period can definitely be set. Those who show precocious mental development prior to their seventh year in life are exceptions. For this reason it may be stated that a person who has a normal mental and physical development from the time of his birth usually has attained a sufficient use of reason for the performance of human acts when he is about seven years of age. A person who has never passed through this normal state of mental development, even though he has made normal progress physically and has achieved the physical development of a mature man, is considered to be still an infant mentally.

As may be seen very easily, there are varying stages of mental development both before and after the so-called age of reason. Experience shows this even apart from further scientific investigations into the matter. It is probable that the absence of actual legislation in the matter of exempting from ecclesiastical laws those who lacked the use of reason was caused by the fact that the ordinary person could for the greater part in his own experience detect the lack of normal reasoning power in mentally sub-normal human beings, and could thus readily realize that they were not entirely responsible for their acts and hence not amenable to law as a rational norm for the regulation of their actions.

As has been stated previously, the use of reason connotes the employment of the intellect and the free will in the performance of a human act. The lack of the power to do this indicates that one does not have the use of reason—the amount of the deficiency varies with each abnormal individual. Hence it is evident just how complicated a matter confronted the legislator. To avoid these complications as far as possible the treatment of this article will stress only the practice of the Church in dealing with various kinds of mentally deficient persons.

Those who were not perpetually without the use of reason, i. e., insane persons who had lucid intervals, as a general rule were obliged to human laws although there were several ways in which their obligation was explained. They were not absolutely excused from obeying the law, for at times they were capable of obeying it when they had lucid intervals. At the moment when they were really insane, of course, they were not responsible for their actions. Those, however, who were perpetually insane were not held to human laws for they were perpetually incapable of using the powers of their reason.[1] These are the generally accepted basic divisions according to which authors determine the exemption of adults who do not have the use of reason.

The distinction between those who are habitually insane and those who have lucid intervals was made already in Roman Law.[2]

One of the first instances of legal restrictions on insane persons in the use of the benefits acknowledged by law is found in a decree of Pope Fabian (236-250).[3] The Pope stated therein that *furiosi,* i. e., the violently insane, could not contract marriage. That probably meant that he for-

[1] Ferraris, *Bibliotheca,* V, s. v. "lex", nn. 9, 10.

[2] C. (6.22) 9; C. (5.70) 6.

[3] J K, n. 97; Mansi, I, 785.

bade them to marry. But he added that if they nevertheless entered upon marriage they were not to be separated. By this he probably meant that, if they really contracted marriage by giving a true marital consent during a lucid interval, they were not to be separated.

In 441 the I Council of Orange [4] passed a regulation about the mentally deficient, but as it stands the meaning is not clear. The canon reads: " Amentibus quaecumque pietatis sunt conferenda." These same words appeared in a canon of the Council of Arles (443) a few years later: [5] " Subito obmutescens baptizari potest: et amentibus quaecumque pietatis sunt conferenda." In these words there seemed to be an acknowledgment of the right of a disabled person because of the connection with the right to Baptism of the person who had become mute suddenly. Still the meaning is not clear. Both the councils may simply have been directing that all pious offices be performed towards insensible persons.

Pope Nicholas I (858-867) in an answer to the Archbishop of Sens (ca. 858) [6] indicated indirectly that, if a certain accused Bishop was not of sound mind, he should not be punished for the grave offenses of which, on several occasions, he had been accused.

Gratian in his *Decretum* has a section treating of insane persons and offers some general principles concerning the imputability of their actions. There is one canon [7] which stated that a *furiosus* cannot perpetrate a true injury, i. e., one which is morally imputable, because he is not *capax doli.* Gratian in his *dictum* to this canon gave the reasons: One who is *non sui compos* cannot contract any guilt, be-

[4] Canon 13—Mansi, VI, 438.

[5] Canon 38—Mansi, VII, 883.

[6] C. 14, C. III, q. 9; J E, n. 2674.

[7] C. 2, C. XV, q. 1.

cause he does not have the faculty of deliberating over what he is about to do.

In another chapter[8] it was noted that certain persons who had become suddenly insane and thereupon had harmed and even killed people could not be held responsible inasmuch as they did not act voluntarily. They were moved by impulses which caused them to act without a knowledge of what they were doing. The canon concluded with a rhetorical question which asked how a person could be considered as a culprit if he did not know what he had done.

Farther on in the *Decretum*[9] it was stated that those acts which did not involve the mind or bind the conscience could not be considered evil. This decision, like the others, concerned the imputability of outwardly evil actions performed by insane persons, and indicated that the insane could not place morally evil actions because they did not advert to what they were doing and did not act contrary to their consciences.

Gratian's conclusions regarding the imputability of the external crimes of insane persons are contained in several of his *dicta* in this section of his work. In one such *dictum*[10] he stated: "Cum itaque qui invitus hominem interfecerit minister Dei sit, cum innocentem furore perimens morti nequaquam obnoxius sit, cum subito dementes eorum, quae faciunt, reatum minime gestent, patet hunc sacerdotem homicidii reum non esse, unde nec sacerdotio privari debet."

He then contraposed to this conclusion an objection taken from the Penitential of Theodore:[11] "Si quis insaniens aliquem occiderit, si ad sanam mentem pervenerit,

[8] C. 5, C. XV, q. 1.

[9] C. 6, C. XV, q. 1.

[10] Ad c. 11, C. XV, q. 1.

[11] Ad c. 12, C. XV, q. 1.

levior ei poenitentia imponenda est." But he upheld his original conclusion that the violently insane are not responsible for their actions by replying thus:

> Sed hoc forte de eo intelligitur, quem propria culpa ad furorem perduxit. Item objicitur: Sunt quaedam, quae, etsi non imputentur ad poenam, tamen impediunt sacramenti signaculum. Ambitio namque parentum filio non imputatur ad poenam, cui tamen obest ad ecclesiae munus accipiendum. Sic quae mente alienata fiunt, etsi non imputentur ad poenam, tamen sacri muneris executionem impediunt.

On the matter of the imputability of crimes performed by insane persons Kuttner[12] treats at length the opinions of the earlier Glossators of Gratian's Decree. In his work he notes the opinion of Huguccio († 1210): [13] " Huguccio dicit quod si furiosus ignoret factum in essentia, non imputatur ei, sed si sciat factum in essentia et non modum facti, bene imputatur ei . . ." Also: [14] ". . . tempore furoris nec matrimonium potest contrahere nec aliquem contractum, qui consensum exigat, celebrare; nec tempore intermissionis, quia furiosi nullus est consensus." Kuttner also quotes the opinion of Vincentius Hispanus who taught from 1212-1230: [15] ". . . saepe enim furiosi sunt in umbrata quiete, et tunc qui tali tradit possessionem, non transfert eam; . . . si tamen in dilucidis intervallis contraheret, valeret matrimonium."

In a letter to the Bishop of Vercelli on December 28, 1205,[16] Pope Innocent III (1198-1216) noted a case in which

[12] *Kanonistische Schuldlehre von Gratian bis auf die Dekretalen Gregors IX*, Studi e Testi, n. 64 (Città del Vaticano: Bibliotheca Apostolica Vaticana, 1935), pp. 94, 95, footnotes 1 and 2.

[13] Ad c. 5, C. XV, q. 1.

[14] Ad c. 5, C. XV, q. 1.

[15] Ad c. 4, Comp. III, *De Spon. et Matr.*, IV, 1.

[16] C. 24, X, *de sponsalibus et matrimoniis*, IV, 1; Potthast, n. 2634.

a woman had married a *furiosus*. He plainly indicated that a violently insane person could not give the required marital consent. As a result he instructed the Bishop to separate the parties, if the fact of the man's insanity was established.

Abbas Panormitanus (1386-1453) in his gloss [17] to this letter of Pope Innocent III considered the reasons which barred the insane person from contracting marriage: "Si tempore contracti matrimonii taliter laborat, non fuit matrimonium . . . Potest dici quod ille tempore contractus erat furiosus, et pater iste et filia ignorabant illum furiosum: Saepe enim furiosi sunt constituti in conspectu umbrae quietis . . . nec tamen sunt mentis sanae, licet videantur: et tunc mulier ista quae cum eo contraxit, non tenuit matrimonium et si hoc probaverit, separabuntur."

A National Synod of Strigonia (ca. 1114) [18] ruled against idiots being ordained priests. The apparent reason seemed to point to their inability to acquire the necessary knowledge, but the language is not altogether clear and it is not unmistakably evident in what sense the word *idiotae* may have been used. At the Council of Vienne (1311-1312) Pope Clement V (1305-1314) enacted a ruling [19] which excused a violently insane person from incurring the irregularity which was contracted by the mutilating or killing of a man. But in the twelfth century Gratian seems to have held the opposite opinion in the matter of incurring an irregularity for such a crime. He, however, may have been referring rather to the irregularity of insanity than to the irregularity that arose from the commission of homicide.

In 1693 the Provincial Synod of Benevento [20] distinguished between insane persons who had the partial use of their reason and could show a certain amount of devotion

[17] Ad v. *furore*.

[18] Cap. 6—Mansi, XXI, 99.

[19] C. un., *de homicidio voluntario vel casuali*, V, 4, in Clem.

[20] Title XXXV, cap. 12—*Collectio Lacensis*, I, 68-b.

for the Holy Eucharist on the one hand and insane persons who were totally deprived of the use of their reason and could show no such devotion on the other. Only in relation to the former did the Council decree that Holy Communion could be given.

With regard to the administration of the sacrament of extreme unction, the Provincial Synod of Naples (1699) ruled that it should not be denied to those who were insane from infancy if in the course of their lives they had lucid intervals.[21] In the year 1850 the Provincial Council of Sens[22] permitted the Holy Eucharist to be given to the insane at those times when they had lucid intervals.

Regulations regarding the administration of Baptism to those not having the use of reason were passed by the II Plenary Council of Baltimore in 1866.[23] In them the Council noted that those who were insane from birth and never had lucid intervals were to be considered as infants and were to be baptized as such. If, however, they had lucid intervals, they had to express a desire for Baptism during one of those intervals before they could be baptized. If before they became insane they had expressed a desire for Baptism and later they were in danger of death, they were to be baptized, even though they were not of sound mind. The same Council[24] ruled that the sacrament of extreme

[21] Title III, cap. 6, n. 6—*Collectio Lacensis,* II, 188-a.

[22] Title III, cap. 4—*Collectio Lacensis,* IV, 890-b.

[23] *Concilii Plenarii Baltimorensis II Acta et Decreta* (Baltimorae, 1868), n. 230; *Collectio Lacensis,* III, 459-c: "Amentes et furiosi non baptizentur, nisi tales a nativitate fuerint; tunc enim de iis idem judicium faciendum est, quod de infantibus, atque in fide Ecclesiae baptizari possunt. Sed si dilucida habeant intervalla, dum mentis compotes sunt, baptizentur, si velint. Si vero antequam insanirent, suscipiendi Baptismi desiderium ostenderint, ac vitae periculum immineat, etiamsi non sint compotes mentis, baptizentur . . ."

[24] *Concilii Plenarii Baltimorensis II Acta et Decreta,* n. 309; *Collectio Lacensis,* III, 481, b, c.

unction was not to be administered to the perpetually insane.

In 1899 the Sacred Congregation of the Council [25] declared null a marriage in which the woman was mentally unbalanced both before and after the ceremony. The decision was based on the inability of an insane person to elicit the consideration and advertence of the intellect and the deliberation of the will necessary for marital consent.

Just prior to the promulgation of the present Code of Canon Law the Sacred Roman Rota [26] declared null a marriage in which one party was insane prior to and following the ceremony. In giving the legal background of the decision the Rota indicated what was required in the consent that makes a valid marriage: There must be a free choice by the will preceded by rational cognition or understanding of what is about to be done. These are necessary for any human act. Then it was noted that the insane are incapable of such a mental procedure, and therefore must be prevented from attempting to contract marriage. In substantiation of this statement the Rota quoted from the above-mentioned letter of Pope Innocent III to the Bishop of Vercelli (Dec. 28, 1205).[27]

From these various citations it may be noted that the distinction between those who were perpetually insane and those who at times enjoyed lucid intervals was plainly indicated several times. The reasons for the nullity of the acts performed by insane persons were connected with the following factors: insufficient use of reason and of free will; inability to realize that acts are good or bad; inability to give true consent; no ability to elicit a desire for Baptism;

[25] S.C.C., *Treviren.*, 22 iul. 1899—*Analecta Ecclesiastica*, VII (1899), 343-349.

[26] S.R.R., *Nullitas matrimonii*, 15 maii 1915, coram R.P.D. I. Prior, *AAS*, VII (1915), 572-587.

[27] C. 24, X, *de sponsalibus et matrimoniis*, IV, 1; Potthast, n. 2634.

no capacity for distinguishing the Holy Eucharist from common bread.

These factors constitute also self-evident reasons on account of which such persons were exempted from ecclesiastical legislation except for some specific cases as noted in the law. The very fact, for example, that the perpetually insane were not permitted to receive Holy Communion actually exempted them from the law which required the reception of Paschal Communion even though fundamentally they were still bound to the law by reason of their previous Baptism. Other reasons exempting them from subjection to the law based on the causes just noted were the inability of such persons to understand either the law itself or its purpose, and the inability to direct their actions toward obedience to the law.

Some of the decisions noted in this section ignored the lucid intervals as being only *umbrata quies.*[28] Such a view would probably hold a man perpetually insane whose lucid intervals were few and transient, whereas he whose periods of insanity were few and transient would be regarded as competent and subject to the law, except of course when it was evident that he was insane when he performed an action.

[28] E. g., the opinion of Vincentius Hispanus on c. 4, Comp. III, *De Spon. et Matr.*, IV, 1, as noted on page 69.

PART II

CANONICAL COMMENTARY

CHAPTER IV

The Unbaptized Not Bound by Strictly Ecclesiastical Laws

Article A. Explanation of Terms

In the canonical commentary on canon 12 of the present Code of Canon Law the text of the canon will be divided according to its three principal clauses and each clause will be developed separately. This is necessary because of the amount of material to be treated in connection with each clause, and it will at the same time tend to offset the confusion that might arise if the canon were treated as a whole.

The first of these clauses gives consideration to the unbaptized and the question of their obligation to purely ecclesiastical laws:

" Legibus mere ecclesiasticis non tenentur qui baptismum non receperunt. . . ."

It is to be learned partly from divine law and partly from the will of the human legislator who are subject to ecclesiastical laws. By divine law only those who have been baptized validly are members of the Church of Christ on earth and subject to its laws. This is true because Baptism is the door by which one enters the House of God, i. e., the Church.[1] But over those who have never received Baptism or who have not received it validly the Church does not have jurisdiction. This was aptly phrased by Saint Paul[2] in these words: ". . . For what have I to do with judging those outside? ", i. e., those who are not members of the Church. And the reason is that unbaptized persons have

[1] Blat, *Commentarium Textus Codicis Iuris Canonici,* (6 vols., Vol. I, Romae: ex Typographia Pontificia in Instituto Pii IX, 1921), I, 85. (Hereafter quoted as Blat, *Commentarium*).

[2] I Cor. V: 12.

never become members of this ecclesiastical society and hence have never submitted themselves to the Church's authority, which of course can be exercised only over those who are within its membership.[3] Canon 12, therefore, states that those who are not baptized [validly] are not subject to purely ecclesiastical laws.

By the word *legibus* the canon points to laws in the strict sense, that is, to laws enacted by a duly-recognized law-giver, and not merely to precepts, regulations or ordinances given for particular groups whose superior has not strict law-making power or authority. The term connotes laws of any kind, whether they be affirmative or prohibitive; universal or particular; preceptive or purely penal.[4]

The phrase *mere ecclesiasticis* indicates that the power of obligating in the laws in question comes directly from ecclesiastical authority alone. The Code by mentioning *merely ecclesiastical laws* intends to distinguish them from natural and positive divine laws as well as from those which, though formulated or more closely determined by human authority, are reflexively called divine laws, e. g., the threefold division of the clergy into bishops, priests and ministers (Canon 108, § 3). As examples of merely ecclesiastical laws there are irregularities, clearly determined penalties, certain matrimonial impediments, and the law of fasting and abstinence on certain days.[5] The canon treats of only purely ecclesiastical laws and not of the natural or positive divine laws by which the unbaptized are bound and by

[3] C. 8, X, *de divortiis,* IV 19—Potthast, n. 1325: ". . . qui [pagani] constitutionibus canonicis non arctantur . . . ;" Conc. Trident., sess. XIV, *de poenitentia,* c. 2. (Both of these citations quote the phrase of Saint Paul just noted above).

[4] Cicognani, *Canon Law* (2. ed., revised [Authorized English Version by Rev. Joseph M. O'Hara and Rev. Francis Brennan], Philadelphia: Dolphin Press, 1935), pp. 530, 531.

[5] Augustine, *A Commentary on the New Code of Canon Law* (8 vols., St. Louis, 1918-1922), I, 87.

which those who are without sufficient use of reason as well as children below the age of seven are obliged at least potentially.[6]

Continuing with the explanation of the words of Canon 12 one must note that the words *non tenentur* indicate that infidels are not obliged directly by strictly ecclesiastical laws, but that they may be obliged indirectly by reason of the subjection to ecclesiastical laws on the part of baptized persons with whom the infidels enter into certain relationships. Purely ecclesiastical matrimonial impediments, therefore, even though only the baptized party may have incurred them, render his marriage with an unbaptized person either illicit or invalid,[7] i. e., unless a dispensation is obtained.

Likewise certain natural bonds or civil impediments which form the basis of ecclesiastical impediments if they were contracted while the parties were still infidels, will not give rise to an ecclesiastical impediment so long as these unbaptized parties remain infidels, but if they receive Baptism these natural bonds or civil impediments will become ecclesiastical impediments also, and then affect the convert the same as they do any other baptized person, e. g., the impediment of consanguinity in the second or third degree of the collateral line.[8]

Baptismum here means valid Baptism of water (*Baptismus fluminis*) and Baptism in regard to its juridical effects only.[9] But when there is a question of juridical effects the idea of juridical personality must be considered. A human person, insofar as he is subject to the law of nature, may be juridically defined as the subject of rights and duties. And

[6] Van Hove, *De Legibus Ecclesiasticis,* p. 194.

[7] Canon 1036, § 3.

[8] Van Hove, *De Legibus Ecclesiasticis,* pp. 196-197.

[9] Coronata, *Institutiones Iuris Canonici,* I, 132.

this definition may be applied to every man.[10] In civil law today, except in regard to certain political rights, all persons whether they be subjects or externs are persons in law.[11] In the United States, however, there is an exception inasmuch as aliens cannot own property. As far as certain political rights are concerned, citizenship is required.[12] But in order that one may be designated as a *persona Christiana* in the Catholic Church valid Baptism is required.[13]

ARTICLE B. PRELIMINARY NOTIONS

a) *Various Kinds of Baptism*

Among theologians three kinds of baptism are recognized —baptism of water (*fluminis*); baptism of desire (*flaminis*); and baptism of blood (*sanguinis*).[14] But the only one of these that constitutes the sacrament is baptism of water—by immersion, infusion, or aspersion.[15] Baptism of desire or of blood is sufficient for salvation, but neither of these two makes one a member and a subject of the visible Church on earth. Baptism of blood purifies a man through his act

[10] Claeys-Bouuaert et Simenon, *Manuale Juris Canonici ad Usum Seminariorum* (3 vols., Gandae et Leodii: prostat apud Auctores in Seminariis Gandavensi et Leodiensi, 1930-1931), I, 137. (From now on quoted as *Manuale Juris Canonici*).

[11] Cocchi, *Commentarium in Codicem Iuris Canonici ad Usum Scholarum,* (5 vols. in 8, Vol. II, 4. ed., Taurinorum Augustae: Marietti, 1937), II, 14; (quoted hereafter as *Commentarium*); Maroto, *Institutiones Iuris Canonici ad Normam Novi Codicis,* I, 456, n. 391 and footnote 2. (In future quoted as *Institutiones Iuris Canonici*).

[12] Claeys-Bouuaert et Simenon, *Manuale Juris Canonici,* I, 137. (Such a right, e. g., is the right to vote).

[13] Canon 87; Claeys-Bouuaert et Simenon, *Manuale Juris Canonici,* I, 137; Cocchi, *Commentarium,* II, 14.

[14] Tanquerey, *Synopsis Theologiae Dogmaticae* (3 vols., Vol. III, 23. ed., Parisiis: Typis Societatis Sancti Joannis Evangelistae [Desclée et Socii], 1934), III, 318.

[15] Canons 758; 737, § 1.

of martyrdom for his faith; baptism of desire cleanses the soul through the internal act of perfect love or of perfect contrition which has united with it the earnest desire to receive baptism of water.[16] But, as has already been stated in the preliminary discussion preceding the historical part of this work, entrance into the visible society established by Christ as His Church is effected solely by means of a visible ceremony, namely, by the reception of valid baptism of water. This baptism must be received not only as a factual ceremony but also as a valid sacramental rite.[17] Baptism of blood and desire, although they may be sufficient for supplying the theological effects of baptism of water, are certainly not sufficient for producing the juridical effects because they surely are not Sacraments and do not imprint an indelibile character on the soul.[18]

b) *Classes of Non-Baptized Persons*

In relation to Canon 12 the unbaptized include: Pagans who have no formal religion even though they may believe in the existence of some kind of a supreme being; infidels who profess some formal religion but who have never received Christian Baptism. Such are chiefly the Mohammedans and the Jews; the Buddhists, the Confucianists and members of the smaller non-Christian religions; finally, Catechumens [19] who, although in a theological sense, they may have been favored with the gift of Faith, are nevertheless considered in a juridical sense as infidels inasmuch as they have not as yet been visibly united to the Church by the sacramental bond of baptism.

16 Tanquerey, *Synopsis Theologiae Dogmaticae,* III, 318; Claeys-Bouuaert et Simenon, *Manuale Juris Canonici,* I, 137.

17 Canon 87; Blat, *Commentarium,* I, 85.

18 Coronata, *Institutiones Iuris Canonici,* I, 132.

19 Payen, *De Matrimonio,* II, n. 1843.

There may be an objection raised that catechumens are bound to the Church's regulations concerning the catechumenate or the time of preparation for Baptism. At first consideration this objection may appear to have some foundation. Still an explanation of the binding force of the law prescribing the procedure is easily made by this distinction: These regulations of the catechumenate bind the priests of the Church *per modum legis,* but they bind the catechumens only *per modum conditionis.*[20] That is, the few rules governing the present-day catechumenate are laid down as conditions that must be fulfilled by the prospective convert before he may be admitted to Baptism. And his admission into the Church depends upon his fulfillment of these conditions. Hence it can be seen that these rules of the catechumenate have no *legal* force for those who wish to enter the Church.

One of the chief proofs that catechumens are considered as infidels is obtained from the response of the Sacred Congregation for the Propagation of the Faith.[21] It stated that a woman catechumen could not take advantage of the Pauline Privilege even though her infidel husband had repudiated the Christian religion which she wished to embrace. The reason given was that there was no reason for the dissolution of the marriage as long as Baptism has not been conferred.

Another indirect evidence that catechumens are still considered as being outside the true fold seems to be given in canon 1239, § 2, of the Code. The law expressed in that canon grants them the special privilege of Christian burial if through no fault of their own they have died without receiving the sacrament of Baptism. The very fact that

[20] Michiels, *Normae Generales Juris Canonici* (2 vols., Lublin [Polonia]: Universitas Catholica, 1929), I, 284. (In future quoted as *Normae Generales*).

[21] S. C. de Prop. Fide (C. P. pro Sin.—Pekin.), 16 ian. 1803—*Fontes,* n. 4671; *Collect. S. C. de Prop. Fide,* n. 665.

they are specially mentioned in this matter is an indication that they had no inherent legal right to Christian burial. The law suggests that even the baptism of desire, which in all probability they received, does not entitle them to the legal right which is granted only as a consequence of sacramental baptism.[22] If they had to be considered as Catholics in this matter they would not only enjoy the right of Christian burial without a special concession but there would also be the duty to grant it to them,[23] and there would be no need of explicitly granting them that right, as is done in canon 1239, § 2, in the event of their inculpable failure to receive baptism before they died.

It may be stated, therefore, that pagans, infidels and catechumens as here defined are exempt, by virtue of the first clause of canon 12, from strictly ecclesiastical laws. They are all bound, however, by divine laws, for they are God's creatures and are subject to Him. One of the chief divine laws that has reference to them in this matter is the one which requires them to hear the word of God and to embrace the Catholic religion when they realize their obligation.[24] As has been stated already in the historical section this precept was formulated by Christ Himself when He sent His Apostles out to preach to every creature and to baptize them.[25] It was repeated by Him during His instructions to Nicodemus: "Unless a man be born again of water and the Spirit, he cannot enter into the kingdom of God." [26]

[22] Canon 87.

[23] Vermeersch-Creusen, *Epitome,* II, n. 526; Cappello, *Summa Iuris Canonici* (3 vols., Vol. II, 3. ed., Romae: Apud Aedes Universitatis Gregorianae, 1939), II, p. 384, n. 706.

[24] Canon 1322, § 2; Claeys-Bouuaert et Simenon, *Manuale Juris Canonici,* I, p. 136, n. 237.

[25] Mark, XVI: 15, 16.

[26] John, III: 5.

Hence by baptism of water one becomes a member of the body of the Church—the visible society established by Christ on earth. While He was here among men He decreed that one must use the means stipulated in order to enter the Church, for to the Church are entrusted the means whereby man may enter heaven. And since the Church on earth seeks and finds its culmination in heaven, the gaining of heaven is to be effected by one's entrance into the Church on earth. Such an entrance can be effected only through the reception of the sacrament of baptism.

ARTICLE C. SOME PRACTICAL APPLICATIONS OF THE PRINCIPLE: THE NON-BAPTIZED ARE NOT BOUND BY PURELY ECCLESIASTICAL LAWS

a) *Preliminary Notions*

How this rule of the first clause of canon 12 operates in practice may be deduced from a consideration of the laws formulated by the Church solely on its own authority and without any immediate dependence upon the divine positive or natural laws. Before doing this, however, one finds it advisable to look at the matter of the indirect subjection of the unbaptized to ecclesiastical law, namely, through direct subjection to the divine natural or positive law and through relations with one baptized.

The supreme ecclesiastical authority, i. e., the Pope alone or together with all the Bishops assembled in an ecumenical council,[27] does have exclusive right to declare authentically when the divine law impedes or invalidates marriage.[28] Such a declaration binds both the baptized and the unbaptized.[29] That the unbaptized are bound by such au-

[27] Canons 218, § 1; 228, § 1.

[28] Canon 1038, § 1; cf. De Smet, *De Sponsalibus et Matrimonio*, p. 378, n. 437bis, and note 1, where it is stated that by *ius divinum* in canon 1038, § 1, is meant both the natural and the positive divine law.

[29] Petrovits, *The New Church Law on Matrimony* (Philadelphia, 1919), p. 77.

thentic interpretations of the divine law is implied by the very wording of the first clause of canon 12 which, in dealing with the question of exemption, refers to purely ecclesiastical laws. The canon, of course, indirectly stresses the fact that divine law does not offer a basis for exemption inasmuch as the canon employs a phrase which points to solely ecclesiastical laws.

Again, when there is a request for the application of the Pauline Privilege the Church seems to exercise direct jurisdiction over the valid *marriages* contracted by two infidels by reason of the divine positive law promulgated by Saint Paul.[30] In such cases the Church's authority over the *baptized party* is *direct* by reason of his subjection to ecclesiastical jurisdiction through baptism; over the *unbaptized party* it is *indirect* in view of his association with the baptized party.[31] This distinction between the infidel *marriage* and the *parties* to that marriage seems to be warranted by the double source of the Church's authority in the matter of the Pauline Privilege, namely, the divine law as promulgated by Saint Paul and the divine law which subjects the baptized to the Church's jurisdiction.

One of the ways in which an infidel may become subject *indirectly* to the ecclesiastical authority is occasioned by his desire to contract marriage with one of the faithful. This obtains because in regard to strictly ecclesiastical laws the validity or licitness of a matrimonial contract in which one of the parties is a Catholic depends upon the freedom of the Catholic party from strictly ecclesiastical diriment or impeding impediments and upon the observance of the canonical form of marriage. If the Catholic party is hampered by one or more such impediments then both

[30] I Cor. VII: 8-15; De Smet, *De Sponsalibus et Matrimonio*, p. 292, n. 341.

[31] De Smet, *De Sponsalibus et Matrimonio*, p. 284, n. 333.

parties are affected by the nullifying or prohibitive character of the impediments which obtain in the case. The Catholic party is affected directly; the other party indirectly.[32]

The same regulations apply to the canonical form of marriage. The Catholic party must observe this form and the unbaptized party must adhere to it also if he does not want the marriage to be invalid in the eyes of the Church. This *indirect* subjection of infidels to the Church's authority, however, is evidently not contrary to the rule of Canon 12, which is interpreted as meaning that infidels are not *directly* subject to strictly ecclesiastical laws.[33]

b) *Practical Applications Involving the Marriage Law*

After the foregoing considerations of the infidel's direct subjection to the divine law (including interpretations of it made by the supreme ecclesiastical authority) and of his indirect subjection to purely ecclesiastical laws, come the practical applications of the first clause of Canon 12 to some of the most pertinent questions regarding the Church's jurisdiction over infidels in the matter of strictly ecclesiastical matrimonial impediments. Usually these questions arise when unbaptized persons are converted to the Catholic religion and receive valid Baptism.

First of all, there are certain bonds which may be present or be contracted by infidels and which, as long as these persons remain infidels, have no influence on their marriages, but as soon as these persons are baptized validly and desire to marry, they are bound by the purely ecclesiastical impediments that arise from these previously contracted

[32] De Smet, *De Sponsalibus et Matrimonio,* p. 380, note 1; Ayrinhac-Lydon, *Marriage Legislation in the New Code of Canon Law,* pp. 56, 57, n. 61.

[33] Beste, *Introductio in Codicem* (Collegeville, Minn.: St. John's Abbey Press, 1938), p. 68.

bonds. These bonds may be natural ones or only juridic ones introduced by the civil law.[34]

Among the natural bonds which have a juridic effect upon a converted infidel is consanguinity within the degrees which entail a strictly ecclesiastical impediment. As has been stated previously, as long as such a person would remain an infidel and there was no civil law or legitimate custom establishing an obstacle for marriage such a natural bond would not be a hindrance to a valid marriage between him and one of his unbaptized blood relations if there be question merely of such a degree of relationship in connection with which the presence of an impediment is indicated solely by a law which is exclusively ecclesiastical in character. As an infidel he was not and is not subject to strictly ecclesiastical laws. Upon his conversion, however, he would be bound immediately by the purely ecclesiastical impediments governing this matter should he desire to contract marriage with a person related to him within all the degrees of kindred which the Church regards as connoting a purely ecclesiastical impediment to intermarriage.

Thus far consideration has been given to the strictly ecclesiastical impediments based on consanguinity. The natural law impediments have not been considered because infidels would be bound to them both before and after their conversion. But what of the impediment of consanguinity in the first degree of the collateral line about which there is much controversy—some say that the natural law invalidates marriages between parties related in this degree, while others deny this and say that the natural law would make them only gravely illicit.[35]

[34] De Smet, *De Sponsalibus et Matrimonio*, p. 381, n. 438[bis].

[35] For a fuller treatment of this discussion confer: Payen, *De Matrimonio*, I, n. 1441; Wernz-Vidal, *Ius Canonicum*, V, n. 348, and footnotes; De Smet, *De Sponsalibus et Matrimonio*, p. 530, n. 607 and footnotes; Benedict XIV, ep. *Aestas*, 11 oct. 1757, n. 13—*Fontes*, n. 445; Wahl, *The Matrimonial Impediments of Consanguinity and Affinity*, pp. 28-40.

The doubtful extent of the divine law in the matter of consanguinity in the first degree of the collateral line begets more serious difficulties in connection with its application to infidel marriages than it does in connection with marriages between two Catholics or between a Catholic and an infidel inasmuch as Catholics are subject also to the ecclesiastical law which in its own right establishes with certainty that an impediment is present. For instance, if a brother and sister, both infidels, were to marry, and later were converted to the Catholic rèligion, their infidel marriage might be treated in various ways:

If there was no civil law or legitimate custom which invalidated such infidel marriages, the two parties upon their baptism would not necessarily have to be separated even though there is a probability that their marriage was invalidated by the natural law.[36] If these two baptized infidels wished to remain together their wish should be granted. They are not forcibly to be separated without consulting the Holy See,[37] because of the *dubium juris* about the natural law having an invalidating effect upon the marriage of a brother and sister. And this decision is in accord with the principle *in dubio standum est pro valore matrimonii.*[38]

But, as Wahl states,[39] if, after they were both baptized, these same two parties desired to separate and to remarry, the *Privilegium Fidei*[40] would favor their freedom to do so, for it has application in cases like this wherein the existing marriage is doubtfully valid.

[36] Payen, *De Matrimonio,* I, n. 1441, and footnote 1.

[37] Gasparri, *Tractatus Canonicus de Matrimonio* (2 vols., Civitate Vaticana: Typis Polyglottis Vaticanis, 1932), I, n. 711.

[38] Canon 1014.

[39] *The Matrimonial Impediments of Consanguinity and Affinity,* p. 40. This is substantiated by Gasparri (*Tractatus Canonicus de Matrimonio,* I, p. 434, n. 711) and Payen (*De Matrimonio,* I, p. 1014, n. 1448).

[40] Canon 1127: *In re dubia privilegium fidei gaudet favore iuris.*

De Smet, however,[41] seems to offer another solution, namely recourse to the Holy See which, besides being able to apply Canon 1127, has the right and power of dissolving a marriage contracted in infidelity and not consummated after the Baptism of both parties.

Since the whole discussion hinges on whether the natural law has an invalidating effect on such a union it affords clear evidence that these infidels prior to Baptism were not bound by strictly ecclesiastical laws. If they had been then there would be no need for a discussion inasmuch as ecclesiastical law now states that marriage between persons related by consanguinity up to the third degree of the collateral line are invalid.[42]

If one were to disregard the controversy just discussed and consider the case in which two infidels, a brother and his sister, married each other in defiance of a civil law or of a legitimate custom that invalidated marriages between such close relations, then, upon the valid Baptism of these two infidels, they are to be separated because their marriage is invalid also in the eyes of the Church [43] even though they were not bound by the Church law in this matter when they contracted marriage. The Church recognizes the authority of the State over the marriages of the unbaptized and, normally, even after such persons had been baptized they could not be married validly to each other because the Church as a matter of general practice never dispenses from the impediment of consanguinity in the first degree of the collateral line.[44]

41 *De Sponsalibus et Matrimonio,* p. 532, n. 608.

42 Canon 1076, § 2.

43 Payen, *De Matrimonio,* I, n. 1448.

44 Chelodi, *Ius Matrimoniale iuxta Codicem Iuris Canonici* (3. ed., Tridenti: Libr. Edit. Tridentum, 1921), p. 104, n. 97; De Smet, *De Sponsalibus et Matrimonio,* p. 532, n. 608.

According to the pre-Code conception a certain bond of affinity arose from licit or illicit sexual intercourse.[45] Hence, if two infidels had sexual intercourse they contracted with each other's closely related kin a certain bond of affinity which, in the absence of any civil law or legitimate custom to the contrary, did not have an invalidating effect upon the subsequent marriage of either one of them with the near relatives of the other, provided that both parties to that marriage were still infidels,[46] even though this bond of relationship may have bound them within degrees that would have made two baptized persons incapable of contracting valid marriage in the eyes of the Church. The reason is that these infidels were not bound by the strictly ecclesiastical law governing affinity.[47]

But if either or both were converted, then that certain bond of affinity would furnish the basis for the ecclesiastical impediment of affinity. If before their Baptism they had been validly married to some one related to them by affinity in degrees that were covered by the ecclesiastical impediment, their subsequent Baptism and the consequent subjection to Church law would have no effect upon that former marriage and they should not be separated. Nevertheless, the impediment would have to be taken into consideration if the marriage were to take place only after conversion be-

[45] Cf. Wernz, *Ius Decretalium,* IV, n. 430.

[46] This is based on the opinion of the majority of pre-Code canonists who regarded the impediment of affinity as being of purely ecclesiastical origin. Cf. Benedict XIV, ep. *Aestas,* 11 oct. 1757, n. 14—*Fontes,* n. 445; Schmalzgrueber, *Jus Ecclesiasticum Universum,* lib. IV, tit. 14, n. 103; Sanchez, *Disputationum de Sancto Matrimonii Sacramento Libri Tres,* lib. VII, disp. 66, nn. 3, 7.

[47] S. C. S. Off., instr. (*ad. Archiep. Quebecen.*), 16 sept. 1924, ad 2: ". . . quippe impedimentum affinitatis, praesertim ex copula illicita, ut in casu, cum non habeatur ut iuris divini, aut naturalis, sed tantum ecclesiastici, infideles ex mente Ecclesiae non afficit, quia Ecclesiae non subditos . . ."—*Fontes,* n. 866.

tween these converts, related as they are within degrees of affinity that invalidate marriage in the Church.

So, while as infidels they were not bound directly by this strictly ecclesiastical impediment of affinity, they could acquire a certain bond that will make them subject to the disqualifying effects of the ecclesiastical law if they ever become Catholics and desire to marry some one related to them within degrees of affinity that invalidate marriage in the Church.[48]

Under the law of the Code [49] the manner in which the relationship of affinity arises has been changed. Now affinity arises only from a valid marriage, either ratified only, or ratified and consummated. In other words it arises from the valid marriage of two baptized persons.[50] Hence, two unmarried infidels who under the pre-Code law were related by affinity in the degrees recognized by the Church as begetting an impediment may now marry each other validly when they both are baptized, inasmuch as the present ecclesiastical impediment of affinity would have no invalidating effect upon their sacramental marriage. The reason is that there is no longer any exclusively natural basis for the impediment, but rather a legal one in virtue solely of ecclesiastical law,[51] and by such a law, according to canon 12, infidels are not bound prior to their Baptism.[52]

Should there be a civil law covering this matter of affinity and it had an invalidating effect upon the marriages of those who are related in the degrees of affinity covered by Church law, even so two infidels could still be validly married after

[48] S. C. C. Off., instr. (*ad Vic. Ap. Nankin.*), 26 aug. 1891—*Collect. S. C. de Prop. Fide* (2. ed.), n. 1766; *Fontes*, n. 1145.

[49] Canon 97.

[50] Cf. Canon 1015, § 1.

[51] Canon 1077.

[52] Cf. De Smet, *De Sponsalibus et Matrimonio*, p. 382, n. 438bis, footnotes 2 and 3.

they were baptized even though they are related in degrees of affinity that invalidate marriage according to the civil law. This would also be true if one infidel after his Baptism desired to marry an unbaptized infidel related to him by affinity. The reason is that the Church does not recognize the State's authority to legislate for the marriages of baptized persons, except insofar as the civil effects are concerned.[53]

The interpretation of canon 97 just noted above is based on the opinion that, according to the strict meaning of the word "*ratum*" in this canon, affinity arises only from the valid marriage of baptized persons.[54] There are, however, other opinions on the interpretation of the word "*ratum*" in canon 97. These give the word a wider meaning than its definition in canon 1015.[55]

One of these opinions is based on the jurisdiction of the Church over marriages in which at least one party is baptized.[56] Hence, according to this opinion the bond of affinity does not arise from the marriage of two infidels; and the reason is that the purely ecclesiastical law on affinity does not apply to the marriage of two infidels.

Another opinion in this matter is based on the consummation or non-consummation of a valid marriage.[57] If the valid marriage of two infidels is consummated, this opinion

[53] Canon 1016.

[54] Payen, *De Matrimonio,* I, n. 1485; Claeys-Bouuaert et Simenon, *Manuale Juris Canonici,* I, n. 249; II, n. 281; Ayrinhac-Lydon, *Marriage Legislation in The New Code of Canon Law,* p. 77, n. 166; Genicot-Salsmans, *Institutiones Theologiae Moralis,* II, n. 505.

[55] Cf. Wahl, *The Matrimonial Impediments of Consanguinity and Affinity,* pp. 58-65 for a full discussion of these opinions. Cappello, *De Sacramentis,* III, n. 538 notes three opinions and defends the opinion based on the strict interpretation of the word "ratum" of canon 97.

[56] Michiels, "De Vera Impedimenti Affinitatis Natura,"—*Jus Pontificium,* V (1925), 142-159, esp. 158.

[57] Wernz-Vidal, *Ius Canonicum,* V, n. 367.

holds that a certain bond of relationship arises between each party and the blood relatives of the other party. It states that this bond is perpetual and should one or both parties to this marriage contracted in the state of infidelity later be baptized, this bond of relationship would form the basis for the ecclesiastical impediment of affinity. This opinion then continues by stating that, if the marriage of two infidels is not consummated, this bond of relationship does not arise. As is evident, this opinion preserves the principle that infidels are not directly subject to purely ecclesiastical laws as long as they remain infidels. It holds that a certain bond of relationship arises from valid, consummated infidel marriages but does not state that the ecclesiastical bond of affinity, referred to in Canon 97, arises from such marriages.

A third opinion emphasizes the word "valido" in canon 97.[58] It holds that even from the valid, legitimate marriages of the unbaptized a bond of affinity arises between one party and the blood relatives of the other. This bond, the opinion states, is a juridical one which arises from any valid marriage, even an unconsummated one. Further this opinion holds that this bond of affinity that arises from the legitimate marriages of the unbaptized does not of itself invalidate marriages between those who are "*affines*" from such a marriage (excluding, of course, the case where such affinity would be a civil diriment impediment) but when those related by affinity from such a marriage become subjects of the Church through Baptism, that affinity will form the basis of the ecclesiastical impediment of affinity. Like the others, this opinion excludes the possibility of infidels being subject to the ecclesiastical law on affinity as long as they remain infidels.

[58] Ojetti, "Ex Infidelium Matrimonio Legitimo An Affinitas Oriatur?"—*Jus Pontificium,* V (1925), 71-76, esp. 76; Chelodi, *Ius Matrimoniale,* p. 105, n. 99; Chelodi-Bertagnolli, *Ius de Personis,* n. 95.

From these considerations of the various opinions on the matter of affinity it may be seen that none of the opinions held that infidels were directly subject to the purely ecclesiastical laws governing affinity.

Now the question of whether the bond of affinity arises from the valid marriage of a baptized person and an infidel must be considered in the light of the four opinions noted above.

According to the opinion that gives a strict interpretation to the word "*ratum*" in canon 97 and holds that affinity arises only from the valid marriage of two baptized persons, Wahl states that it is doubtful whether the bond of affinity would arise from the valid marriage of a baptized person and an infidel.[59] Payen [60] states that it is more probable that the affinity does not arise from such a marriage. If Wahl's statement is taken into consideration then, by virtue of canon 15, the impediment of affinity practically does not arise from the case under consideration.

If the other three opinions are followed, namely, that the bond of affinity arises from a marriage over which the Church has jurisdiction by reason of the fact that one of the parties is baptized; that the bond of affinity arises from a valid marriage that has been consummated; and that the bond of affinity arises from any valid marriage, then the bond of affinity would arise from a valid marriage between an infidel and a baptized person provided the conditions stated in these three opinions were present. As a result the impediment of affinity would arise:

a) directly between the baptized party and a baptized relative of the infidel party;

b) indirectly between an unbaptized relative of the infidel party and the baptized party;

[59] Wahl, *The Matrimonial Impediments of Consanguinity and Affinity,* p. 58.

[60] *De Matrimonio,* p. 1044, n. 1485.

c) indirectly between the unbaptized party and a baptized relative of the baptized party;

d) The impediment would not arise between the unbaptized party and an unbaptized relative of the baptized party.

Hence, it is evident from what has just been stated, that where the impediment of affinity does arise as the result of a disparate marriage that impediment binds the infidel "*affinis*" only indirectly by reason of association with a baptized person.

Since legal relationship may be a diriment or an impeding impediment of the civil law, two infidels may contract it. And, if after their conversion they wish to marry each other, this legal relationship would be an ecclesiastical impediment to their marriage, even though at the time that they contracted the legal relationship they were not subject to the ecclesiastical law. The reason is that the Church "canonizes" the civil law in this matter if such a civil law exists.[61]

It may be said, therefore, that under the law of the Code, in the matter of consanguinity (in the degrees touched solely by ecclesiastical law) and legal relationship (when it is an impediment of the civil law) infidels are not bound directly by the strictly ecclesiastical laws, but only potentially, insofar as these two bonds constitute the basis for ecclesiastical impediments if the infidels who have contracted these natural and legal bonds ever become Catholics and desire to marry.

Although the general principle of canon 12 exempts the non-baptized from all purely ecclesiastical laws, they are specifically released from the law regarding the canonical form of marriage[62] whenever they contract marriage with other unbaptized persons, or with those who were baptized in a non-Catholic sect, or even with those who were bap-

[61] Canons 1059; 1080.

[62] Canon 1099, § 2.

tized in the Catholic Church but who were born of non-Catholics, or of apostates, or of a mixed or disparate marriage, and then were reared from infancy in heresy, schism, infidelity or without any religion.

Because of the exemption noted in the first clause of canon 12 the strictly ecclesiastical impediment of public propriety has no binding force on infidels.[63] It is possible, however, to suppose a case involving public concubinage in which the marriage of the infidel would be perfectly valid according to legal principles but in which it would seem to be contrary to propriety and the mind of the Church.[64] Such a case would arise if an infidel woman were living in public concubinage with a Catholic man who had a Catholic son from a former marriage. Suppose that the unbaptized woman desired to marry this son of her illicit consort. She certainly is not bound by the ecclesiastical impediment of public propriety and, as far as is known, it is not possible for the father to transmit the disqualifying effects of his impediment to his son. Therefore, there seems to be no legal obstacle to the marriage of this woman and the son, provided that the latter was not bound by any other impediments, and provided that the Church would grant a dispensation from the impediment of disparity of cult. But, as has been noted already, such a marriage would seem to be contrary to propriety and the mind of the Church.

Another strictly ecclesiastical impediment — *crimen* — would not affect the civil marriage of two infidels even though they had fulfilled the various conditions necessary to constitute the crime which eventuates in the ecclesiastical impediment,[65] because the unbaptized are not bound directly by such laws. Nor would those actions, committed

63 Gasparri, *De Matrimonio,* n. 744.

64 Petrovits, *The New Church Law on Matrimony,* pp. 277-278.

65 Canon 1075.

in the infidel state, give rise to the impediment if the same persons later were validly baptized and then desired to marry, since such crime does not constitute a natural but only a legal bond according to the law of the Church.[66]

Even in the supposition that the adultery took place before the conversion of the infidel parties but the promise of marriage was given after their conversion the impediment of *crimen* would not be present.[67] And the reason is that one of the conditions necessary to constitute the crime was actualized when these parties were still infidels and therefore not bound by the ecclesiastical impediment, even though the other condition was added after these parties had received valid baptism, that is, at a time when they were bound by the ecclesiastical law. The two things that must concur, therefore, in order to produce the impediment did not both occur at the time when the parties were capable of being bound by the ecclesiastical impediment and as a result they would not incur the impediment.[68] The same conclusion would hold, of course, if only one of the parties was converted.

There is, however, a dissenting opinion[69] holding that the impediment would be present in such circumstances, but this view seems to be incorrect because the mere promise of marriage alone is not sufficient to cause this impediment of *crimen*[70] and, according to this dissenting opinion, no

[66] Gasparri, *De Matrimonio,* p. 413, n. 681; De Smet, *De Sponsalibus et Matrimonio,* p. 381, n. 438[bis]; Petrovits, *The New Church Law on Matrimony,* p. 217.

[67] This is founded on the more probable opinion as stated by Gasparri, (*De Matrimonio,* p. 414, n. 681).

[68] Sanchez, *Disputationum de Sancto Matrimonii Sacramento Libri Tres,* Lib. VII, disp. 79, n. 43; Schmalsgrueber, *Jus Ecclesiasticum Universum,* Lib. IV, tit. 7, n. 3; *Ius Decretalium,* IV, n. 521.

[69] Cf. Cappello, *Tractatus Canonico-Moralis de Sacramentis* (3 vols. in 6, Vol. III, 4. ed., Taurinorum Augustae: Marietti, 1933), III, n. 501, ad 4.

[70] Gasparri, *De Matrimonio,* p. 403, n. 671; Wernz-Vidal, *Ius Canonicum,* V, n. 325.

further basis for the impediment is alleged. Canon 1075, n. 1 indicates that two factors, the adultery and the promise of marriage, must be present in order to constitute the impediment. If, therefore, only one of these necessary factors takes place when at least one of the parties is a Catholic and bound to purely ecclesiastical laws, the impediment of *crimen* is not present. Both factors must take place when at least one of the parties is bound to ecclesiastical law. Cappello [71] thinks that since there is a *dubium iuris* here, the opinion that denies that the impediment arises in the above circumstances is certain.

There is another opinion touching the impediment of *crimen* which Vlaming [72] seems to base on the situation wherein the promise of marriage was given while the parties were still infidels, and then after their baptism the adultery was committed. Vlaming seems to contend that the promise of marriage made while the parties were unbaptized (and not bound by ecclesiastical laws) virtually perseveres and after their baptism is, as it were, renewed by the commission of the adultery.

This is the interpretation that Payen [73] puts on the words of Vlaming and he says that this opinion is not to be accepted. He also states that it was expressly rejected by Schmalzgrueber [74] and Sanchez,[75] although Vlaming uses the same section of Sanchez's work to prove his contention. And together with it he also quotes another section of Sanchez's same work.[76] A check of these two sections from

[71] *Loc. cit.*

[72] *Praelectiones Iuris Matrimonii ad Normam Codicis Iuris Canonici* (3. ed., 2 vols., Bussum in Hollandia, 1919), I, n. 327, c.

[73] *De Matrimonio,* I, n. 1321.

[74] *Jus Ecclesiasticum Universum,* Lib. IV, tit. 7, n. 3.

[75] *Disputationum de Sancto Matrimonii Sacramento Libri Tres,* Lib. VII, disp. 79, n. 43.

[76] *Disputationum de Sancto Matrimonii Sacramento Libri Tres,* Lib. VII, disp. 78, n. 3.

Sanchez seems to indicate that Vlaming was using one reference from Sanchez [77] only as an indication of where his (Vlaming's) opinion might be found, because Sanchez actually does reject Vlaming's opinion as proposed by several of the older writers. In the other reference from Sanchez [78] noted above there seems to be under consideration the case in which one party is an infidel and the other a baptized person. And, therefore, Vlaming seems to have here an incorrect reference.

In rejecting Vlaming's contention Payen [79] puts forth the following reasons:

1) Adultery is not necessarily a tacit renewal of the previous promise.[80]

2) Since the promise of marriage which preceded the baptism of both parties was made at a time when they were not juridically capable of being bound by the impediment of *crimen*, it is not only a virtual but an express promise of marriage that is required to create the impediment after the baptism of the parties.

It is this second reason which is the more important one in a study of the first clause of canon 12. For its principle seems to be upheld more consistently by the opinion based on this argument, namely, that both elements that constitute the impediment of *crimen* must occur and concur when at least one of the parties is baptized and, of course, while the legitimate spouse of one of the parties is still living.

In the species of the impediment of *crimen* which involves both the sin of adultery and the crime of spouse-murder on the part of one of the culprits but solely the sin of adultery on the part of the other, a case might occur in which no impediment would arise even though one party is already

[77] *Op. cit.*, Lib. VII, disp. 79, n. 43.

[78] *Op. cit.*, Lib. VII, disp. 78, n. 3.

[79] *De Matrimonio*, I, n. 1321.

[80] Cf. Chelodi, *Ius Matrimoniale*, p. 97, n. 93, 2°.

baptized and the other is an infidel, provided that it is the infidel party who is guilty of the combined factors of adultery and of spouse-murder.[81] If, of course, the above situation were reversed and the baptized party were guilty of the combined factors of adultery and of spouse-murder then the impediment of *crimen* would result.

The impediment of abduction is also of purely ecclesiastical origin and, therefore, does not affect directly the non-baptized.[82]

Infidels can in no way be affected by the impediment of spiritual relationship, not even indirectly, since this impediment can affect only the baptized.[83] Even if an infidel were the extraordinary minister of baptism he would not contract the spiritual relationship which is the basis for the impediment.[84] There may be some objections raised against this last statement but this is the contention of all the authors who were consulted on this point.[85] The only question that is raised is whether the infidel minister noted above would be held by the impediment of spiritual relationship if he were later baptized. One opinion [86] holds that he would not be bound by this impediment after his conversion. Another [87] holds that he would be bound by this impediment but because of the *dubium iuris* the impediment is not binding in practice.

81 Wernz, *Ius Decretalium,* IV, n. 521.

82 De Smet, *De Sponsalibus et Matrimonio,* p. 563, n. 652.

83 Canons 765; 768; 1079.

84 De Smet, *De Sponsalibus et Matrimonio,* p. 558, n. 642 and footnote 3; Gasparri, *De Matrimonio,* n. 762.

85 Cf. Payen, *De Matrimonio,* I, p. 1099, n. 1569; Claeys-Bouuaert et Simenon, *Manuale Juris Canonici,* II, n. 283; Vermeersch-Creusen, *Epitome,* II, n. 364; Ayrinhac-Lydon, *Marriage Legislation in the New Code of Canon Law,* p. 185; Cappello, *De Sacramentis,* III, p. 660, n. 558.

86 Cf. Cappello, *De Sacramentis,* III, p. 660, n. 558.

87 Cf. Claeys-Bouuaert et Simenon, *Manuale Juris Canonici,* II, p. 280, n. 283 and footnote 2.

Since the impediment of age springs from a double source—from the natural law in relation to the period which extends up to the time when a party has sufficient use of reason to give true marital consent; and from the ecclesiastical law for the ages in excess of that period[88] a distinction must be made in the treatment of this impediment in its relation to infidels. If two infidels have the mental maturity necessary for them to give true marital consent, then they may be married validly. They are not subject to the impediment of age which springs exclusively from the Church's law.[89] The reason is the same as that which already has been given for their exemption from the other purely ecclesiastical impediments—the lack of that subjection to the Church which is produced by the reception of valid baptism.

c) *Practical Applications Involving the Law on Irregularities*

The principle that non-baptized persons are exempted from purely ecclesiastical laws has practical application also in relation to the canons that govern irregularities. These irregularities properly so-called affect only those who, according to divine positive and natural laws, are capable of receiving Holy Orders, but whom the Church by its law on irregularities restricts from receiving or exercising these Orders.[90]

Since canon 986 states definitely that an irregularity *ex delicto* arises from a grave, external sin, either public or occult, committed after baptism, this type of irregularity cannot be incurred by an infidel. Even though he may

88 Gasparri, *De Matrimonio*, n. 492.

89 Gasparri, *op. cit.*, n. 497.

90 Genicot-Salsmans, *Institutiones Theologiae Moralis* (12. ed., 2 vols., Louvain: Museum Lessianum, 1931), II, p. 571, n. 629; p. 572, n. 631; Vermeersch-Creusen, *Epitome*, II, p. 145, n. 254.

have committed the deed, e. g., voluntary homicide, that would give rise to an irregularity in a baptized person, and then was baptized, he would not incur the irregularity *ex delicto* because the sin would be taken away by the subsequent baptism; and with the sin the basis for the irregularity.[91] The same effect, of course, would not come about if a Catholic who had incurred an irregularity *ex delicto* were to have the sin forgiven in confession because he had already incurred the irregularity which is of its very nature permanent.

There is one exception to the rule that the sin must have been committed *after* baptism. It obtains when an infidel in his act of conversion to the Church gives permission for baptism to be conferred on him by a non-Catholic in any manner when there is not a case of extreme necessity.[92] This, of course, presupposes that the infidel would not be in good faith when he permitted the baptism to be given by the non-Catholic because there must be a *delictum* present. In an instance where baptism is conferred under these conditions the sin is committed *in* the act of receiving baptism [93] or simultaneously with its administration, that is, the sin is completely perpetrated only when the baptism is completely conferred. Hence, the sin is not taken away by the baptism and the irregularity is incurred. But it is actually incurred only when the infidel has become a baptized person. The very nature, therefore, of all irregularities *ex delicto* prevents them from being incurred by infidels even though prior to baptism they may have committed the deeds that would give rise to irregularities in baptized persons.

[91] Hickey, *Irregularities and Simple Impediments in the New Code of Canon Law*, The Catholic University of America Canon Law Studies, n. 7 (Washington, D. C.: The Catholic University of America, 1920), p. 15.

[92] Canon 985, n. 2.

[93] Hickey, *Irregularities and Simple Impediments in the New Code of Canon Law*, p. 71.

With regard to the irregularities *ex defectu,* however, there are some defects that may be present or that occur prior to baptism and constitute a basis for irregularities after the infidel is converted and baptized. The reason is the perseverence of the defects that were present when the person was an infidel. This means that although the defect which would cause a baptized person to be subject to an irregularity is present in the unbaptized person, he is immune from the irregularity as long as he remains an infidel, and is not subject to the purely ecclesiastical law in this matter.

An example of an action which may be performed before baptism and which gives rise to an irregularity after baptism is the following: The contracting of two successive legitimate and consummated marriages.[94] Prior to the promulgation of the present Code of Canon Law Gasparri [95] indicated that all the irrgularities *ex defectu* that existed then arose when an infidel who had these defects was baptized and became capable of incurring an irregularity. Hence, it seems as though all the irregularities *ex defectu* enumerated in Canon 984, except *infamia juris* may be incurred, after baptism, by an infidel who had these defects also prior to his reception into the Church. This conclusion is based on what has been noted about the irregularity that arises from the contracting of two successive legitimate and consummated marriages.

Here it should be pointed out that the question whether infidels are subject to the disqualifying effects of irregularities before and after the reception of valid baptism does

[94] Canon 984, n. 4; Gasparri, *Tractatus Canonicus de Sacra Ordinatione* (2 vols., Parisiis, 1893-1894), I, p. 238, n. 377; Vermeersch-Creusen, *Epitome,* II, n. 254, § 2; Hickey, *op. cit.,* p. 35.

[95] *Tractatus Canonicus de Sacra Ordinatione,* I, p. 122, n. 198: ". . . sed defectus permanent, ex quibus jam oritur irregularitas, cum subjectum capax evaserit per baptismum."

not seem to have the same practical importance as the question whether infidels are subject to the effects of strictly ecclesiastical matrimonial impediments before and after the reception of valid baptism, because irregularities pertain to the regulation of the reception and exercise of Holy Orders which is strictly a Sacrament and intended only for Catholics. Matrimonial impediments on the other hand govern the reception of matrimony which is not only a Sacrament which as such may be received only by the baptized but also a contract which may be entered into by the unbaptized.[96]

These practical applications of the clause of canon 12 which exempts infidels from purely ecclesiastical laws are not intended to be exhaustive. They have touched principally marriage legislation because it seems that infidels may be affected by such legislation more than by any other. These examples serve as indications of how the Church applies this principle of canon 12 and adheres to it strictly.

[96] Cf. Wernz-Vidal, Ius Canonicum, V, 47-52, nn. 41, 42, for a discussion of the question: Whether baptized non-Catholics actually receive the Sacrament when they contract valid marriages among themselves, or whether the baptized party in a disparity-of-cult marriage (dispensation obtained) actually receives the Sacrament.

CHAPTER V

Status of Validly Baptized Non-Members of the Church in Regard to Strictly Ecclesiastical Laws

ARTICLE A.—PRELIMINARY DISCUSSION

In this and succeeding articles the terms *fundamentally* or *fundamental subjection* will be used in the sense that all those who have received valid baptism and consequently the indelible mark that baptism imprints on the human soul are by that very fact permanently and irrevocably made subjects of the Church and bound by its laws. Also when the word *actually* or the phrase *actual subjection* is used in connection with subjection to ecclesiastical law it will mean that a baptized person who is fundamentally bound to that law is here and now, in this case, and under these circumstances *actually* bound by the ecclesiastical law. The necessity for such a distinction becomes evident when it is recalled that in some circumstances one may, while remaining *fundamentally* subject to ecclesiastical law, be excused or dispensed from actual subjection to a certain section of the law.

Since canon 12 states that certain categories of persons *are not* bound by strictly ecclesiastical laws, the question may be raised: Is it permissible to infer from the words of this canon that all those persons who belong to categories which are not enumerated there *are bound* by strictly ecclesiastical laws?

Michiels [1] mentions an opinion which seems to indicate that one cannot with certitude conclude from canon 12 that all those not enumerated there (including the validly

[1] *Normae Generales,* I, 290, footnote 1.

baptized) are *always actually* bound by the ecclesiastical laws. The opinion then states that from canon 12 it is proved that the baptized are *fundamentally* bound by such laws, but that since such persons may, at the will of the legislator, be exempted or dispensed from these enactments, it is necessary to have recourse to other canons to prove the *actual subjection* of baptized non-Catholics to purely ecclesiastical laws.[2]

Van Hove[3] writes, however, that canon 12 in a negative manner determines who are subject to purely ecclesiastical laws and, therefore, those not actually excepted by the canon are held to these laws. [Among those not excepted by the canon are the baptized—both Catholics and non-Catholics. Hence, they are bound by ecclesiastical laws].

He continues[4] by stating that no one denies that heretics are *fundamentally* subject to ecclesiastical laws and that the Church *can* bind them because they are subjects of the Church. He bases this statement on the general principle that all who have received valid baptism are subjects of the Church. Then he remarks that it is clear, in view of the evidence given in the pre-Code law, that the Church also *wishes* to bind them; that the same is manifest from the fact that canons 12 and 87 state a general principle; and that one may readily deduce this from certain canons which explicitly exempt heretics from definitely specified obligations.[5]

Claeys-Bouuaert and Simenon[6] in speaking of canon 12 hold that one may, by way of elimination, conclude just who is regularly bound by ecclesiastical laws: "Negativa

[2] One of those canons, and an important one, is canon 87; others will be noted in the course of this chapter.

[3] *De Legibus Ecclesiasticis*, p. 194.

[4] *Op. cit.*, p. 201.

[5] Canons 1070, § 1; 1099, § 2.

[6] *Manuale Juris Canonici*, I, p. 91, n. 159.

fit enumeratio eorum qui non tenentur. Ergo e contrario concludere licet quinam positive, regulariter tenentur. . ."[7]

In view of these statements the words of canon 12 should not of themselves lead to the inference that all baptized persons who have the sufficient use of their reason and are seven years of age are *actually* bound by strictly ecclesiastical laws. Such an inference is permitted, however, when canon 12 is considered together with canons 87, 88, § 3, and the exemptions made in canons 1070, § 1 and 1099, § 2.

Even though this be so it seems that the topic of baptized non-members of the Church may still be treated as an important incidental point whose discussion depends on the general principles of subjection to law rather than upon any direct connection with canon 12.[8]

ARTICLE B.—HERETICS AND THE BINDING FORCE OF STRICTLY ECCLESIASTICAL LAWS

a) *Introduction*

After the Pseudo-Reformation had become an acknowledged fact that the Church had to accept,[9] there arose many

[7] Cf. also Ojetti, *Commentarium in Codicem Iuris Canonici,* I, 102; Blat, *Commentarium,* I, 86.

[8] Cf. Cicognani, *Commentarium ad Librum I. Codicis,* p. 95: "Peculiaris quaestio est heic exponenda de excommunicatis, haereticis, et schismaticis."

[9] The most evident proof of this was the calling of the Council of Trent (1545-1563). Its decrees show clearly that the Church saw the menace of Protestantism and took measures to guard against it. It is a well-known historical fact that the Church had to contend with heretics from its earliest years and that many questions arose as to the status of heretics in regard to the binding force of Church laws. The ecclesiastical authorities settled these questions as they arose but, since many of the questions about heretics and the binding force of ecclesiastical laws that are discussed at the present time have arose as a result of the Protestant revolt of the sixteenth century, this article will begin with an historical background that dates from January 26, 1564. On that day official confirmation was given to the decrees of the Council of Trent which inaugurated the Counter-Reformation.

perplexing questions about the status of those who had accepted the heretical doctrines originally and of their descendants who were now being born into the heretical sects and were being reared as heretics. Chief among these questions, of course, was that of the binding force of ecclesiastical laws on these heretics.

In order to throw some light on the matter of baptized heretics and their subjection to ecclesiastical laws the general principles of law must be consulted before anything else. It is conceded by all that the subjects of a society are all those who have been united to it by some external sign which indicates admittance into that society and sets up a bond of union between the society and those whom it has admitted.[10] As a result of this bond, all the subjects and only the subjects are obliged by the laws of that society, for a lawmaker can normally bind only his own subjects.[11]

As has been noted already,[12] in the Church which is a perfect society the external ceremony that creates this bond of union is Baptism. But because of the peculiar effect of valid Baptism, namely, the imprinting of an indelible character or mark on the human soul, the bond of union with the Church takes on a special quality of permanence.[13] Hence, this union can never be broken. Even though a baptized person may cease to be a *member* of the Church by separating himself from the number of the faithful, juridically he will still be *subject* to the Church's jurisdiction. Also those persons who are validly baptized outside

[10] Wernz, *Ius Decretalium,* I, n. 103, footnote 78.

[11] Santi, *Praelectiones Juris Canonici,* I, n. 30: ". . . Prima conditio est ut homo sit subditus legislatoris; obligatio enim legis enascitur ex relatione jurisdictionis ex una parte et dependentiae ex altera . . . Hinc de legis natura est, ut ab eo feratur qui communitatis curam habet. Quare lex non urget eos quorum legislator curam non habet, idest non subditos. . . ."

[12] P. xiii.

[13] Sägmüller, *Lehrbuch des katholischen Kirchenrechts* (1 vol., Freiburg im Breisgau, 1900), I, 56.

of the Church and never are *members* of the Church, are juridically subject to the jurisdiction of the Church because of the indelible mark of baptism, which every valid baptism imprints on the soul. This same effect occurs whether the valid baptism is administered in the Catholic Church or in an heretical sect. Under the proper conditions, the sacrament of baptism is administered by anyone who uses the valid matter and form and has at least the intention of doing what Christ wanted done when He instituted the sacrament.

In order to understand, therefore, how one can be separated from the Church and still be under its jurisdiction, one must keep in mind the permanence of the bond of union with the Church because of the indelible mark imprinted on the soul by Baptism. And then one must make a clear distinction between a person who is a *member* of the Church and one who is *merely* a *subject* of the Church. This distinction is given very clearly by Wernz.[14] All heretics, therefore, by reason of being separated from the true Church are not actual *members* of that organization. They do not profess externally the Catholic faith, participate in the same Sacraments or are they [visibly] subordinated to the Catholic hierarchy.[15] But because of the indelible mark of Baptism they are still *subjects* of the Church and fundamentally under its jurisdiction. Hence, Catholic writers are agreed that juridically all heretics are fundamentally subjected to the laws of the Church.[16] The discussion here, therefore, will concern principally the

[14] *Ius Decretalium,* I, n. 103, footnote 78: ". . . Tandem cum homo baptizatus ratione characteris indelebilis vero vinculo cum Ecclesia aliqua ex parte sit coniunctus, etiam potestati legiferae, iudiciariae, coactivae Ecclesiae manet subjectus. Quare notio *subditi* Ecclesiae latius patet quam *membri* corporis Ecclesiae; multi enim sunt vere subditi Ecclesiae velut haeretici, schismatici, excommunicati, qui *membra* Ecclesiae simpliciter non iam existunt." (Italics added).

[15] Michiels, *Normae Generales,* I, 287.

[16] Van Hove, *De Legibus Ecclesiasticis,* p. 201.

actual subjection of heretics to purely ecclesiastical laws. The Church, of course, as all law-makers, may exempt such persons from its laws under certain definite circumstances.

b) *Pre-Code Legislation, Opinions, Decisions, and Decrees*

1. Preliminary Notes

Because of the fact that circumstances sometimes cause exceptions to be made to general principles, authors have tried to make various distinctions in ecclesiastical laws and by so doing they have attempted to prove exceptions for heretics. But before these are taken up it is necessary to make a distinction between heretics who have deliberately separated themselves from the Church and heretics who were baptized in a non-Catholic sect and have remained in it thereafter for various reasons.

As far as the first group is concerned, they have formally separated themselves from the Church. These seem to be the heretics who are mentioned in canon 1325, § 2.[17] There is no doubt that they are fundamentally bound to purely ecclesiastical laws [18] because, as stated above, they have received baptism and with it the indelible spiritual character which binds them irrevocably to Christ's visible society on earth. They may have rebelled against the Church and separated themselves from actual membership in it, but that does not mean that they have freed themselves from its jurisdiction. Such validly baptized persons can never be separated absolutely from this authority either by their own private determination or by a universal liberation on the part of the Church itself.[19] Whether the Church *actually*

[17] Cf. Coronata, *Institutiones Iuris Canonici,* II, p. 247, n. 911, and footnote 7.

[18] Van Hove, *De Legibus Ecclesiasticis,* p. 201.

[19] Wernz-Vidal, *Ius Canonicum,* V, p. 72, n. 58; Tarquini, *Iuris Ecclesiastici Publici Institutiones* (Romae, 1862), p. 76, n. 63; Bellarmine, *Opera Omnia* (8 vols., Neapoli, 1872), (Nova Editio iuxta Venetam Anni 1721 dicata Xisto R. Sforza), Tom. II, Lib. III (*De Ecclesia Militante*), cap. IV, 77, 78.

desires to bind them to the observance of all its laws is another question. Still it seems to be the unanimous opinion [20] that the Church, besides having the legal right, also *wishes* to bind such persons to its laws [actually] since it is not fitting that anyone should profit by his own evil deeds.

The members of the second class (those who never were Catholics), who comprise the great majority of baptized non-Catholics today, are the ones who are considered chiefly in the question of the actual subjection of heretics to purely ecclesiastical laws. They, too, are fundamentally bound to the Church's laws provided they have received valid baptism, but there is the controverted question of whether in practice the Church wishes them to remain actually subject to all its laws.

2. Legislation prior to the Nineteenth Century

Because of the important and intimate connection between the pre-Code treatment of the questions on heretics and the treatment given them in the Code and after it, it seems most useful and appropriate to place here in the commentary an historical outline of the matter.

After the great defection of the sixteenth century there arose large heretical sects protected by civil rulers. And because the Church, checked by these civil authorities, was unable to make any concerted attempts at that time to bring these people back into the true fold, the theologians and canonists began to discuss the question of the actual subjection of these persons to the Church's laws to which they were fundamentally bound. As time went on there were sharp controversies about whether the Church as a

[20] Michiels, *Normae Generales,* I, 287; Cicognani, *Commentarium ad Librum I. Codicis,* p. 95, § 4; Vermeersch-Creusen, *Epitome,* I, 78; Maroto, *Institutiones Iuris Canonici,* I, n. 196.

matter of fact desired to bind these heretics to the observance of all of its laws at all times.[21]

Some of the decrees of the Council of Trent (1545-1563) left little doubt as to the mind of the Church in this matter. The very fact that the Church enacted and approved the following decrees of that Council seems to indicate that she wished to contradict and refute opinions that evidently were beginning to be voiced at least among heretics.

She condemned anyone who asserted that the baptized are by baptism made debtors only to faith and not to the observance of the entire law of Christ; [22] or that the baptized are free from all the precepts of the Church, either written or handed down by Tradition, so that they are not bound to observe them unless they wish to submit themselves to them of their own accord.[23]

The two preceding definitions do not expressly state that heretics as such do not have to obey ecclesiastical laws, but they are used by authors to show that the Church wishes to bind heretics to the observance of its laws. The second one is cited by Maroto [24] for that purpose, and Cicognani [25] mentions both of them as being employed by authors to prove that heretics in good faith, born and brought up in a non-Catholic sect are actually bound even by the purely ecclesiastical laws which are enacted for the benefit of man's

[21] De Schepper, "De Haereticis Relate Ad Leges Ecclesiasticas,"—*Collationes Brugenses,* XXIV (1924), 209; Michiels, *Normae Generales,* I, 287.

[22] Conc. Trident., sess. VII, *de baptismo,* can. 7: "Si quis dixerit baptizatos per baptismum ipsum solius tantum fidei debitores fieri non autem universae legis Christi servandae, A. S."

[23] Conc. Trident., sess. VII, *de baptismo,* can. 8: "Si quis dixerit baptizatos liberos esse ab omnibus sanctae Ecclesiae praeceptis, quae vel scripta vel tradita sunt, ita ut ea observare non teneantur, nisi se sua sponte illis submittere voluerint, A. S."

[24] *Institutiones Iuris Canonici,* I, 203, n. 196, footnote 2.

[25] *Canon Law,* pp. 568-569.

personal sanctification. He does not, however, agree with the opinion. Still he does not say that they cannot be used to show that heretics are bound to some of the laws of the Church. He also admits that they may refer to heretics in bad faith. The point is that these canons of the Council of Trent are cited here to give evidence of the Church's general attitude toward heretics at that time, and in particular toward their subjection to ecclesiastical laws. The matter of the subjection of heretics to the various kinds of ecclesiastical laws will be treated later.[26]

Although there was much uncertainty about the binding force of this same Council's decree *Tametsi*,[27] which forbade clandestine marriages, it was generally agreed that this law also governed the marriages contracted by two heretics in places where this decree had been promulgated in the manner prescribed in the decree itself.[28]

Pope Benedict XIV, however, declared [29] valid those marriages which heretics had already contracted in the Federated States of Belgium without the observance of the form prescribed by the Council of Trent, and granted that such marriages contracted in those localities in the future without adherence to the same Tridentine form were to be considered as valid, provided there was not present any other canonical impediment. The Pope issued this declaration because it seemed clear to him that the Council of

[26] P. 124 seq.

[27] Conc. Trident., sess. XXIV, *de ref. matrim.*, c. 1.

[28] S. C. C. (*ad Ep. Tricarien.*), 18 ian. 1663—*Collect. S. C. de Prop. Fide*, n. 149; Feye, *Dissertatio Canonica de Matrimoniis Mixtis* (Lovanii, 1847), p. 99: ". . . non obligare decretum nisi in iis parochiis, in quibus fuit promulgatum, in his vero eo obligari ipsos etiam haereticos . . . ;" Carberry, *The Juridical Form of Marriage*, The Catholic University of America Canon Law Studies, n. 84 (Washington, D. C.: Catholic University of America, 1934), pp. 31, 34.

[29] S. C. C., declar. *Matrimonia*, 4 nov. 1741—*Bullarium Benedicti XIV* (3 vols. in 4, Prati, 1845-1847), I, 111; *Fontes*, n. 3527.

Trent did not intend to bind heretics to this law when the heretics were already united and organized into a society with churches and ministers.[30] This declaration was later extended to other places.

The juridical nature of the Benedictine Declaration is this: For the parts of the United Provinces of Belgium where heretics were organized as a distinct society the Declaration was a simple announcement that the Fathers of the Council of Trent did not intend to subject them to the decree. For other sections of the United Provinces, however, where Catholicism prevailed and heretics were in the minority, the Benedictine Declaration contained a dispensation (at least *ad cautelam*) from the common law.[31]

Pope Benedict XIV in his Declaration indicated that heretics were bound to ecclesiastical laws regarding matrimonial impediments for he said that the future marriages of heretics in the United Provinces of Belgium were valid if the Tridentine form were not observed but only provided that no other canonical impediment were present.

3. Opinions prior to the Nineteenth Century

The attitude that the Council of Trent took toward heretics was continued in the writings of contemporary authors.

Suarez (1548-1617),[32] for example, in his *Tractatus de Legibus* treated of formal heretics whom he called apostates in the wide sense of any one who left the Church for another

[30] Benedict XIV, const. *Singulare Nobis*, 9 febr. 1749—*Fontes*, n. 394.

[31] Carberry, *The Juridical Form of Marriage*, pp. 34, 35.

[32] *Opera Omnia*, Tom. V, Lib. IV (*De Lege Positiva Canonica*), Cap. XIX, n. 2: ". . . Respondeo negando consequentiam: supponimus enim sermonem esse de haereticis baptizatis qui generalius apostatae dici possunt; sive ad judaismum, sive ad paganismum, sive ad propriam haeresim translati sint. De his ergo omnibus negatur consequentia, quia sunt vere subjecti ecclesiasticae jurisdictioni: nam retinent characterem baptismalem quod est fundamentum hujus subjectionis . . . Unde fit ut ejus praeceptis obligentur et contra illa peccent illa non servando."

religion or for paganism, but some of the things that he said about them apply also to material heretics. This is especially true of the passages wherein he treated of their subjection to ecclesiastical jurisdiction as a consequence of the reception of valid baptism.

Saint Robert Bellarmine († 1621) [33] also referred to the same type of heretic and likened him to a stray sheep. He said that the indelible mark of baptism is not a means which unites one with the Church but it is a sign of union with the Church and the power of the Church over those who possess this mark. In stating this he clarified the difference between a member of the Church and one who is but a subject of the Church.

As recorded by De Lugo (1583-1660),[34] there arose in the seventeenth century a discussion about the obligation of heretics to observe the decree on annual confession which had been enacted by the Fourth Lateran Council (1215) [35] and renewed by the Council of Trent (November 25, 1551).[36]

Some theologians at that time taught that heretics were not bound by that law, particularly in view of the use of the word *fidelis,* which they claimed referred only to Catholics. And, besides, they contended that it would not seem prudent or reasonable to extend this law to heretics who certainly would not observe it, and thus there would be occasions given for new sins when the law was violated by

[33] *Opera Omnia,* Tom. II, Lib. III (*De Ecclesia Militante*), Cap. IV, p. 77: ". . . Ad illud de charactere dico, haereticos retinere extra Ecclesiam characteres illos indelebiles . . . sed non propterea sunt de Ecclesia, quia non sufficiunt characteres illi ad constituendum aliquem in Ecclesia; . . . Praeterea non proprie unit character hominem cum capite, *sed est signum potestatis et unionis cujusdam. . . .*"

[34] *Disputationes Scholasticae et Morales* (Nova Ed., 8 vols., Parisiis, 1868-1869), Tom. IV (*Tract. De Sacramento Poenitentiae*), Disp. XV, Sect. VII, n. 144.

[35] Canon 21—Denzinger-Bannwart, *Enchiridion,* n. 437.

[36] Sess. XIV, *de poenitentia,* c. 5.

these heretics. This law was probably the occasion for one of the first attempts, after the Council of Trent, to treat of exemptions of heretics from ecclesiastical laws, even though the law of annual confession can not be considered as simply an ecclesiastical law inasmuch as it is based on the divine law itself.

In answer De Lugo showed that the word *fidelis* was used in contradistinction to the word *infidelis,* and hence included all baptized persons. Then he rejected the second part of the objection thus:

> . . . Nec etiam obstat confirmatio adducta ex eo, quod lex illa esst inutilis, et nociva, si ad haereticos extenderetur: hoc enim argumentum multo magis probaret de aliis legibus ecclesiasticis quod non debeant haereticos obligare, atque adeo ipsos non peccare contra legem jejunii, vel abstinentiae a carnibus, nec incurrere excommunicationem, et censuras latas pro variis criminibus. *Quae tamen omnia absurdissima sunt.* Ratio autem est, quia ad hoc, ut lex aliqua universalis sit prudens et justa, non debemus attendere, an sit futura utilis huic personae, vel illi, sed toti communitati; cui si utilis sit, lex est rationabilis, nec debet restringi ad solas illas personas, quae eam probabiliter observabunt: nam per hoc daretur ansa, ut multi malitione se subtrahrent a legum obligatione, ponendo se in tali statu, in quo propter ipsorum perversitatem non crederentur observaturi legem, et sic non intelligerentur obligati . . .

Thus, even though he treated of an ecclesiastical law based on a divine precept, he adduced a powerful argument against all who tried to exempt heretics from any Church laws. In the course of his answer he did mention some purely ecclesiastical laws to which they were bound. And it seems that his view may be applied to the consideration of a heretic's obligation to observe purely ecclesiastical laws, since his argument is based on the fact that heretics have received baptism. It is principally for these reasons that this section from De Lugo was quoted.

In reference to the general principles of the subjection of heretics to ecclesiastical laws, it is interesting to note that some important writers in the seventeenh and eighteenth centuries make no reference to any opinions that may have existed in their times about reasons for exempting all heretics from ecclsiastical laws, but stated simply the principle that heretics are fundamentally bound to ecclesiastical laws. As far as could be ascertained, they made no distinction between *fundamental* and *actual* subjection, or between ecclesiastical laws in general and purely ecclesiastical laws.

Gibalini (1592-1671) [37] stated: ". . . Non sequitur porro ex eo quod haeretici sint extra Ecclesiam, eos non teneri legibus Ecclesiae, eiusque subduci jurisdictioni. . . ."

And in the next century Schmalzgrueber (1663-1735) [38] noted:

> . . . legibus non tantum naturalibus, et divinis, sed tiam ecclesiasticis *per se* subjectos manere haereticos et apostatas a fide; licet enim, ut putrida membra, per excommunicationem ab ecclesia corpore abscissi sint, ob indelebilem tamen baptismi characterem eidem subjecti manent. Haec certa.

He, however (as will be noted later), aside from this general principle held to the exemption of heretics in Germany from ecclesiastical marriage impediments.

Pichler (1670-1736) [39] added that heretics are often excused because of ignorance of their subjection to and their obligation to obey ecclesiastical laws. In this he went a little further than Schmalzgrueber who spoke only of fundamental subjection.

[37] *Scientia Canonica et Hieropolitica* (2 vols., Lugduni, 1670), Tom. I, p. 65, n. 27.

[38] *Jus Ecclesiasticum Universum,* Lib. I, tit. 2, n. 35. (Italics inserted).

[39] *Jus Canonicum Secundum Quinque Decretalium Titulos Gregorii Papae IX Explicatum* (Ravennae, 1741), Lib. I, Tit. II, n. 46.

Reiffenstuel (1641-1703)[40] held to the fundamental subjection of heretics to Church laws, but also noted that invincible ignorance or any other just cause may excuse them just as it would excuse Catholics. He also quoted De Lugo's observation, which has been noted already, about the absurdity on the part of anyone to deny that heretics are bound by ecclesiastical laws.

During this period there arose a discussion about the subjection of heretics to matrimonial impediments. The opinions on the matter are recorded by Schmalzgrueber.[41]

One side denied the validity of the marriages of heretics when they were contracted in the face of an impediment of strictly ecclesiastical law which the heretics did not accept. The other (the one to which Schmalzgrueber adhered) held that heretics in Germany were not bound by such impediments, but only because of a contrary custom.

Schmalzgrueber[42] also adhered to the stand that heretics in Germany were fundamentally obliged to obey the Tridentine law against clandestine marriages in consequence of their valid baptism, but that it could be presumed that the Church tolerated clandestine marriages which were contracted, especially on account of the great evil and danger that would come if such marriages were regarded as invalid. Hence, there were beginning at that time attempts to find reasons for exempting heretics from strictly ecclesiastical laws.

The opposite opinion which insisted on the binding force of the law of the Council of Trent which forbade clandestine marriages seems to be more in keeping with the policy of the Church which did not usually permit exceptions to its laws unless it expressly stated that it wanted to give a

40 *Jus Canonicum Universum,* Lib. I, tit. 2, n. 274.

41 *Jus Ecclesiasticum Universum,* Lib. IV, Tit. I, nn. 378-380.

42 *Op. cit.,* Lib. IV, Tit. III, n. 99.

general exemption. This is noted implicitly in the Declaration of Benedict XIV[43] which was issued shortly after Schmalzgrueber's time. Here the Pope gave definite expression to his contention that the Fathers of the Council of Trent did not wish to bind heretics to the canonical form of marriage which they had commanded in their decree *Tametsi* when those heretics had been established into a definite community with churches and ministers. The Pope's declaration was an explicit pronouncement that heretics in the Federated States of Belgium were not subject to the law just noted. He acknowledged, however, in this same declaration that these heretics were bound by the laws that treated of matrimonial impediments. Hence, it seems as though there could be no sanction given to that opinion of Schmalzgrueber according to which heretics in Germany were admitted to be fundamentally bound by the law of the decree *Tametsi* but by a presumption could be considered as having contracted their marriages validly apart from the observance of the canonical form particularly in view of the great evil and impending danger that would be present if such marriages were to be regarded as invalid.[44]

In treating of punishments, Schmalzgrueber[45] noted that corporal and temporal punishments could not be inflicted on heretics in Germany and in other parts of the Holy Roman Empire because of a pact to that effect between the Holy See and the Protestant German rulers. This seems to be the only reason assigned by him, for he stated that elsewhere such punishments could be inflicted by the Church. He admitted, however, that spiritual ecclesiastical punishments could be meted out to all heretics, even to

[43] *Matrimonia*, 4 nov. 1741—*Bullarium Benedicti XIV*, I, 111; *Fontes*, n. 3527.

[44] Schmalzgrueber, *Ius Ecclesiasticum Universum*, Lib. IV, tit. 3, n. 99.

[45] *Op. cit.*, Lib. V, tit. 7, n. 171.

those in Germany. Thus he upheld the principle that heretics are still under the Church's jurisdiction.

In all thees citations it should be noted that heretics are held to be fundamentally bound to ecclesiastical laws because of the reception of valid baptism; and although most of the citations seem to be treating of heretics who have previously been Catholics, their evidence is of such a nature that it may be applied to all heretics who have received valid baptism. Also from these foregoing citations it should be noted that, even though there were attempts to find reasons for exempting heretics from ecclesiastical laws, there were no distinctions made in the types of laws, e. g., there were no distinctions made between laws that were enacted for preserving the public order or for promoting personal sanctification. It remained for later writers to do that.

4. Pre-Code Decisions and Decrees

In the following official pronouncements of the Popes and of the Congregations there are clear indications of the Church's official stand in the matter of heretics' obligation to observe its laws.

Pope Benedict XIV in his Declaration *Matrimonia* [46] stated that heretics in the Federated States of Belgium were not subject to the Council of Trent's regulation regarding the canonical form of marriage but that they were subject to the ecclesiastical laws that treated of the canonical impediments to marriage.

The same Pope in 1748 [47] treated of a dispensation granted for the marriage of two heretics in Poland, thus indicating that heretics must be subject to ecclesiastical impediments, else there would be no point to their seeking a dispensation from ecclesiastical laws in this matter. The

[46] 4 nov. 1741—*Bullarium Benedicti* XIV, I, 111; *Fontes,* n. 3527.

[47] Ep. encycl. *Magnae Nobis,* 29 iun. 1748—*Fontes,* n. 387.

Pope did not seem to be objecting to the actual granting of the dispensation, but to the fact that the petition did not contain the information that the two parties were heretics and that, therefore, the dispensation should not have been executed.

Again in the same year Pope Benedict XIV [48] in a letter to the Primate, Archbishops and Bishops of Poland, discussed a dispensation granted for the marriage of two Lutherans related in the second degree of affinity—a purely ecclesiastical impediment. It seems that a certain Polish bishop, without having any authority from Rome, granted the dispensation to the two Lutherans in question. The Pope admitted that such dispensations were granted by the Holy See, but, since the bishop had acted without having authorization, the marriage of the two heretics in question was invalid. Hence, there are two indications from this letter that the Pope considered heretics as bound by this ecclesiastical law not only *fundamentally* but *actually*. These two indications are: The fact that dispensations were granted to them by the Holy See and the fact that the Pope declared the marriage invalid because of the presence of an ecclesiastical impediment.

In regard to the strictly ecclesiastical impediment of disparity of cult, there was published a most important document by the same Pope.[49] In treating of the marriage of a Jew with a woman heretic, he asserted that baptism when conferred validly by a heretic on an infant, who naturally is not able to make a profession of faith, imprints the indelible character and makes the baptized child a member of the Catholic Church. If, however, that child, after he reaches the age when he can distinguish between right and wrong, accepts the erroneous doctrine of the heretical sect, he is

[48] Ep. *Ad tuas manus,* 8 aug. 1748—*Fontes,* n. 389.

[49] Benedict XIV, ep. *Singulari Nobis,* 9 febr. 1749, nn. 13, 14—*Fontes,* n. 394.

to be dismissed from union with the Church, but he is not thereby freed from the Church's authority or laws. From this the Pope concluded that the marriage in question —between a Jew and a heretic—was invalid. Certainly the points enumerated by the Pope—baptism in infancy by a heretic and the acceptance of heretical errors when able to distinguish between good and evil—would apply to a very large number of heretics. Therefore, it seems safe to say that he considered all heretics as actually bound to ecclesiastical laws in general and to the strictly ecclesiastical law concerning the disparity of cult impediment in particular.

About thirty years later there was a response of the Sacred Congregation of the Council[50] that held as invalid those marriages which were contracted in Hungary between heretics who were related within prohibitive degrees of relationship if a dispensation had not been procured previously.

Shortly afterwards Pope Pius VII[51] in an absolute manner recorded the subjection of heretics to the Church's laws in consequence of the reception of Baptism.

The Sacred Congregation of the Holy Office in 1860[52] noted that heretics were bound by the matrimonial impedi-

[50] S. C. C., *Rosnavien.*, 20 aug. 1780—*Fontes*, n. 3811.

[51] Breve *Etsi Fraternitatis*, 8 oct. 1803—De Roskovany, *Matrimonium in Ecclesia Catholica Potestati Ecclesiasticae Subjectum, Cum Amplissima Collectione Monumentorum et Literatura* (5 vols., Pestini, 1870-1882), I, 461: "Sed quid dicendum erit de illorum sententia, qui iactant, haereticos Ecclesiae legibus nequaquam subici, atque inde posse illos novo coniugii foedere copulari, si primum publicae auctoritatis iudicio solutum fuerit, praepostere inferunt? Adversus illam clamant Scripturae, Concilia, traditio denique universa. Omnium instar sit Tridentina Synodus, quae Sess. 14, cap. 2 non baptizatos a baptizatis distinguens illos tantum Ecclesiae iudicio proinde legibus non subiici affirmat, cum Ecclesia in neminem iudicium exerceat, qui non prius in ipsam per baptismi januam ingressus. Si baptizati ergo Ecclesiae filii—quamquam rebelles et transfugae—qui eiusdem Ecclesiae legibus subiiciuntur; quare suam in illos potestatem exercere numquam praetermisit Ecclesia, potestate sibi divinitus tradita. . . ."

[52] Instr. *ad Vic. Ap. Gallas*, 28 mart. 1860—*Fontes*, n. 957; *Collect. S. C. de Prop. Fide*, n. 1188.

ments enacted in the law of the Catholic Church.

From the consideration of the foregoing documents, the Church's official stand in regard to heretics is clear. In not every instance is it evident whether or not the heretics in question were formerly Catholics. But, since no distinction was made, it may be stated that the Popes and the Congregations did not think any distinction was necessary. Even where former Catholics may have been spoken of, the examples would have value because the basis for the subjection to ecclesiastical laws was valid baptism which could be received even from heretics. And since these documents and answers referred to specific instances they treated of the *actual* subjection of heretics to ecclesiastical laws. In instances where ecclesiastical laws were mentioned without limitation it may be concluded that the phrase included also the purely ecclesiastical laws—no distinction was made.

In the beginning of the twentieth century there were two decisions that indicated the mind of the Church in regard to the subjection of heretics to its laws. One [53] concerned two heretics, born and educated in heresy. They had a domicile at Paris, but attempted marriage before a minister in England. The marriage was declared null on the grounds of clandestinity. The Sacred Congregation of the Council, therefore, by this decision that heretics, even those born and reared in heresy, were obliged to obey the Church's law on the canonical form for marriage showed that it considered them bound to at least this purely ecclesiastical law.

The other decision was given by the Sacred Roman Rota [54] in the following case: Two Wesleyans, related supposedly in the fourth degree of the collateral line of consanguinity, were married without any Protestant rite, lived

[53] S. C. C., *Causa Parisiensis,* 18 iul. 1903—*Analecta Ecclesiastica,* XI (1903), 284.

[54] *Causa Trincomalien,* 1 febr. 1913—*AAS,* V (1913), 201.

together a year and had a child. Then the man married his sister-in-law, had a child and this second woman divorced him because he became a Catholic. The case concerned the nullity of the first marriage. It was not declared null because consanguinity could not be proved but the very fact that the Rota tried to prove that the consanguinity existed and that, if it did, the marriage was null, indicates that these two heretics were bound by the strictly ecclesiastical law on consanguinity.

Finally there was a general exception made for the marriages of heretics in regard to the canonical form of marriage when these heretics contracted among themselves.[55] And this is proof that prior to that date the Church considered heretics bound by the law and, if consideration is given to the general principle that all validly baptized persons, including heretics, are fundamentally subject to ecclesiastical jurisdiction, it seems to offer proof that the Church considered them as actually bound at least to all marriage laws and probably to all her laws since she made only this exception. It is a well-known axiom that the exception attests the rule in those things that are not excepted.

5. Nineteenth and Early Twentieth Century Opinions

Commentators in the nineteenth century [56] still adhered to the incontrovertible principle of fundamental subjection of heretics to the Church's jurisdiction, but they express diverse opinions about whether the Church desired that

[55] S. C. C., decr. *Ne temere*, 2 aug. 1907—*Fontes*, n. 4340; *ASS*, XL (1907), 525-530.

[56] Tarquini, *Iuris Ecclesiastici Publici Institutiones*, pp. 75, 76, nn. 62, 63, 64; De Angelis, *Praelectiones Juris Canonici ad Methodum Decretalium Gregorii IX Exactae* (4 vols. in 8, Romae, 1877-1887), Tom. I, Pars I, pp. 54, 55, 56, n. 13; Sanguineti, *Iuris Ecclesiastici Privati Institutiones ad Decretalium Enarrationem Ordinatae* (Romae, 1884), p. 26, n. 58; Santi, *Praelectiones Juris Canonici*, I, 22, n. 31.

they be *actually* bound by its laws in all circumstances and cases.

Some made distinctions by stating that heretics and schismatics were bound to obey those Church laws which were enacted for correcting abuses or for safeguarding public order and morals, e. g., matrimonial impediments. But as for laws whose direct purpose was that of personal sanctification, e. g., the observance of fast and abstinence, they held that heretics and schismatics were not bound since the Church perceived that in such matters these persons would in all probability remain contumacious and that nothing would be accomplished but the multiplication of sins, if they were held to the observance of the law.[57]

This opinion, of course, referred to actual subjection to ecclesiastical laws, for all admitted the fundamental subjection in view of the reception of valid baptism. This opinion made, however, no distinction between the types of heretics. Still it must be kept in mind that formal heretics who left the Church were bound by all ecclesiastical laws, for they were not to receive any advantage from their evil deeds. This was held unanimously.

Opposed to the above explained opinion seems to be that which held that heretics were bound to all ecclesiastical laws unless they were expressly exempted by the Church.[58]

According to Feye,[59] the common opinion in the nineteenth century was that heretics were bound by the diriment matrimonial impediments and that the Church did not wish to exempt them. That doctrine naturally bore out the opinion that heretics were bound to ecclesiastical laws governing matrimonial impediments. In addition Feye stated[60]

[57] De Angelis, *Praelectiones Juris Canonici*, p. 56, n. 13; Santi, *Praelectiones Juris Canonici*, I, 22, n. 31.

[58] Sanguineti, *Iuris Ecclesiastici Privati Institutiones*, p. 26, n. 58.

[59] *Dissertatio Canonica de Matrimoniis Mixtis*, p. 89.

[60] *Op. cit.*, pp. 89, 90.

that all heretics were bound by ecclesiastical marriage laws and that no reasons strong enough had been advanced to show that they were exempted by law, dispensation, prescription, lack of observance of the laws or by custom.

Just prior to the promulgation of the Code of Canon Law there were two important authors who treated the topic of the obligation on the part of heretics to observe ecclesiastical laws.

Cavagnis (1841-1906),[61] in referring to heretics who were born and educated in heterodoxy, stated that the Church did not wish to enforce its laws which pertained to personal sanctification, but that the Church did not evince a similar passive attitude with regard to laws which were directed to the common good.

Wernz (1842-1914),[62] on the other hand, noted this opinion of Cavagnis and of others, but rejected it with these words:

> At haec distinctio cum partiali et generali quadam immunitate acatholicorum *hucusque in fontibus iuris, qui generatim et indiscriminatim loquuntur, nullum habet fundamentum.* Ratio autem a patronis istius sententiae ex praesumptione petita nititur coniectura cum textibus iuris vix conciliabili et in aliquo argumento, quod, cum de omnibus legibus ecclesiasticis valeat, nimium probat, et insuper non attendit, quod lex quaedem iusta et prudens debeat esse utilis toti communitati, non solis personis, quae illam probabiliter sint observaturae.

Then Wernz stated as a conclusion that it was no wonder that De Lugo[63] and others rejected entirely the arguments

61 *Institutiones Iuris Publici Ecclesiastici* (4. ed., 3 vols., Romae, 1906), I, p. 360, n. 564.

62 *Ius Decretalium,* I, n. 103, footnote 80.

63 *Disputationes Scholasticae et Morales,* Tom. IV (*Tract. De Sacramento Poenitentiae*), Disp. XV, Sect. VII, n. 144. (For the text of De Lugo the reader may turn to p. 116, *supra*).

which he himself criticized adversely. He did, of course, admit without a doubt that many heretics and schismatics on account of their ignorance were in good faith and therefore they at least did not sin by their transgressions of ecclesiastical laws. But any more immunity than that Wernz did not recognize as being established and proved.

From all that has been noted and said thus far it appears that, even though some authors tried to give reasons for exempting heretics from actual subjection to certain ecclesiastical laws, the weight of evidence from the Church's official stand in the matter was against their contentions. Mention has also been made of authors who refuted these contentions for exemption. There was one official declaration [64] which applied exclusively in the law on the form required for marriage and which stated that heretics in the Federated States of Belgium were not bound by this law when they married among themselves.

Later in 1907 [65] an exemption from the Catholic form of marriage was extended to all heretics when they contracted marriage among themselves. But for mixed marriages the Catholic form of marriage was necessary, unless the Holy See had determined otherwise in some particular place. There were two such particular places, namely, Germany and Hungary, where the exemption from the Catholic form of marriage was still in force for marriages between a heretic and a Catholic.[66] These two exceptions to the decree *Ne temere* remained in force until the promulgation of the Code of Canon Law.

[64] *Matrimonia,* 4 nov. 1741—*Bullarium Benedicti XIV,* I, 111; *Fontes,* n. 3527.

[65] S. C. C., decr. *Ne temere,* 2 aug. 1907—*Fontes,* n. 4340; *AAS,* XL (1907), 525-530.

[66] Cf. Litt. Ap., *Provida* of Pope Pius X, 18 ian. 1906—*ASS,* XXXIX (1906), 81-84.

In the light of what has been noted up to this point, therefore, it may be stated that validly baptized heretics are *fundamentally* subject to all ecclesiastical laws in view of the indelible mark of baptism upon them and, unless they be given an express, official, exemption, they are also *actually* subject to these laws. Those reasons, of course, which are valid for excusing individual Catholics from the actual observance of some law are also valid for excusing individual heretics from observing Church laws. But even in such circumstances the basic, fundamental subjection to Church laws remains with the Catholic and the heretic, for it stands certified through the indelible character of baptism inherent in their souls.

c) *The Code of Canon Law and Heretics*

1. Introductory Explanation

It is necessary now to show in some way how the opinion that heretics are actually bound to purely ecclesiastical laws unless they are expressly and officially exempted is strengthened by the present law of the Church.

By way of introduction one may well state the Code's official definition of a heretic: [67] " If anyone, after having received baptism and while retaining the name Christian, pertinaciously denies any of the truths that must be believed with divine and Catholic faith, or doubts about them, he is a heretic." This definition of course, indicates a formal heretic through its use of the word *pertinaciter*, which presupposes knowledge of the wrongdoing on the part of the heretic.[68]

As treated by the authors since the beginning of the so-called Reformation, the question of whether heretics are bound by the laws of the Church is not explicitly or abso-

[67] Canon 1325, § 2.

[68] Coronata, *Institutiones Iuris Canonici*, II, pp. 247, 248, n. 911.

lutely settled in the present Code.[69] This is shown by the fact that authors even today have diverse opinions in the matter. In various canons of the Code, however, there are certain points which help one to some kind of practical solution.

From what has been recorded already about the general principles of subjection to laws there can be no doubt that all validly baptized persons are fundamentally bound to all ecclesiastical laws. The Church, therefore, can bind validly baptized heretics to its laws. The Code indicates for the greater part that she wishes to do so. This is noted definitely in Canon 87, which gives the juridic effects of baptism as officially stated by the Church. It also implicitly notes the important difference between a *member* of the Church and a *subject* of the Church. In translation it reads: " By baptism a human being is made a person in the Church of Christ with all the rights and duties of Christians, unless, inasfar as rights are concerned, there is some obstacle impeding the bond of communion with the Church or a censure inflicted by the Church." And its sense is this: By baptism a human being is given juridic personality (capacity) in the Church with all the rights and duties that accompany it, unless there is some obstacle or ecclesiastical censure hindering the exercise of the rights.

A *member* of the Church possesses complete (*plena*) juridic personality (capacity), because he not only is bound by the obligations imposed by the Church, but he may also enjoy the corresponding rights which are granted to the members of the various states of life that exist in the Church, e. g., the clerical state, the religious state, the lay state. One who is only a *subject* of the Church, on the other hand, possesses incomplete (*minus plena*) juridic personality (capacity), because he is generally held to all the

69 De Schepper, " De Haereticis Relate Ad Leges Ecclesiasticas,"—*Collationes Brugenses,* XXIV (1924), 209.

obligations, but is deprived of the rights, either entirely or partially.[70]

It should be noted that Canon 87 very definitely states that some obstacle [like adherence to an heretical or schismatical sect],[71] or an ecclesiastical censure [such as excommunication] may hinder the exercise of the *rights* that accompany juridic personality in the Church, but it states nothing about such an obstacle or censure as excusing a baptized person from fulfilling his Christian *duties*. Hence these duties are fundamentally and actually binding on all validly baptized persons, even though some obstacle or ecclesiastical censure prevents them from exercising their Christian rights. This is a general rule which under special circumstances may suffer an exception in an individual case.

Heretics are not now members of the Church and, therefore, they are temporarily deprived of any rights that they may have had by reason of valid baptism. But, as Canon 87 notes, they are still subject to all the juridic obligations that arise from the reception of valid baptism [even if it were administered by an heretical minister or any one else].[72]

Just as a person who is convicted of a crime against the State loses many of the privileges of citizenship and is barred from exercising many of his rights, he is nevertheless still subject to the authority of the State. So it is with the baptized non-Catholic—he commits an offense against the Church by adhering to an heretical doctrine. But because he can never erase the indelible mark of baptism, he still remains subject to the Church unless the Church sees fit to exempt him from her own laws for special reasons.

[70] Cf. Maroto, *Institutiones Iuris Canonici*, I, p. 455, n. 390-b; p. 457, n. 392-B.

[71] Claeys-Bouuaert et Simenon, *Manuale Juris Canonici*, I, 137, n. 237; Chelodi-Bertagnolli, *Ius de Personis*, p. 162, n. 91.

[72] Woywod, *A Practical Commentary on the Code of Canon Law* (5. ed., 2 vols., New York: Joseph F. Wagner, Inc., 1939), I, p. 37, n. 64.

2. Legislation concerning Heretics

That the Church prior to the Code wished heretics to remain subject to her laws was demonstrated by various citations. And that she still wishes them to give obedience to her laws and that she still considers them as subject to her jurisdiction is also amply evidenced in the Code:

In Canon 167, § 1, 4°, she definitely excludes heretics from casting votes in canonical elections. This canon, however, treats only of heretics who by positive action have joined a sect. This is noted by the use of the phrases *nomen dederunt* and *publice adhaeserunt.* The first phrase refers to those who knowingly and willingly are admitted into some sect with or without a special rite. And *publice adhaeserunt* refers to those who not only publicly inscribe their names on the rolls of a non-Catholic sect but who publicly and repeatedly communicate *in sacris* in a non-Catholic place of worship with members of that non-Catholic sect.[73]

Vermeersch-Creusen[74] state that the phrase *publice adhaeserunt* may be taken as denoting the passing from the true religion to a sect, according to the interpretation made on October 16, 1919, by the Pontifical Commission for the Authentic Interpretation of the Canons of the Code, in regard to Canon 542, n. 1,[75] even though the phrase *nomen dederunt* precedes the phrase *publice adhaeserunt* here in Canon 167, § 1, 4°.

Hence it must be concluded that this section of Canon 167 refers only to heretics who have actually joined a sect and take part publicly in its religious ceremonies. Accordingly,

[73] Coronata, *Institutiones Iuris Canonici,* IV, p. 289, n. 1863; Vermeersch-Creusen, *Epitome,* III, p. 263, n. 513.

[74] *Epitome,* I, 165, n. 245.

[75] *AAS,* XI (1919), 477; Bouscaren, *The Canon Law Digest* (2 vols. and two supplements [1938, 1941], Milwaukee: The Bruce Publishing Co., 1934-1941), I, 298.

other heretics are not excluded from casting votes in canonical elections except by the general principle of Canon 87 as to certain obstacles, such as heresy, that prevent the use of Christian rights. The point, however, in citing this section of Canon 167 is still valid, for the actual consideration of heretics in an ecclesiastical law is an indication that the Church still considers herself as having jurisdiction over them, since a lawgiver can normally make laws only for those under his jurisdiction. And there would not be much point to restricting the right of someone who never had any claim to such right, as in the present case the casting of votes in canonical elections.

This section of Canon 167 seems to be just a specific application of the general principle of Canon 87. It probably was included under Canon 167 in order to emphasize the general disability in the specific instance of the right to vote in canonical elections.

The same observations about heretics' being under the Church's jurisdiction apply to other juridic regulations referring to heretics. Thus it is forbidden to administer the Sacraments to them even when they err in good faith. Unless they reject their errors and are reconciled with the Church, they have no claim upon the reception of the Sacraments.[76] In Canon 731, § 2, the Code implies the distinction between heretics who are such in bad or in good faith, but it includes both of these classes under the same prohibition. The very object of the prohibition demands that all heretics be included in the prohibition, for the reecption of the Sacraments is a prerogative of members, not of mere subjects, of the body of the faithful.

Because of this prohibition heretics who might be physically capable of fulfilling the obligations of annual confession [77] and of Paschal Communion,[78] are not directly and

[76] Canon 731, § 2.

[77] Canon 906.

[78] Canon 859, § 1.

actually bound by these two laws.[79] In their root and of themselves, however, these obligations remain and therefore continue in their binding force, for they are entailed by the very reception of valid baptism. They are not fundamentally removed when a heretic has ceased to be a member of the body of the faithful, or when in view of such non-membership he is prohibited from the use of the right which alone makes it possible for him to fulfill these obligations.

Heretics cannot act validly as sponsors at baptism,[80] or at confirmation.[81]

The Code also treats of heretics in connection with one of the irregularities which arises *ex delicto,* that is, the irregularity which attaches to a person who is guilty of the delict of heresy.[82] Hence, canon 985, n. 1, does not refer to heretics who are such through no fault of their own and remain in good faith, but it rather refers to those heretics who have joined an heretical sect, or to those who were born and reared in heresy, and who, after they reached the age of reason and knew of their obligation of submitting to the Catholic Church, still remained in heresy. That this is the situation is indicated by the fact that an irregularity *ex delicto* arises from an action which is seriously wrong in the internal and external forums. In order to beget an irregularity *ex delicto* an action must be a serious sin committed after baptism, except in the case noted in Canon 985, n. 2; it must be an external act, but it can be such when the act is occult, and it necessarily is such when the act is public.[83] A heretic in good faith would not

79 De Schepper, "De Haereticis relate ad Leges Ecclesiasticas,"—*Collationes Brugenses,* XXIV (1924), 211.

80 Canon 765, n. 2.

81 Canon 795, n. 2.

82 Canon 985, n. 1.

83 Canon 986; cf. Gasparri, *Tractatus Canonicus de Sacra Ordinatione,* p. 122, n. 200: ". . . ad irregularitatem ex delicto contrahendam requiritur delictum grave tum in foro interno tum in foro externo. . . ."

in his heretical conduct have fulfilled these conditions.

Vermeersch-Creusen[84] hold that even a heretic who in good faith has been enrolled in a sect will normally need a dispensation *ad cautelam* from the irregularity of Canon 985, n. 1. Hickey[85] holds that heretics, even upon their conversion and reconciliation are still subject to this irregularity: "Since perpetuity is an essential characteristic of irregularity (Canon 983), an apostate, heretic or schismatic, even subsequent to his conversion, *remains* irregular, and must obtain a dispensation before he can be advanced to Orders, or exercise the same." Genicot-Salsmans also state[86] that the heretics or schismatics referred to in canon 985, n. 1, are those who are enrolled in a sect or were enrolled in one.

Gasparri, when treating of those who are capable of incurring this irregularity, simply mentions *viros baptizatos*[87] among whom, of course, are included all men who are validly baptized heretics. He also states that it is certain that heretics are irregular and that as a result after their conversion they are prohibited by ecclesiastical law from being promoted to orders or to exercise the orders that they have received.[88] Later, when treating of the actual irregularity that arises from one's adherence to a condemned sect, he states that the irregularity affects those who belonged to such a sect either as a result of their own action or as a result of being ascribed to that sect when an infant. But, in regard to the latter class, since the irregularity is one of those which arises *ex delicto* he evidently means such persons who as infants received baptism in an heretical sect

[84] *Epitome*, II, p. 149, n. 257.

[85] *Irregularities and Simple Impediments in the New Code of Canon Law*, p. 46.

[86] *Institutiones Theologiae Moralis*, II, p. 574, n. 633: "Intelliguntur haeretici et schismatici qui sectae ascripsi *sunt* vel ferunt."

[87] *Op. cit.*, p. 122, n. 200.

[88] *Op. cit.*, p. 289, n. 461.

and later refused to acknowledge their known obligation of submitting to the Church. Gasparri then notes that this irregularity affects these heretics when they come into or return to the Church, that is, their conversion furnishes the occasion for the Church to advert to the previous delict which is assumed as having given rise to the irregularity.

Hence it may be seen that heretics are subject to the ecclesiastical law that governs irregularities, at least in regard to this one that arises from adherence to an heretical sect, but only after they have been converted.

That the Church wishes to bind heretics actually even by her purely ecclesiastical laws which govern marriage is also evident, for after she claims for herself the exclusive right to declare authentically when the divine law impedes and invalidates marriage,[89] she asserts her exclusive right to institute, by means of universal or particular laws, impeding or diriment impediments for the marriages of *all* baptized persons.[90] By using simply the unqualified term *baptizatis* she includes all validly baptized persons, even heretics,[91] for when the Church wishes heretics to be exempt from any of her marriage laws she gives them express exemption.

In corroboration of this contention that the Church claims jurisdiction over heretics in regard to marriage, it will be noted that she asserts her exclusive right to hear, to consider and to judge all marriage cases between baptized persons.[92] In canon 1960 the law again contains the unrestricted word *baptizatos* which, as has been said, includes all validly baptized persons within its scope.[93]

89 Canon 1038, § 1.

90 Canon 1038, § 2.

91 De Smet, *De Sponsalibus et Matrimonio*, p. 373, n. 430; Ayrinhac-Lydon, *Marriage Legislation in the New Code of Canon Law*, pp. 56, 57, n. 61.

92 Canon 1960.

93 Coronata, *Institutiones Iuris Canonici*, III, p. 414, n. 1478, 2°: "Causae matrimoniales in iudicio ecclesiastico tractandae sunt causae agitatae inter

A striking example of the Church's exercising this right to judge a marriage case in which heretics were concerned is found in the famous Vanderbilt-Marlborough case. It involved two heretics. Their case was decided by the Holy Roman Rota on July 29, 1926.[94] And the following words of the Dean of the Sacred Roman Rota in referring to that case [95] express plainly what may be taken as the Church's attitude in regard to the marriage cases of all baptized persons, including heretics: "The accusation has been made against us that we undertook the adjudication of matrimonial causes between non-Catholics . . . But such a charge is devoid of all foundation. For in the first place everyone knows that *the Church openly claims for herself the right to decide matrimonial causes between baptized persons* [96] (as is clear from the law of Canon 1960 of the Code) . . . It is very evident that non-Catholics by appealing to the ecclesiastical authority recognize by that very fact the competence of the Church, which (inasmuch as their petition has for its purpose, as Canon 1564 declares, the averting of spiritual harm) does not refuse to give such non-Catholics a hearing."

Since that time, however, a decision [97] has been given that a non-Catholic, either baptized or unbaptized, cannot act as plaintiff [*actor*] in a marriage case; and even if there are special reasons for admitting such non-Catholics as plain-

baptizatos. Baptizati autem omnes in hac re subduntur Ecclesiae, sive haeretici ii sint sive schismatici, exclusis infidelibus."

[94] *AAS*, XVIII (1926), 501-506; *Jus Pontificium*, VII (1927), 30; Cicognani, *Canon Law*, p. 565, footnote 9.

[95] Cicognani, *Canon Law*, p. 565, footnote 9. These words, the translation of which is given here, were spoken at the opening of the juridical year, October 1, 1927.

[96] Italics not in the original.

[97] S.C.S. Off., 27 ian. 1928—*AAS*, XX (1928), 75; Bouscaren, *Canon Law Digest*, I, 762-763; Ayrinhac-Lydon, *Marriage Legislation in the New Code of Canon Law*, p. 356–c.

tiffs, the Holy Office must be consulted in each case. As is evident, this refers only indirectly to the Church's right over the marriage cases of heretics; directly it restricts the heretics' right to have their cases brought before an ecclesiastical tribunal. This is in accord with Canon 87 (noted especially in the response) which states that baptized persons may not use their Christian rights when an obstacle prevents them from exercising these rights. Such an obstacle, as noted previously, is the profession of heretical doctrines. The very fact that the Holy Office may give permission is an evidence that it does consider itself as having jurisdiction over the marriages of the heretics in question. The instruction just noted seems to be a regulation for enabling the Holy Office to exercise the greatest vigilance in this matter.[98]

In the Code notorious heretics are deprived specifically of the right of Christian burial.[99] Though Kerin by convincing arguments shows that canon 1240 applies only to Catholics who have left the Church, and that heretics are deprived of this right simply by the general restriction of Christian rights expressed in canon 87,[100] this canon 1240 shows at least that some heretics are specifically deprived of a Christian right and offers an indication that at least they had a claim to the right of Christian burial by reason of their baptism for one cannot be deprived of something that he does not possess. The very word used by canon 1240 is *privantur*. The important point about this, however, is that the canon indicates the Church's jurisdiction

[98] Cf. *Periodica*, XVII (1928), 54, where reference is made to a similar decision of the Holy Office (8 apr. 1925). This, however, was not published officially in the *Acta Apostolicae Sedis*.

[99] Canon 1240, § 1, 1°.

[100] Kerin, *The Privation of Christian Burial*, The Catholic University of America Canon Law Studies, n. 136 (Washington, D. C.: The Catholic University of America Press, 1941), pp. 180, 182, 185, 188.

over heretics, since the deprivation of something can be done legitimately only by one who has jurisdiction over the person affected. And if the person is under the Church's jurisdiction the Church can bind him by its laws.

Finally, excommunication could not be inflicted on a person who becomes a heretic [101] unless he were still considered as being subject to the Church even after his defection, for the delict for which this punishment is inflicted must be perfected [102] before the censure is incurred. And the censure and its consequences bind the culprit until he becomes reconciled with the Church.[103] Hence, he must be considered by the Church as being capable not only of incurring this censure, but also of remaining under it for a time. And that indicates that she considers him as being actually subject to her laws, even when he is separated from the body of the Church.

That the Church wishes validly baptized heretics to remain subject to its laws, not only fundamentally but also actually, has been shown already from Canon 12, which may be taken in its positive form to mean that all those who are baptized validly are bound also by purely ecclesiastical laws.[104] One may regard this general principle as receiving full corroboration from canon 87.

In order to vindicate sufficiently the contention that this general principle derived from canon 12 applies to all validly baptized persons, even to heretics, and that the Church wishes them to be subject actually to its laws unless express exemptions are given, it seems that it is necessary only to point out specific exemptions from certain purely ecclesiastical laws which the Code has granted to heretics.

[101] Canon 2314.

[102] Canons 2228; 2242.

[103] Canons 2241; 2248.

[104] De Schepper, " De Haereticis relate ad Leges Ecclesiasticas "—*Collationes Brugenses*, XXIV (1924), 210.

The basis for the proof is furnished by the legal axiom: *Exceptio firmat regulam in iis quae non excipiuntur.*

First, those heretics who have been validly baptized in an heretical sect and have never been actual members of the Catholic Church are exempted from the impediment of disparity of cult, which has been restricted to persons baptized in the Catholic Church or converted to it from heresy or schism.[105]

Secondly, the same class of heretics is exempted from the use of the Catholic form of marriage when they marry among themselves.[106] That this is a very special concession and a derogation from the general rule of the actual subjection of all validly baptized heretics to the Church's laws is evident from the fact that those who have left the Church to become heretics are not included in this exemption from the Catholic form of marriage.[107]

Canon 1099, § 2, also extends this exemption from the canonical form of marriage to a class of persons born of non-Catholic parents and baptized in the Catholic Church, but reared in heresy, schism, infidelity or even without any religion. Hence the Code considers them in the same class as those mentioned in the first clause of Canon 1099, § 2. Further, the Pontifical Commission for the Authentic Interpretation of the Canons of the Code by several responses has included in this exempt group, under the same conditions, those born of parents one of whom is a Catholic and the other a non-Catholic, even though the *cautiones* had

105 Canon 1070, § 1; cf. private replies on this canon: S. C. de Prop. Fide, 26 febr. 1924, reply to the pro-Vicar Apos. of Hankow—Sartori, *Enchiridion Canonicum* (6. ed., Vicetiae: ex Typographia Commerciali, 1938), p. 238; S.C.S. Off., 21 dec. 1924, reply to the Archbishop of Freiburg—*AKKR*, CV (1925), 202; Payen, *De Matrimonio*, I, p. 759, n. 1097; De Smet, *De Sponsalibus et Matrimonio*, p. 114, n. 140; p. 513, n. 586 and footnote 6.

106 Canon 1099, § 2.

107 Canon 1099, § 1.

been signed according to Canons 1061 and 1071,[108] and also those born of apostates.[109]

The exemption from the canonical form of marriage, therefore, has been given to almost every validly baptized person who is not a member of the Church; it has not been shared, of course, with Catholics who have deliberately separated themselves from the Church.

It is these two exemptions just recorded that strengthen and corroborate the general rule and make plain the Church's official attitude toward heretics. The very fact that these exemptions are granted though the Church enacted the general principle contained in canons 12 and 87 shows that they are the only general exceptions that she wishes to make for heretics.[110] She has not given any exemptions from her laws which are enacted for man's personal sanctification. Hence it may be concluded that she does not wish to make any even for heretics in good faith.

The Church, of course, may make other exceptions for heretics in particular cases, just as she does for Catholics. But, just as such dispensations in particular instances do not withdraw Catholics from actual subjection to the rest of the Church's legislation, so these *de jure* exemptions noted above do not excuse validly baptized heretics from actual subjection to all other ecclesiastical laws, including those which are enacted for man's personal sanctification.

108 *AAS*, XXI (1929), 573.

109 *AAS*, XXII (1930), 195.

110 Van Hove, *De Legibus Ecclesiasticis*, p. 201: "Quod autem Ecclesia velit illos [haereticos] obligare, patet tum ex iure superiore tum ex can. 12 et 87, qui principium generale ponunt, tum ex ipsis canonibus qui haereticos eximunt a quibusdam obligationibus (can. 1070, § 1; 1099), nam exceptio firmat regulam in iis quae non excipiuntur. . . . Quia exceptiones statuuntur, inde clare patet alias leges ligare haereticos, quod iam a nemine in dubium vocatur."

d) *Post-Code Opinions on the Obligation of Heretics to Observe Ecclesiastical Laws*

Writers since the publication of the Code of Canon Law have unanimously held to the fundamental subjection of heretics to all ecclesiastical laws.[111] Van Hove states[112] that there is no one who denies that heretics are fundamentally subject to ecclesiastical laws. And the reason given by most of those just noted, and at least presupposed by the others, is the reception of the indelible mark of baptism, which makes one a permanent subject of the Church, bound by all its laws.[113]

After admitting this fundamental subjection of heretics to ecclesiastical laws, many post-Code writers make the same distinctions concerning certain types of laws as proposed just prior to the promulgation of the Code.[114]

There seem to be no objectors to the opinion that heretics are actually bound by those laws which pertain to the preserving of the public order or the safeguarding of the ecclesiastical community, or which are conducive to the public good.[115] In one or the other such category are in-

111 Augustine, *A Commentary on the New Code of Canon Law*, I, 87, 88; Bargilliat, *Praelectiones Juris Canonici*, I, 62, 63, n. 70; Berutti, *Institutiones Iuris Canonici* (Vol. I, Taurini-Romae: Marietti, 1936), I, 78; Cicognani, *Commentarium ad Librum I. Codicis*, p. 95, n. 4; De Schepper, "De Haereticis Relate Ad Leges Ecclesiasticas,"—*Collationes Brugenses*, XXIV (1924), 209; Leroux, "Le Sujet Des Lois Ecclésiastiques,"—*Revue Ecclésiastique de Liège*, XVI (1924-1925), 331; Maroto, *Institutiones Iuris Canonici*, I, p. 203, n. 196; Michiels, *Normae Generales Juris Canonici*, I, 286; Van Hove, *De Legibus Ecclesiasticis*, p. 201.

112 *De Legibus Ecclesiasticis*, p. 201.

113 Michiels, *Normae Generales*, I, 286.

114 Let it be brought to mind again that the discussion is not about heretics who were once Catholics and left the Church. Hence, when the unqualified word *heretic* is employed in this section it does not include these persons who left the Church. Express mention of them will be made if it is necessary.

115 Bargilliat, *Praelectiones Juris Canonici*, I, 63; Chelodi-Bertagnolli, *Ius de Personis*, p. 113, footnote 2; Cicognani, *Commentarium Ad Librum I.*

validating and disqualifying laws and the general laws which concern delicts and punishments,[116] and also the enactments pertaining to human acts, such as contracts, and the juridical effects of fear and of ignorance.[117]

In regard to the ecclesiastical laws that tend primarily to secure man's personal sanctification, such as those on fast and abstinence, the observance of feasts, or the prohibition of books, there is a difference of opinion. Some [118] contend that the Church is presumed to act more mildly with heretics in regard to these laws and does not wish to oblige them actually in this matter. One of the reasons given is: That the Church foresees that heretics, by their contumacy, will violate these laws and multiply their sins. Hence, these authors give a benign interpretation of the will of the Church. Others [119] admit the probability of that opinion and teach that it may be held, but they attack it for various reasons.

First of all, and probably as the most important consideration, the pre-Code Law and the Code itself do not contain any positive indication of this tacit or presumed exception of non-Catholics from actual subjection to such

Codicis, p. 95, n. 4; Claeys-Bouuaert et Simenon, *Manuale Juris Canonici*, I, 91; De Schepper, *Collationes Brugensis*, XXIV (1924), 211; Leroux, *Revue Ecclésiastique de Liège*, XVI (1924-1925), 331; Michiels, *Normae Generales*, I, 288, 289. Cf. also Onclin, *De Territoriali vel Personali Legis Indole*, Universitatis Catholicae Lovaniensis Dissertationes ad Gradum Magistri in Facultate Theologica vel in Facultate Iuris Canonici Consequendum Conscriptae, Series II, n. 31 (Gambloci: J. Duculot, 1938), p. 298.

116 Michiels, *Normae Generales*, I, 288, 289.

117 Cicognani, *Canon Law*, p. 566.

118 Bargilliat, *Praelectiones Juris Canonici*, I, 63; Cicognani, *Commentarium Ad Librum I. Codicis*, p. 95, n. 4.

119 Cance, *Le Code de Droit Canonique* (16. ed., 3 vols., Paris: J. Cabalda et Fils, 1930), I, 49, n. 41; Chelodi-Bertagnolli, *Ius De Personis*, p. 113, footnote 2; Leroux, *Revue Ecclésiastique de Liège*, XVI (1924-1925), 332, 333; Michiels, *Normae Generales*, I, 289, 290; Van Hove, *De Legibus Ecclesiasticis*, pp. 201, 202.

laws.[120] Hence it is said that there is no solid canonical foundation for the distinction between laws for the public and private good.[121] Secondly, against the point raised from the multiplication of sins, it is asserted that in the majority of cases these heretics are already excused from formal sin by their ignorance or by their persuasion of immunity from such laws.[122] This, however, does not exempt them from the laws, inasmuch as there is a substantial difference between being exempted from observing a law and being excused from complying with it, either by ignorance or through some other reason, so that the material transgression does not become a formal sin.

Since it is a unique departure from the strict principles of law that have been set down thus far, further consideration must be given to this opinion that heretics are exempted, in view of the benevolence of the Church, from laws that pertain to man's personal sanctification. One must also keep in mind that the term "heretics" refers to those who never formally have left the Church,[123] i. e., to those who were baptized and reared in heretical sects, and perhaps to those who were born of Catholic parents and baptized in the Catholic Church and then, because of the defection of their parents, were reared and educated in heresy or schism, so that they are excused from personal guilt in being heretics.[124]

Some of the reasons on account of which the liberal opinion is rejected have just been recorded, but it is useful to examine the opinion itself more closely.

120 Michiels, *Normae Generales*, I, 289, 290.

121 Coronata, *Institutiones Iuris Canonici*, I, p. 27, n. 14.

122 Leroux, "Le Sujet Des Lois Ecclésiastiques,"—*Revue Ecclésiastique de Liège*, XVI (1924-1925), 329-334.

123 Michiels, *Normae Generales*, I, 287.

124 Maroto, *Institutiones Iuris Canonici*, I, p. 204, n. 196.

Its proponents state that the Church does not wish to bind heretics, schismatics and excommunicates because she sees that they will be contumacious in regard to these laws and the only effect of her insistance upon the principle that heretics are subject to all ecclesiastical laws without exception would be to multiply sins. Thus they say the Church would be using her power rather for destruction than edification.[125]

The argument which is drawn from the alleged multiplication of sins seems to presuppose that these heretics are not in good faith and know that they are bound by the laws in question, otherwise no formal sin would be committed by their transgression of these laws. The opposite, as noted before, contends that these heretics are either in good faith, or in a state of ignorance, or in a condition of persuasion regarding their immunity from obedience to these laws, and hence they are excused from formal sin and there is no need for a general exemption from these laws on the part of such persons.[126] Some say that even those who remain in a non-Catholic sect through doubtful faith or even bad faith are excused from formal sin by ignorance or by the persuasion of immunity from the Church's authority.[127] It is evident that this can be true since it is possible for a heretic to be in bad faith or doubtful faith regarding the correctness of his own religious creed, but yet

[125] Maroto, *Institutiones Iuris Canonici*, I, p. 204, n. 196; De Angelis, *Praelectiones Juris Canonici*, Tom. I, Pars I, p. 56, n. 13; Genicot-Salsmans, *Institutiones Theologiae Moralis*, I, p. 86, n. 111; cf. also Cocchi, *Commentarium in Codicem Iuris Canonici*, I, 173.

[126] Coronata, *Institutiones Iuris Canonici*, I, p. 27, n. 14; Leroux, "Le Sujet Des Lois Ecclésiastiques,"—*Revue Ecclésiastique de Liège*, XVI (1924-1925), 332; Michiels, *Normae Generales*, I, 289-290; Van Hove, *De Legibus Ecclesiasticis*, p. 202.

[127] Vermeersch-Creusen, *Epitome*, I, p. 61, n. 78; Vermeersch, *Theologia Moralis* (3. ed., 4 vols. in 3, Romae: Università Gregoriana, 1933-1937), I, pp. 253-254, n. 253.

feel persuaded that he is not subject to the creed or the authority of the Catholic Church.

An examination of the opinion holding for exemption made in a practical manner, seems to indicate this: Most of the members of heretical denominations today know about some of these laws of the Church intended for personal sanctification, e. g., that there is such a regulation as the Lenten Fast; that Catholics are not permitted to eat meat on Fridays; that they are bound to go to Mass on Sundays and Holy Days of Obligation; and, at least with the better-educated among them, that certain books are forbidden. There is probably only a small group that is not aware of any of these laws. But do those who are cognizant of them consider themselves as bound by them? It seems that it may be said safely that the vast majority of heretics are convinced that they are not bound by the laws of the Catholic Church in view of their separation from the body of that Church. It may be safely conjectured that there are very few non-Catholics today who think that they are committing sin every time they do not comply with one of these laws—for example, every time they do not abstain from meat on Friday.

Hence it appears that this argument for the exemption of heretics by the Church because otherwise sins would be multiplied is not based entirely on the facts of the case, for it presupposes that all or at least the majority of non-Catholics are in bad faith. This does not seem to be the case; and even if some small number of heretics is in bad faith, it does not seem that the Church should exempt them from actual subjection to her laws lest they cannot be saved by being permitted to remain in bad faith. Why should the Church have any more concern for such heretics than it has for Catholics who steep themselves in sin because of their bad faith? The Church does not exempt such Catholics from actual subjection to its laws.

The writers already cited as favoring the opinion under discussion seem to give evidence that they are referring to the multiplication of *formal* sins, for they speak of the Church as urging its laws for personal sanctification upon validly baptized heretics for their destruction rather than unto their edification.[128] But, if some of them perhaps refer to material sins, then it seems that their argument is even weaker, for the heretics would not be harmed spiritually by committing material sins, and certainly no scandal would be given to Catholics today by heretics not obeying the laws of the Catholic Church. Most of the Catholics probably never advert to the fact that validly baptized non-Catholics are still bound by the laws of the Catholic Church, and many probably do not consider any non-Catholics as bound by these laws. That these authors seem to have in mind the commission of formal sins is deducible from the counter-arguments of those who assert that heretics are excused from formal sin as long as they are in good faith or as long as they are convinced that they are not bound by the laws of the Church.[129]

The strongest argument for this benign opinion, therefore, does not seem to be its insistence on the subsequent multiplication of sins, but rather that which is based on charity toward heretics,[130] if not possibly that which alleges the benefits that come from holding to this opinion, namely,

[128] Cf. Bargilliat, *Praelectiones Juris Canonici*, I, 63.

[129] Cf. Leroux, *Revue Ecclésiastique de Liège*, XVI (1924-1925), 332, 333; Vermeersch-Creusen, *Epitome*, I, p. 61, n. 78.

[130] Cavagnis, *Institutiones Iuris Publici Ecclesiastici*, I, p. 360, n. 564: ". . . . quoniam non est praesumendum Ecclesiam velle haereticos et alios heterodoxos (natos et educatos in heterodoxia), obligare ad suas leges cum certa praevisione transgressionis absque necessitate aliqua (etenim esset occasionem praebere multiplicandis peccatis, quod etsi liceat ex gravi causa, non licet ex charitate absque ea), hinc communiter et cum veritate respondetur huic quaestioni Ecclesiam non urgere leges suas quando diriguntur primario ad sanctificationem individui. . . ."

the lessening of the alienation of non-Catholics who are in good faith and the obviating of many anxieties in the cases of conversion. Another point in its favor is that it has been taught for a long time openly by many important writers, without any official contradiction by the Church, and that it has not been expressly reprobated by the Code.[131]

Still, when it is considered from a strictly juridical standpoint that opinion does not have any firm foundation. But because of the weight of authority behind it, it is considered as probable and may be held in practice.[132] Hence in practice it is not necessary, when heretics are converted, to question them concerning violations of the laws of the Church in regard to the observance of Sundays and Holy Days, fast, abstinence,[133] and Catholics are permitted to cooperate with heretics who wish to perform actions that are forbidden to Catholics, e. g., to serve meat to a non-Catholic on a day of abstinence. All the adherents to this benign opinion, however, warn that Catholics are forbidden to induce non-Catholics to perform such actions either by persuading or enjoining them to do so.[134]

There is one author[135] who holds that this opinion *ex benevolentia Ecclesiae* is based on the principle of canon 5 regarding centenary custom contrary to law. He also states that recourse is had to *epikeia* and asks: Why must the law remain in force when it is admitted that it is not to be observed?

131 Claeys-Bouuaert et Simenon, *Manuale Juris Canonici*, I, 92; De Schepper, *Collationes Brugenses*, XXIV (1924), 212, 213.

132 Claeys-Bouuaert et Simenon (*Manuale Juris Canonici*, I, p. 91, n. 160) think that it is *communior*.

133 Vermeersch-Creusen, *Epitome*, I, p. 61, n. 78.

134 De Schepper, *Collationes Brugenses*, XXIV (1924), 213; Cicognani, *Canon Law*, p. 569.

135 Cicognani, *Canon Law*, p. 568.

In answer to the first argument based on centenary custom contrary to law, as arising under canon 5, it should be said first of all that if a custom did exist whereby heretics exempted themselves from the ecclesiastical laws in question it was indeed not expressly reprobated by the Code. But the next part of canon 5 speaks of contrary custom, centenary and immemorial, which may be tolerated by the bishop if circumstances are such that these customs cannot be done away with prudently. This takes in all kinds of custom whether general or particular. The question here is about a universal custom since the practice of almost all heretics is included.

In a treatment of a claim based on a contrary custom the intention required to begin a custom must not be overlooked. There are two opposing opinions as to the necessity of this intention. If the more common opinion is held that a custom contrary to the law can be introduced only by those who have the intention of establishing such a custom,[136] then it seems that heretics who have been in good faith and have not considered themselves bound by the Church's laws certainly have not introduced a custom of fact against the law, even though they have not been obeying the Church's laws for personal sanctity.[137] Those who do not think they are bound by laws certainly cannot be said to be committing actions against them when they do not obey such laws. Hence, it does not seem that such

[136] Cf. Cicognani, *Commentarium Ad Librum I. Codicis*, p. 161; Chelodi-Bertagnolli, *Ius De Personis*, p. 128, n. 72; Beste, *Introductio in Codicem*, p. 95; Maroto, *Institutiones Iuris Canonici*, I, p. 269, n. 252; Cocchi, *Commentarium in Codicem Iuris Canonici*, I, p. 218, n. 135; Claeys-Bouuaert et Simenon, *Manuale Juris Canonici*, I, p. 105, n. 183.

[137] A custom of fact is formed by the frequent repetition of similar acts by a community. A custom of law proceeds from the custom of fact, that is, a law is formed by the frequent repetition of similar acts. A custom of fact begets no obligation. A custom of law does beget an obligation for it possesses all the conditions required by the legislator and has obtained by his consent the force of law; (cf. Cicognani, *Canon Law*, p. 643).

persons can be said to have introduced a custom of fact against the law in question. If they have not introduced a custom of fact then they have not introduced a custom of law for a custom of law follows from a custom of fact when that custom of fact has the approval of the superior.

Even heretics who, though they have never been Catholics, are now in bad faith because they are convinced of their obligation of becoming a member of the Catholic Church but still remain out of it, could not introduce such a contrary custom as just noted because they would for the greater part be of the opinion that they are not bound by the Church's law since they are still not members of the Church. This is based on the fact that there are very few heretics who are aware that by the reception of valid baptism in an heretical sect they become subject to the Church's laws even though they are not members of the Church. Such persons would, therefore, be in practically the same state as heretics in good faith as far as establishing such a custom was concerned, for the intention of liberating themselves would still be lacking.

The conclusion seems to be that, even if heretics for centuries have not been obeying the Church's laws intended for personal sanctification they have not introduced a custom of fact that might be permitted to become a custom of law that would liberate them from the obligation of observing these laws since they have not had the intention of liberating themselves from these laws. It is certain that they have not introduced a custom of law because that must follow from a custom of fact. A custom of law is a custom of fact that has the sanction of the legislator.

If the opinion is held that no intention is necessary for introducing a custom contrary to the law,[138] then heretics,

[138] Cf. Guilfoyle, *Custom*, The Catholic University of America Canon Law Studies, n. 105 (Washington, D. C.: The Catholic University of America, 1937), p. 109.

even those in good faith, can introduce a custom of fact by not obeying the laws under discussion. But, since a custom receives its legal force from the consent of the legislator, then the consent of the lawgiver must intervene before the usage can supplant the existing law.

It may be objected that a community that is at least capable of receiving a law is capable of introducing a custom which may obtain the force of law.[139] This is true and the community comprised of heretics all over the world may be considered as having the capacity to introduce a custom, because they are capable of receiving a law. But that capability would be restricted by the lack of intention of liberating themselves from the law, if it is admitted that such an intention is necessary for introducing a custom contrary to the law. Even if the opinion that no intention is required in this matter were followed no custom of law could arise unless the legislator gave his consent to that custom. The legislator has not given that consent and it seems as though he will not give it except for the gravest of reasons since it is the realization of their obligation to these laws for personal sanctification that will be a means of leading heretics back into the Church.

If one holds the opinion that heretics are in a state of ignorance or of good faith in relation to their apparent transgressions of ecclesiastical law, then the use of *epikeia* is not necessary to show that they are not bound to the Church's laws for the personal sanctification of its subjects. *Epikeia* is used when a person is bound to a law and knows of his obligation but has grave reasons to think that he is excused at the time from observing that law. In other words, he thinks that his particular case is not within the ambit of this law.[140] It has been stated that heretics in good faith do not know of their obligation to ecclesiastical

[139] Canon 26.

[140] Genicot-Salsman, *Institutiones Theologiae Moralis*, I, p. 97, n. 133.

laws. How then is it possible for them to use *epikeia* to release themselves from an obligation which they think does not exist?

Against the point of some authors that the laws for personal sanctification would not be useful because they would not be observed but would be actually harmful if extended to heretics, it is noted[141] that a law is judged prudent and just, not because it is useful or adaptable to this or that person, but because it is useful and beneficial to the whole community. Hence, if it is for the good of the entire body politic, it should not be restricted to those who probably will observe it. Heretics, because of baptism, are subjects of the Church and, therefore, they are juridically bound by her laws, since the latter are conceived as being made for the universal Church including those who are separated by heresy.

Another opinion which seems to hesitate between both extremes,[142] is that the Church, in the external forum, does not urge the obligation of its laws too strongly. The fact that the Church does not urge the obligation to its laws too strongly is no indication that the Church does not still consider heretics as bound by those laws. The Church in many cases does not insist upon some of its basic rights as a perfect society, inasmuch as prudence in certain circumstances counsels another course of action. This same prudence may enter into the explanation for its not urging heretics to obey its laws. But the Church may still consider heretics as actually bound by its laws, and may still claim authority to force its subjects, even heretics, to obey its laws.[143] Today, however, it uses only certain spiritual

141 De Lugo, *Disputationes Scholasticae et Morales,* Tom. IV (Tract. *De Sacramento Poenitentiae*), Disp. XV, Sect. VII, n. 144; Van Hove, *De Legibus Ecclesiasticis,* pp. 201, 202.

142 Berutti, *Institutiones Iuris Canonici,* I, 78.

143 Cappello, *Summa Iuris Publici Ecclesiastici* (3. ed., Romae: apud Aedes Universitatis Gregorianae, 1932), II, p. 357, n. 362.

punishments against heretics as will be noted in the penal section of the Code.[144] It does not, of course, use such punishments for violations of laws such as the one requiring fast and abstinence on certain days.

In regard to ecclesiastical laws which prescribe certain determined acts for subjects of the Church but which non-Catholics are prohibited from performing, e. g., the laws of annual confession and Paschal Communion and the law regarding the hearing of Mass on Sundays and Holy Days of Obligation, some authors, though maintaining in general that heretics are not directly exempt from laws looking to personal sanctification,[145] hold that non-Catholics are exempted from them indirectly (*per accidens*).

It is to be noted that these examples cannot be classed as strictly ecclesiastical laws, since they are based very directly on divine laws. They are ecclesiastical only insofar as the Church has determined the exact times at which the divine commands are to be obeyed. It has enacted them in order to make sure that Our Lord's commands in these matters are carried out.

Michiels [146] states that it seems that this opinion is to be rejected entirely, for the prohibition which touches non-Catholics in these cases does not in any way remove the obligation, but simply shows their unworthiness and indicates that they should remove this unworthiness in order that they may perform these acts rightfully and legitimately. This seems to be correct as far as general principles are concerned, for the obligation depends fundamentally upon the indelible mark of valid baptism, and since that can never be erased, neither can the consequent

[144] Cf. Canons 2314-2319.

[145] Cicognani, *Commentarium Ad Librum I. Codicis*, p. 95; cf. De Schepper, " De Haereticis relate ad Leges Ecclesiasticas,"—*Collationes Brugenses*, XXIV (1924), 211.

[146] *Normae Generales*, I, 288.

obligation be taken away. The actual obligation is also present inasmuch as no express exemption has been made. And this is what Michiels intimates, even though indirectly the obligations cannot be fulfilled inasfar as those persons are no longer actual members of the Church.

By a *reductio ad absurdam,* Michiels [147] shows that from the above opinion, which he rejects, exemption would be proved for Catholic excommunicates, infamous persons and the publicly unworthy, who also are kept from receiving Holy Communion [148] until they are reconciled to the Church.

A summary of the preceding section will show that the principle of heretics being both *fundamentally* and *actually* bound even to purely ecclesiastical laws unless they are expressly exempted is upheld by important authors.[149] This principle applies even to those heretics who were baptized and educated in non-Catholic sects and are in good faith. It also applies to other heretics who may be in good faith. The question is superfluous as to those who left the Catholic Church to become heretics.

The opinion that heretics are not bound to obey those ecclesiastical laws that pertain to personal sanctification may be held in practice.[150]

147 *Normae Generales, loc. cit.*

148 Canon 855, § 1.

149 Coronato (*Institutiones Iuris Canonici,* I, p. 27, n. 14) expresses the opinion most succinctly: ". . . . Codex supponit omnes valide baptizatos legibus Ecclesiae ligari; quare nullo solido fundamento canonico nititur distinctio ab aliquibus fieri solita circa leges bonum publicum aut bonum privatum respicientes, excusando ab his haereticos et schismaticos in bona fide educatos. Summum concedi poterit istos excusari ex ignorantia; nisi specialis exceptio probatas. . . ."

150 De Schepper, "De Haereticis relate ad Leges Ecclesiasticas," *Collationes Brugenses,* XXIV (1924), 213.

ARTICLE C.—SCHISMATICS, APOSTATES, AND EXCOMMUNICATES—THEIR OBLIGATION TO OBSERVE ECCLESIASTICAL LAWS

a) *Schismatics and Apostates*

Besides heretics there are other classes of baptized persons who are separated from the Church, namely, excommunicates, schismatics and apostates. The Code[151] gives the official definition of an apostate and a schismatic as follows: An apostate—one who after having received baptism rejects totally the Christian Faith; a schismatic—one who after having received baptism refuses to remain subject to the Supreme Pontiff or to communicate with the members of the Church who are subject to the Supreme Pontiff. These definitions refer to formal schismatics and apostates.[152]

The obligations of formal heretics to the observance of ecclesiastical law have been treated already—they are bound by all ecclesiastical laws, for it is not to be assumed that such persons should profit by their own evil-doing. The same rule applies to apostates, for the moral malice of apostasy is of the same character as that of heresy. There is no formal difference between them. Both have for their motivating causes contempt of divine wisdom and veracity and disobedience to the divine precept of obeying the Church.[153] The sin in each case is against faith. Hence, the only difference between apostasy and heresy is one of degree: heresy consists in the denial of one or more dogmas that must be believed *fide divina et catholica,* while apostasy consists in the denial of all the dogmas that must be believed *fide divina et catholica.*[154]

[151] Canon 1325, § 2.

[152] Coronata, *Institutiones Iuris Canonici,* II, pp. 247, 248, n. 911.

[153] Coronata, *Institutiones Iuris Canonici,* II, p. 248, n. 911.

[154] Canon 1325, § 2; MacKenzie, *The Delict of Heresy in Its Commission, Penalization, Absolution,* The Catholic University of America Canon

The definition of a schismatic given above by way of translation of the text of canon 1325, § 2, is that of a person who is guilty of *pure* schism, which is not so easily found today when almost all schism tends to be *mixed* schism, i. e., pure schism mixed with heresy. At the present time it is difficult to adhere to the dogmas of the primacy and infallibility of the Pope and still remain separated from him or from his subjects simply because they are his subjects.[155]

Those formally guilty of both *pure* schism and *mixed* schism are to be considered in the same category as formal heretics in relation to ecclesiastical laws—they are subject to all ecclesiastical laws for the reason that no one who has been validly baptized is ever to be permitted to profit by his own evil actions. In other words, the same principles of subjection to ecclesiastical laws that apply to formal heretics apply also to apostates and to formal schismatics. And what has been set down about material heretics may be applied to material schismatics. There cannot be a material apostate. Material schismatics, therefore, are bound actually to all ecclesiastical laws unless they are expressly exempted.[156]

An excommunicate is a baptized person who is under a censure that excludes him from communion [communication] with the faithful.[157]

From all that has just been said it can be gathered that heretics, apostates, schismatics and excommunicates have certain characteristics in common: They have received the sacrament of baptism validly; they are now separated from

Law Studies, n. 77 (Washington, D. C.: The Catholic University of America, 1932), p. 17.

155 Coronata, *Institutiones Iuris Canonici*, II, pp. 248, 249, n. 911; MacKenzie, *The Delict of Heresy*, pp. 16, 17.

156 Cf. pp. 111, 140.

157 Cf. Canon 2257, § 1.

the members of the Church; and they are still subjects of the Church by reason of their baptism. This subjection causes them to be bound *fundamentally* and *actually* to ecclesiastical legislation, unless expressly exempted.

b) *Excommunicates*

Special consideration must now be given to excommunicates in the light of some of the legal effects of excommunication. Although excommunicates are fundamentally and actually bound by all ecclesiastical laws, there are some obligations that they seem to be unable to fulfill, for one of the effects of their delinquency is that they are deprived of the means, or of the right to use the means, necessary for satisfying these obligations.

Any excommunicate [*toleratus aut vitandus*] lacks all right of assisting at any of the divine offices [services; functions] except the preaching of the Word of God.[158] These divine offices, as listed in the Code,[159] are denoted by those functions of the power of Orders which, by the institution of Christ or of the Church, are ordained for divine worship and can be performed only by clerics. Among these are: The Holy Sacrifice of the Mass, the administration of the sacraments and sacramentals, ecclesiastical burial, the singing of the canonical hours in choir, liturgical processions, consecrations, blessings and preaching; they are not identified with any private devotions.[160]

But, because of the difficulty of interpreting the phrase of canon 2259, § 1—*caret iure assistendi divinis officiis*—it

[158] Canon 2259, § 1.

[159] Canon 2256, n. 1.

[160] Cocchi, *Commentarium in Codicem Iuris Canonici*, V, p. 142, n. 84; Roberti, *De Delictis et Poenis* (1 vol. in 2, Romae: Apud Custodiam Librariam Pontificii Instituti Utriusque Iuris, 1938), I, pars II, pp. 390, 391, n. 331; Coronata, *Institutiones Iuris Canonici*, IV, p. 187, n. 1766.

is doubtful whether or not excommunicates are absolutely forbidden to attend such divine offices. The canon certainly does not exempt them from any laws that may require attendance at divine offices.

If the phrase is given one interpretation it means that excommunicates are forbidden to assist at the divine offices.[161] Noldin-Schönegger[162] hold that this prohibition binds under grave sin if the excommunicate is present at a notable part of the divine offices, unless the necessity of avoiding scandal or some other grave inconvenience excuses him in his presence at the service. Sole[163] holds that *tolerati* either commit a slight sin or no sin at all if they are present at divine offices, even if they stay for the entire function. Another view takes the phrase—*caret iure*—to mean that the excommunicates simply lose the right to attend divine offices and that they are not prohibited to attend.[164]

These two interpretations have practical application in the question of whether or not an excommunicate is still bound by the laws which require attendance at Mass on Sundays and Holy Days of Obligation; and annual con-

161 Cappello, *Tractatus Canonico-Moralis de Censuris iuxta Codicem Iuris Canonici* (2. ed., Taurinorum Augustae: Marietti, 1925), p. 147, n. 149-c; Chelodi, *Ius Poenale et Ordo Procedendi in Iudiciis Criminalibus iuxta Codicem Iuris Canonici* (4. ed., Tridenti: Libraria Moderna Editrice A. Ardesi, 1935), p. 49, n. 37.

162 *De Censuris* (26. ed., Oeniponte: Typis et Sumptibus Fel. Rauch, 1933), p. 38, n. 39.

163 *De Delictis et Poenis* (Romae, 1920), p. 152.

164 Coronata, *Institutiones Iuris Canonici*, IV, p. 194, n. 1772; Hyland, *Excommunication—Its Nature, Historical Development and Effects*, Catholic University of America Canon Law Studies, n. 49 (Washington, D. C.: Catholic University of America, 1928), pp. 62, 64; Ayrinhac-Lydon, *Penal Legislation in the New Code of Canon Law* (New York: Benziger Bros., 1936), p. 89, n. 115: "More probably a *toleratus* should attend."

fession and Communion.[165] According to the first opinion, the prohibition of passive assistance at divine offices contains a kind of dispensation or indirect excuse from the precept of hearing Mass on Sundays and Holy Days.[166] Accordingly, an excommunicate would commit a sin if he attended.[167]

It should be noted, however, that there is no mention of excommunicates not being bound to the law which requires attendance at Mass on Sundays and Holy Days. The very use of the phrase *dispensation from the precept*, as noted in the opinion of the authors above, indicates that the law in itself still binds but that indirectly it is relaxed in this particular case—that is the very nature of a dispensation.[168] It seems to these authors that in this case the special prohibition in regard to attendance at Mass takes precedence over the general obligation to attend Mass on Sundays and Holy Days. In other words, excommunicates are still bound to the law, but *per accidens*, in this particular instance, they are not bound to fulfill the obligation imposed by the law.

The other opinion in this matter, namely, that excommunicates simply lose the right of assisting at divine offices, holds that they are not prohibited to assist at or are they directly excused from the observance of the actual obligation of assisting at Mass.[169] Some of the protagonists of

165 Cf. Canon 1248.

166 Cappello, *De Censuris*, p. 147, n. 149-c; Chelodi, *Ius Poenali*, p. 49, n. 37.

167 Noldin-Schönegger, *De Censuris*, p. 38, n. 39.

168 Canon 80: "Dispensatio, seu legis in casu speciali relaxatio. . . ."

169 Vermeersch-Creusen, *Epitome*, III, p. 232, n. 461. In the same place these authors say that an occult excommunicate should satisfy this precept, but that a public excommunicate should not assist when there is danger that he will be ejected.

this opinion, however,[170] hold that only an excommunicate *toleratus* is not prohibited from attending and is not absolved from the obligation of hearing Mass.

This latter opinion is based on the more obvious interpretation of the phrase—*excommunicatus quilibet caret iure assistendi divinis officiis*—of canon 2259, § 1. The literal translation of the phrase—*caret iure*—is, *he lacks a right* to do something; but this is not the same as being prohibited from doing something. One may lack a right to do something and still be permitted to do it or even be ordered to do it.

This opinion also seems to be more consonant with the general principle that all validly baptized persons are bound by all ecclesiastical laws, fundamentally and actually, unless they are expressly exempted by the Church, for by not being absolved from the obligation that arises from the law requiring attendance at Mass on Sundays and Holy Days an excommunicate is surely still bound by the law that imposes that obligation. It is also in accord with Canon 87 which is interpreted as meaning that baptized persons under censure have their Christian rights temporarily suspended but are held to the fulfillment of all their Christian obligations.

The discussion thus far has considered the question with regard to paragraph 1 of Canon 2259, which includes all excommunicates [*tolerati et vitandi*], since no express distinction is made in the canon and the word *quilibet* is used. Now, however, paragraph 2 of this canon must be considered.

First of all, there is offered support to the view that *tolerati* are not prohibited from attending divine offices inasmuch as the canon states that they are not to be expelled

170 Genicot-Salsmans, *Institutiones Theologiae Moralis*, II, 535, n. 583; Coronata, *Institutiones Iuris Canonici*, IV, p. 195, n. 1772.

if they assist passively.[171] With regard to the *vitandi*, the second paragraph of canon 2259 implies a prohibition against the attending of divine offices, for it states that they are to be expelled even when they assist passively. But as stated already, the opinion which holds all excommunicates to be prohibited from attending divine offices still does not say that they are not bound by the law to attend Mass on Sundays and Holy Days, but merely that they are excused from the obligation of attending Mass on those days. Hence, according to that view, even the *vitandi* are bound by this law but possess the equivalent of a dispensation inasfar as they are forbidden to attend.

Because of the difference of opinion in this matter of excommunicates assisting at Mass, there is a doubt of law as far as *tolerati* are concerned, and in practice such persons cannot be compelled to observe the precept of hearing Mass on Sundays and Holy Days of Obligation; [172] nor can they be judged guilty of mortal sin if they do not attend. If they neglect, however, to have the censure absolved with the designed purpose of keeping themselves from this obligation, then they commit the sin of wantonly maintaining the existence of an obstacle relative to the fulfillment of an obligation.[173]

In regard to the *vitandi*, some authors would hold that, since they are prohibited from attending divine offices either actively or passively,[174] they are thereby indirectly

[171] Hyland, *Excommunication*, p. 65; Vermeersch-Creusen, *Epitome*, III, p. 232, n. 461; Genicot-Salsmans, *Institutiones Theologiae Moralis*, II, p. 535, n. 583.

[172] Hyland, *Excommunication*, p. 72.

[173] Maroto, *Institutiones Iuris Canonici*, I, 203, footnote 3; MacKenzie, *The Delict of Heresy*, p. 61 and footnote 26; Cappello, *De Censuris*, p. 101, n. 108: "At si excommunicatus negligat absolutionem praecise in eum finem, ut liber sit ab obligatione Missae, graviter peccat."

[174] Canon 2259, § 2.

excused by a kind of a dispensation from the obligation of assisting at Mass on Sundays and Holy Days. Another opinion, however,[175] would hold that, even though they are not permitted to attend the divine offices either actively or passively, they are not thereby freed from the obligation of assisting at Mass on Sundays and Holy Days; for this prohibition in no way removes their obligation but simply indicates their unworthiness to attend Mass and imposes on them the added obligation of having this unworthiness removed so that they may fulfill these obligations properly. This latter view is more consonant with the principle that excommunicates are still subject to ecclesiastical laws.

Excommunicates are not freed from the obligation of receiving Paschal Communion [176] and of making their annual confession,[177] even though they are prohibited from receiving the Sacraments.[178] Cappello notes [179] that they are not freed from these two obligations because there has arisen a new obligation of seeking absolution from the censure. Excommunicated clerics who by canon 2259, § 2, are not permitted to sing the canonical hours in choir, which implies an active participation in the divine offices, are not excused from the private recitation of the canonical hours.[180]

It should be noted that the laws regarding attendance at Mass, annual confession and the reception of Paschal Communion have some basis in the divine law [181] but the actual

[175] Michiels, *Normae Generales*, I, 288.

[176] Cappello, *De Sacramentis*, I, pp. 428, 429, n. 475.

[177] Cappello, *De Censuris*, p. 148, n. 149.

[178] Canons 855, § 1; 2260, § 1; 2265, § 1, 3°.

[179] *De Censuris*, p. 148, n. 149.

[180] Cappello, *De Censuris*, p. 148, n. 149; Coronata, *Institutiones Iuris Canonici*, IV, p. 195, n. 1772.

[181] Cicognani, *Canon Law*, p. 564.

determinations of when the divine law should be fulfilled are strictly ecclesiastical and it is these ecclesiastical precepts that are important in the present discussion.

A consideration of the preceding discussion on excommunicates shows that the opinion that holds them, both *tolerati* and *vitandi,* to be bound by the obligations of hearing Mass on Sundays and Holy Days; and by the obligations of annual confession and Communion and the recitation of the canonical hours is more in accord with the principle that all validly baptized persons are subject fundamentally and actually to ecclesiastical laws unless they are expressly exempt. This is the general rule.

CHAPTER VI

The Doubtfully Baptized and Their Subjection to Purely Ecclesiastical Laws

ARTICLE A.—INTRODUCTION

Thus far only the unbaptized and the validly baptized have been considered in the discussion concerning those who are subject to purely ecclesiastical laws. But what of those whose baptism is doubtful?

It has been shown that the non-baptized are never directly bound by any strictly ecclesiastical laws and all who are validly baptized, even heretics, are, fundamentally and actually bound by all strictly ecclesiastical laws unless they are expressly exempted. If then one follows a logical procedure, based on the point that valid baptism alone makes one a subject of ecclesiastical jurisdiction, it would seem that, inasmuch as Baptism, which is the basis of the subjection to ecclesiastical laws, is doubtful, the subjection also is doubtful. Practically, however, the matter may not be left in that state. There must be an attempt to resolve the doubt in an individual case. Then if the usual practical investigations fail and the doubt persists, there must be formulated rules for treating such cases. Theologians and canonists have attempted to do this and the result is a difference of opinion as to juridical consequences.

ARTICLE B.—EXTERNAL FORUM—DOUBT OF LAW

In the first place canonists consider how the matter should be treated in the external forum, for the conferring of baptism normally is a public act from which proceed consequences important in the external forum. Van Hove [1] holds that in a doubt of law, namely, when the baptism was conferred but there is a doubt concerning its validity, there is a presumption in favor of the baptism. In such a case the baptism is presumed to be valid and the person who received it should be considered a member of the Church with all the rights and duties that such membership entails.[2] He bases his stand on a response of the Holy Office,[3] which concerned Japanese whose baptism was doubtfully valid. The response reads: *Generatim loquendo, ut christiani habendi sunt ii de quibus dubitatur an valide baptizati fuerint.*

An objection may be raised against such a conclusion inasmuch as it is based upon a decision given in a particular case and, therefore, has only a particular application. But if the words of the response are examined, it will be seen that they are very general and it seems that the Holy Office was stating a generally accepted principle to be used in practice. This contention is borne out by the fact that the second part of the answer refers to the relation of doubtful baptism to the sacrament of matrimony and applies the principle stated in the first part: *Censendum est baptisma validum in ordine ad validitatem matrimonii.*

There was also a previous response [4] which stated that in regard to the validity of matrimony a doubtful baptism was to be considered as valid.

[1] *De Legibus Ecclesiasticis*, pp. 197-198.

[2] Vermeersch-Creusen (*Epitome*, I, p. 61, n. 79) and Beste (*Introductio in Codicem*, p. 70) also hold this opinion.

[3] S.C.S. Off., *Iaponiae*, 9 sept. 1868—*Collect. S.C. de Prop. Fide*, n. 1334; *Fontes*, n. 1007.

[4] S.C.S. Off., 17 nov. 1830—*Fontes*, n. 869; *ASS*, XIII (1880), 457; XXV (1892-1893), 258.

Besides, an instruction of the Holy Office to the Vicar Apostolic of Japan [5] considered the doubtfully baptized as bound by all ecclesiastical diriment matrimonial impediments, except clandestinity which was not in force in Japan at that time. Since these instructions considered such persons as bound by the laws, some of which were purely ecclesiastical, therefore in accordance with the general principle that a person becomes subject to ecclesiastical laws through valid baptism it may be inferred that in a doubt of law the doubtfully baptized are considered in the external forum as validly baptized, by a presumption of law, and are therefore theoretically bound by all purely ecclesiastical laws. This, of course, is substantiated by the fact that Van Hove, Vermeersch-Creusen and Beste, who have been noted on p. 164, hold this.

Speaking of the external forum and of a doubt of law, Michiels [6] adheres to the opinion just noted. In such circumstances, according to him, the baptism is presumed to be valid until a positive reason is adduced not only for doubting but for affirming with certitude that something substantial was lacking either in the matter and form of the sacrament or on the part of the minister or the subject. In substantiation of his contention Michiels cites the following documents of the Holy See. The first [7] is a response used by moral theologians [8] to prove that it is necessary after baptism for converts who had previously been doubtfully baptized to confess sins which they committed since their doubtful baptism. It concerns a certain Karl Wip-

[5] S.C.S. Off., ad Vic. Ap. Japoniae Merid., 4 febr. 1891—*ASS*, XXVI (1893-1894), 63; *Fontes*, n. 1130.

[6] *Normae Generales*, I, 284-285.

[7] S. C. S. Off., 27 iun 1715—*Collect. S. C. de Prop. Fide*, n. 286; *Fontes*, n. 780.

[8] Cf., e. g., Noldin-Schmitt, *Summa Theologiae Moralis iuxta Codicem Iuris Canonici* (22. ed., 3 vols., Oeniponte: Typis et Sumptibus Fel. Rauch, 1934), III (*De Sacramentis*), p. 237, n. 230.

perman von Rostock, a Lutheran Quietist, who desired to be reconciled with the Church but who, because some errors were detected in his first baptism, was considered as doubtfully baptized. Questions were asked about baptizing him conditionally and about his obligation to confess the sins of his past life. The Holy Office replied that he was to be baptized conditionally and then he was to confess the sins of his past life and receive conditional absolution.

After a consideration of this answer it seems that the conditional baptism was required in order to be sure that an indispensable requisite for salvation was really fulfilled. In requiring the confession of sins the Sacred Congregation seems to have presumed that the first baptism was valid, for only in such a case could there arise an obligation of confessing these sins. In the event that the earlier baptism was invalid the petitioner would have been an infidel, not subject to the obligation of confessing these sins. When he was baptized conditionally by the priest any sins that Karl had committed prior to that time would have been taken away by the baptism. The conditional absolution was imparted after the confession of the past sins in order to make sure that the sins were really forgiven if the second baptism was not needed and hence did not take away the sins. It should be noted that the Holy Office was deciding the juridical question of the necessity of submitting the sins to the power of the keys.

The second response cited by Michiels [9] was given to questions similar to those in the response just noted. It [10] even refers back to the answer of June 27, 1715, just cited.[11]

[9] *Normae Generales*, p. 285.

[10] S.C.S. Off., 17 dec. 1868—*Collect. S.C. de Prop. Fide*, n. 1338.

[11] The third document—S.C.S. Off. (ad Vic. Ap. Japoniae Merid.), 4 febr. 1891 [*ASS*, XXVI (1893-1894), 63; *Fontes*, n. 1130]—has been referred to already and some explanation given of it.

Again the objection that these examples are decisions given in particular cases may be raised, but it may be answered as Noldin-Schmitt [12] answer it when they treat of the necessity for converts who had previously been doubtfully baptized to confess the sins of their past life after they have been conditionally baptized by a priest. They say that even though the decrees they are treating (among them the one involving Karl Wipperman von Rostock) refer to particular cases and their circumstances were diverse, and yet they elicited the same decision, the same reason was evidently behind all the decrees—namely, that in a doubt of law in the external forum the doubtfully baptized are to be presumed validly baptized. It is because of this implication that Michiels referred to these decisions.

ARTICLE C.—EXTERNAL FORUM—DOUBT OF FACT

In treating of a doubt of fact in the external forum, namely, as to whether any ceremony of baptism was conferred, Van Hove is not so definite.[13] He states that first of all recourse must be had to the various presumptions which may be used in such matters and from which with more or less probability it may be concluded that the baptism was or was not conferred. Then he says that all such presumptions are of law only and must give way to the truth. He states nothing more definite except to point out the presumption of canon 1070 in favor of the validity of a marriage contracted between an unbaptized person and a doubtfully baptized one even when the fact of the baptism is in doubt. This latter point will be treated later.

From what Van Hove says it seems that it may be concluded that, if from the special circumstances of the case

[12] *Summa Theologiae Moralis iuxta Codicem Iuris Canonici*, III, p. 237, n. 230.

[13] *De Legibus Ecclesiasticis*, p. 198.

a presumption may be established that the baptism was conferred validly, then the person will be presumed to be subject to ecclesiastical laws. If, however, a presumption may be set up that the baptism was conferred, but that its validity is doubtful, then the former doubt of fact will resolve itself into a doubt of law and, as noted above, the baptism is to be presumed as valid. On the other hand, if the presumption is that the baptism was not conferred, then the person is to be considered as exempt from subjection to the purely ecclesiastical laws, for the foundation of that subjection (baptism) is considered as not being present. If such a person in this latter case should disobey ecclesiastical laws, he must be mindful of his duty not to give scandal at any time.[14] And it seems that there is an obligation to have baptism conferred immediately, but conditionally.

Beste [15] holds the same conclusion that, when the doubt concerns the fact of baptism, the doubtfully baptized person is not subject to ecclesiastical laws; but he says nothing about the use of presumptions. He states simply that in a doubt of fact in the external forum it ought to be concluded that the baptism was not conferred. He bases his decision on the rule of law: *In dubio factum non praesumitur, sed demonstrari debet.*

On this point of a doubt of fact in the external forum Michiels [16] is very definite. He states that if the doubt of fact is truly probable and positive and can be resolved neither by direct proofs nor by indirect ones [presumptions] it must be concluded that in such a case the person in question is not subject to the Church's laws since the fact

[14] Claeys-Bouuaert et Simenon, *Manuale Juris Canonici*, I, p. 91, n. 160.

[15] *Introductio in Codicem*, p. 70.

[16] *Normae Generales*, I, 285.

of baptism must not be presumed, but must be proved.[17] And therefore, he says, if the fact that the baptism was conferred cannot be proved, then neither can the obligations that necessarily depend upon the existence of that fact. He cites Vermeersch [18] in corroboration of this.

ARTICLE D.—INTERNAL FORUM—DOUBT OF FACT OR OF LAW

At this point, the matter of doubtful baptism and the subjection to purely ecclesiastical laws must be considered in reference to the internal forum. Here Van Hove [19] asserts that there is an obligation of the divine law that the doubt be resolved and, as long as the doubt persists, the obligation extends to the reception of baptism at least conditionally in order that one may make certain his eternal salvation.[20]

The importance of this procedure is evident; but beyond this fundamental obligation arising from the divine law, are doubtfully baptized persons obliged in the internal forum to obey purely ecclesiastical laws?

In answer Van Hove continues [21] by citing the agreement among writers that a doubtfully baptized person is permitted to abide by the presumptions of the external forum and by citing, on the other hand, the dispute as to whether he must in conscience abide by them. In the point at issue, the dispute touches the question whether he must observe

[17] Vermeersch-Creusen assert the same: ". . . . Factum non praesumitur sed probatur."—*Epitome*, I, p. 61, n. 79.

[18] *Theologia Moralis*, I, p. 254, n. 254.

[19] *De Legibus Ecclesiasticis*, p. 198.

[20] It seems that Van Hove should have qualified that statement by saying that one is thus obliged to make certain of his salvation as far as it depends on the reception of baptism.

[21] *Loc. cit.*

the merely positive laws of the Church. Van Hove concludes that this must be denied because an *obligatio dubia est obligatio nulla.*

After making these general observations, he continues by saying that writers are also generally agreed that such an obligation of the positive law is sustained by neither the principle that baptism is in possession nor by the principle: *in dubio standum esse pro valore actus.* The reasons for this contention will be analyzed in the following paragraphs.

In a doubt of law in the internal forum Van Hove admits that there are a few [22] who hold that the doubtfully baptized are bound by ecclesiastical laws, for when one enters a visible society by means of an external rite prescribed by God, then, by law, he is considered a member of that society until it is proved that the baptism was invalid. He states, however, that on the other hand there are authors who favor freedom in such a doubt of law in the internal forum. He records their opinion as follows: " Incorporation by means of a sensible sign is valid only when no reasonable motives raise a doubt about the validity of the incorporation. But if it is apparent from probable indications that the incorporation was invalid, the society has no right to take to itself authority over a person who probably is not a member of that society." These authors maintain, he says, that there is a principle of the natural law: *Melior est conditio possidentis,* meaning that no one is bound to give a thing which he has to another whose right of possessing it is doubtful. But the one in possession must prove his possession of a thing which *de iure* belongs to no one. In the case in question they say there is no evidence that the society is in possession, since the baptism which is the foundation of the possession is doubtful.

[22] Lehmkuhl, *Theologia Moralis* (9. ed., 2 vols., Friburgi Brisgoviae, 1898), II, p. 237, n. 322; Noldin-Schmitt, *Summa Theologiae Moralis*, III, 238.

These authors, he says, contemplate an objection in the light of the invoked principle: *In dubio standum est pro valore actus.* But they insist that it cannot be invoked in this instance because that principle, no matter how reasonable it is, must be expressly stated by the positive law in specific instances in order that it may prevail against the important principle of the natural law: *Obligatio dubia est obligatio nulla.*[23]

Mannajoli[24] contends that the doubtfully baptized are bound by the obligation of the divine law to submit themselves to ecclesiastical laws. This obligation is postulated by the need to avoid the danger of grave disturbance in society arising from a temptation to escape the law on the pretext of invalid baptism. The danger might even appear in the form of hallucinations, by which persons would be moved, without adequate reason, to doubt about their own baptisms; and, therefore, when there is a doubt, he maintains the validity of the baptism must be upheld or the stability of the status of baptized persons in general and of clerics and regulars in particular would be endangered. He foresees the danger as extending from the first doubting about the validity of baptism to a doubt regarding the valid reception of the other sacraments such as matrimony and holy orders. As a result, many who desired to give up the obligations of those states would immediately be able to do so in view of the excuse of a doubtfully valid baptism.

Van Hove[25] replies to this stand by holding that the danger from the consequences of such an hallucination is not very great, inasmuch as only positive and reasonable

[23] An example of such a statement in the positive law is given in canon 1014: ". . . . in dubio standum est pro valore matrimonii. . . . "

[24] *De Obligationibus Christianorum Propriis Quibus in Genere Dubie Baptizati Obstringuntur* (Romae, 1913), pp. 25-35; 69-73—cited by Van Hove, *De Legibus Ecclesiasticis*, p. 199.

[25] *De Legibus Ecclesiasticis*, p. 199.

doubt is entitled to any theological or juridical attention. Then he states that there are only a few Catholics among the doubtfully baptized and, if there are more frequent instances among non-Catholics, the disturbance in the Church is not caused by the fact that their baptisms are doubtful, but by the fact that they do not recognize the authority of the Church. He contends, therefore, that no such obligation of the divine law can be proved and that the following principle can be observed: *In dubio standum est pro libertate.* It must be admitted that Mannajoli's opinion for the obligation as arising from the divine law, based as it is on the possibility of hallucinations, certainly appears rather unconvincing.

In another place [26] Mannajoli sums up his opinion by stating that the doubtfully baptized, as long as a *dubium juris* or *facti* is present, are bound by the laws of the Church in both forums, whether the laws be preceptive or simply prohibitive. He also says that invalidating laws, as long as the doubt perdures, have the power of obligating the doubtfully baptized in both forums. Thus he gives an all-embracing rule which covers all ecclesiastical laws, both forums and both kinds of doubts.

Another writer, Castillon, in an article [27] gives a criticism of Mannajoli's book on the obligations to which the doubtfully baptized are subject and disagrees with him. This writer holds that, since the doubtful baptism is probably non-existent, the doubtfully baptized person is probably outside the jurisdiction of the Church. He concludes, therefore, that such a person, according to the rules of

[26] *Supplementum Editioni Quintae Summulae Theologiae Moralis Josephi Card. D'Annibale,* (Romae, 1909), p. 86. This work appeared prior to Mannajoli's book on the subject of the obligations of the doubtfully baptized and probably formed the basis for that book.

[27] "Le Baptême de Valeur Douteuse et Les Obligations Qu'il Produit,"—*Nouvelle Revue Théologique,* XLVI (1914), 581-598, especially p. 582.

probabilism, is free from all the obligations that depend for their binding force on the validity of the Baptism.[28] He adopts this rule without any distinctions or qualifications.

Vermeersch-Creusen [29] say that Mannajoli uses scholarly arguments to arrive at his opinion, but admit that he takes the more severe stand in the matter of doubtful baptism and subjection to ecclesiastical laws. They hold that in the internal forum presumptions are not necessary and, therefore, if the baptism is only probable the principle that no one is bound by an uncertain precept is valid.

Chelodi-Bertagnolli [30] also seem to stand by the more liberal opinion which holds without any qualification that the doubtfully baptized are not bound by ecclesiastical laws. And they say that this opinion is widely accepted and solidly probable.

In his consideration of the internal forum Michiels [31] states that the conclusions concerning the subjection of doubtfully baptized persons to ecclesiastical laws seem to be less certain. He says that many authors hold that those whose baptism is truly doubtful, whether the doubt be of law or of fact, are not bound in conscience to ecclesiastical laws because the obligations founded on such a baptism are theoretically doubtful and, therefore, practically non-existent. He quotes Vermeersch [32] as saying that such a solution is based on equity. Then Michiels gives this as his reason for the equitable solution: A probably baptized person in his entire spiritual life cannot promise himself any certain benefit from the reception of the other sacra-

[28] Cf. Beste, *Introductio in Codicem*, p. 70.

[29] *Epitome*, I, p. 61, n. 79.

[30] *Ius De Personis*, p. 113.

[31] *Normae Generales*, I, 285-286.

[32] *Theologia Moralis*, I, p. 254, n. 254.

ments. So why should the obligations that are based on doubtful baptism be made more certain than the benefits that come from it?

Then Michiels notes the opinion of others[33] who contend that the doubtfully baptized are obliged to ecclesiastical laws at least when there is a doubt of law, and he says that they have strong enough reasons based both on decisions of the Holy See and founded in the very nature of things.[34] The latter authors, in holding for greater evidence of the obligation when the doubt is a doubt of law, seem to be considering the fact that when baptism is conferred it can reasonably be presumed to be valid.

ARTICLE E.—DISTINCTION BETWEEN DOUBTFULLY BAPTIZED CATHOLICS AND NON-CATHOLICS

In regard to doubtful baptism a distinction is made between Catholics and heretics.[35] This seems to be necessary in spite of the principle that baptism received either in the Catholic Church or in an heretical sect is valid provided that the proper matter and form were used and the minister had the proper intention.

The rules that have just been discussed apply to Catholics, even though some of the decisions of the Holy See referred to by the authors treated of the reception of converts and the necessity for a confession of sins committed during the time prior to the conditional baptism. The authors did not make a distinction in drawing their conclusions even when they based them on the decisions of the Holy See. Hence, in the case of Catholics who are doubtfully baptized the following rules based on the foregoing opinions seem to apply:

[33] E.g., Lehmkuhl, *Theologia Moralis*, II, n. 426.

[34] Cf. also Beste, *Introductio in Codicem*, p. 70.

[35] Claeys-Bouuaert et Simenon, *Manuale Juris Canonici*, I, p. 91, n. 160.

Where the external forum is considered, if the doubt is one of fact, namely, whether the Catholic rite of baptism has actually been conferred and this doubt cannot be resolved by the usual means, it seems that theoretically the person is free of any obligation to obey strictly ecclesiastical laws provided no scandal would be given by non-observance of them. In such a case, however, the person should be baptized conditionally if he is willing that it should be done.

When the doubt in the external forum is one of law, i. e., when the Catholic rite has been conferred but because of certain circumstances there arises a prudent, positive doubt about its validity, it seems that the person should be bound by the Church's laws even if no scandal would result from non-observance of them, because in such circumstances the baptism is presumed to be valid.[36]

In a treatment of the internal forum the first consideration must be given to the divine law and the absolute necessity of baptism for salvation.[37] Hence, a doubtfully baptized Catholic must be baptized at least conditionally if he is willing.

In the internal forum, when there is a doubt of fact, the doubtfully-baptized Catholic, after all reasonable means have been taken to dispel the doubt, may be considered as exempt from purely ecclesiastical laws, because where the basis of an obligation is doubtful the obligation itself is doubtful and the application of the principle, *obligatio dubia est obligatio nulla,* is warranted.

In a doubt of law in the internal forum, when the doubt cannot be resolved such a person seems to be freed from

[36] Michiels, *Normae Generales,* I, 284-285; Van Hove, *De Legibus Ecclesiasticis,* pp. 197-198; Claeys-Bouuaert et Simenon, *Manuale Juris Canonici,* I, p. 91, n. 160.

[37] Van Hove, *De Legibus Ecclesiasticis,* p. 198.

his obligation to ecclesiastical laws by the principle: *in dubio standum est pro libertate.*[38] But even when this is the case the giving of scandal must be avoided.[39]

These same rules apply to doubtfully baptized heretics in cases which involve members of sects that usually confer valid baptism, e. g., Anglo-Catholic Episcopalians. But when the case involves members of denominations which confer baptism that is always doubtful, e.g., Presbyterians,[40] then in a doubt of law in the external forum such a baptism cannot be presumed valid as it would if a Catholic baptism were in doubt. The reason is that the presumption in a doubtful Catholic baptism is stronger on the side of validity, while in the case of the doubtful Presbyterian baptism the presumption is stronger on the side of invalidity. Hence, such a person would be presumed not to be subject to purely ecclesiastical laws and the same rule would hold for a doubt of law in the internal forum.

In regard to the baptism of heretics in a doubt of fact in either forum it seems that the opinion in favor of freedom from the obligations of ecclesiastical laws should be sustained because of the general attitude of many non-Catholic denominations toward the need of conferring and the necessity of receiving baptism as a means indispensable for salvation. If there is a doubt about whether a person has actually been baptized by some kind of a rite in an heretical sect other than that of the aforementioned Episcopalians or of others who are known to be orthodox in the

[38] Vermeersch, *Theologia Moralis,* I, p. 254, n. 254; Van Hove, *De Legibus Ecclesiasticis,* p. 199; Michiels, *Normae Generales,* I, 285-286.

[39] Claeys-Bouuaert et Simenon. *Manuale Juris Canonici,* I, p. 91, n. 160.

[40] S. C. de Prop. Fide, instr. (*ad Vic. Ap. Siam*), 23 iun. 1830: ". . . . agens de quodam brittano baptizato ab heretico puritano, hoc est presbyteriano, de quo valde dubitabatur, num in Baptismatis collatione orthodoxa forma usa fuisset, dicit, quod cum rationabiliter de hoc dubitari posset sub conditione rebaptizandus erat. . . ."—*Fontes,* n. 4748.

matter of conferring baptism, it seems that such persons may be presumed not to have received baptism. Thus they would not be subject to purely ecclesiastical laws. Still, because of the diversity of ways of acting in non-Catholic sects, each individual case must be investigated. It is only after thorough investigation that the rules just mentioned are applicable in cases that still remain doubtful.

Since the baptism administered by Greek schismatics and Oriental heretics is presumably valid,[41] the rules that have just been noted for doubtfully baptized Catholics would apply for members of these groups whenever there may arise a question of doubtful baptism.

The point to be kept in mind in all this matter of doubtful baptism is that when, after reasonable investigation, the baptism remains doubtful, then it is to be administered conditionally, if it is desired by the person under consideration, in view of the absolute necessity of a valid baptism for eternal salvation.

ARTICLE F.—DOUBTFUL BAPTISM AND THE IMPEDIMENT OF DISPARITY OF CULT

The matter of doubtful baptism had practical importance in relation to the ecclesiastical impediment of disparity of cult in the pre-Code law because *in ordine ad validitatem matrimonii* doubtful baptism was presumed to be valid.[42] Baptized non-Catholics were bound by this impediment on the basis of what has been said about those who are validly

[41] S.C.S. Off., instr. (*Pro. Vic. Ap. ad Gallos*), 8 sept. 1633—*Collect. S. C. de Prop. Fide*, n. 74; *Fontes*, n. 722; 20 iun. 1866, ad 40—*Collect. S. C. de Prop. Fide*, n. 1293; *Fontes*, n. 994; Leroux, "Les Baptêmes D'Adultes,"—*Revue Ecclésiastique de Liege*, XVII, (1925-1926), 341-352.

[42] S.C.S. Off., 17 nov. 1830—*Fontes*, n. 869; De Smet, *De Sponsalibus et Matrimoniis*, p. 515, n. 587; Schenk, *The Matrimonial Impediments of Mixed Religion and Disparity of Cult*, The Catholic University of America Canon Law Series, n. 51 (Washington, D. C.: The Catholic University of America, 1929), p. 131.

baptized as being subject to purely ecclesiastical laws. Hence, a marriage between a doubtfully-baptized Catholic or non-Catholic [43] and an infidel was presumed to be invalid on account of the impediment of disparity of cult.[44]

Today this has been changed.[45] When a doubtfully-baptized Catholic contracts marriage with an infidel the rule is to uphold the validity of the marriage. In other words, now the marriage is favored rather than the baptism. Only a doubtfully-baptized Catholic has been noted in this consideration of the law of the Code, for today baptized non-Catholics who have never been Catholics are exempt from the impediment of disparity of cult.[46]

[43] In regard to the doubtfully baptized non-Catholic the same principle was followed at least in a doubt of law, for the decisions of the Holy Office (17 nov. 1830—*Fontes*, n. 869; 10 iun. 1896—*Fontes*, n. 1180; *Collect. S. C. de Prop. Fide*, n. 1940) refer only to cases involving a doubt of law. But it seems that the spirit of the principle, namely that a doubtful baptism was presumed valid in a case involving the validity of marriage, was such that it included the case of a baptism doubtful for any reason, inasmuch as the principle was formulated to preserve the sanctity of marriage.

[44] Cf. Ayrinhac-Lydon, *Marriage Legislation in the New Code of Canon Law*, pp. 138-140.

[45] Canons 1070, § 2; 1014.

[46] Canon 1070, § 1; Schenk, *The Matrimonial Impediments of Mixed Religion and Disparity of Cult*, pp. 139-140, n. 212.

CHAPTER VII

Baptized Persons Who do not Possess a Sufficient Use of Reason are not Bound by Purely Ecclesiastical Laws

ARTICLE A.—INTRODUCTION

The second clause of canon 12 concerns those who are not bound to purely ecclesiastical laws because they lack a sufficient use of reason. The text of the clause reads:

"*Legibus mere ecclesiasticis non tenentur . . . baptizati qui sufficienti rationis usu non gaudent.*"

This exemption is based on the natural law,[1] which requires that certain conditions be verified in a person before he can be subject to any human laws. He must be able to understand the law in some way, and he must be able to perform the human actions that carry out the purpose of the law.[2] In other words, the person must enjoy the use of intellect and free will,[3] for the use of his intellect enables him to understand the law and the use of his will enables him to carry out the law. If these conditions are not verified in any given person, then that person is exempted from human laws—in the present discussion, from purely ecclesiastical laws. This exemption is based on the very nature of a law as an *ordinatio rationis ad bonum commune.*[4] It is a rule and a measure which directs human

[1] Cicognani, *Commentarium ad Librum I. Codicis*, p. 93.

[2] Michiels, *Normae Generales*, I, 291.

[3] Ojetti, *Commentarium in Codicem Iuris Canonici*, I, 102: "...ex iure tamen naturae, ut singuli obligentur, necesse est eos pollere scientia et libertate. Neque enim potest quis subdi regulae seu normae externae ab auctoritate sociali Ecclesiae propositae, qui eam cognoscere nequit ab eaque duci..."

[4] St. Thomas Aquinas, *Summa Theologica*, 1^a2^{ae}, q. 90, a. 4c.

actions to the definite aim and purpose of the community; and only those who are endowed with the use of reason can be directed by laws in a human manner.[5]

ARTICLE B.—EXPLANATION OF TERMS

The second clause of canon 12 speaks of a *sufficiens rationis usus,* but it makes no attempt to clarify the phrase. Hence it is necessary to try to determine just what should be understood by it.

The very use of the word *sufficienti* indicates that even those who are exempt from ecclesiastical laws by this clause of the canon may have some use of reason, but not enough to meet the requirements for subjection to them.

From the next clause of canon 12 it is learned that, even though some precocious persons may have the use of reason before they reach the age of seven, the lawgiver considers seven years of age as the time at which children usually have a sufficient use of reason to enable them to keep the laws of the Church, though they may be exempted as to certain specific laws, e. g., as to the law of fasting until they are twenty-one years of age.[6] But there are some who even at the age of seven may not have a sufficient use of reason. For that reason, an inquiry as to what constitutes a sufficient use of reason is not inappropriate.

Hence it may be concluded that a sufficient use of reason would be about as much as a child has when it is said to have reached the age of reason or discretion. As has been shown already,[7] the age of discretion is that time at which a person is able to distinguish between right and wrong and is *capax doli.*

In regard to law, therefore, one may be considered as having the use of reason sufficient to bind him to the

5 Bargilliat, *Praelectiones Juris Canonici,* I, 62.

6 Canon 1254, § 2.

7 In the historical section of this dissertation, pp. 59-60.

observance of the law when he is able to see that it is right to keep the law and wrong to break it. This, of course, presupposes some understanding of the law and of the reason for which a regulation is to be obeyed, i. e., some kind of knowledge of the purpose of the law. This is corroborated by the following citations from authors:

Claeys-Bouuaert et Simenon [8] state that a sufficient use of reason is present if the subject can understand the purpose which was intended by the human legislator when he enacted the law, and is able to cooperate substantially in fulfilling this purpose. Cicognani [9] says that they do not have a sufficient use of reason who are incapable of being directed by a fixed rule to the common end of society. And Berutti [10] holds that one has a sufficient use of reason when he understands a law and posits acts that are truly human. A truly human act is one that proceeds from the deliberate will of the person placing the act.[11] But, since the movement of the will follows the deliberation of the intellect, a human act is one that is placed by a man acting under the influence of his intellect and free will.

Because the statements of the cited authors are substantially similar and indicate what is commonly held in this matter, from their doctrine as well as from certain general principles derived from the definition of a law, a *sufficiens usus rationis* in relation to ecclesiastical laws may be defined as: That exercise of intellect and free will which enables a baptized person to understand an ecclesiastical law in such a way, even if not completely, that he can place the actions that will fulfill the purpose of that law.

[8] *Manuale Juris Canonici,* I, p. 92, n. 161.

[9] *Commentarium ad Librum I. Codicis,* p. 93.

[10] *Institutiones Iuris Canonici,* I, 77.

[11] Thomas Aquinas, *Summa Theologica,* $1^{a}2^{ae}$, q. 1, a. 1: "...illae ergo actiones proprie humanae dicuntur, quae ex voluntate deliberata procedunt ..."; cf. Genicot-Salsmans, *Institutiones Theologiae Moralis,* I, p. 10, n. 6.

It is also necessary to explain here the following terms which will be used in this section: A person is said to be subject to a law in *actu primo* when he is *habitually* subject to it; he is said to be subject to a law in *actu secundo* when he is *actually* subject to it. For example, all men without exception are subject to the natural law. Infants and the habitually insane are bound by it in *actu primo*, for they are human beings but, because they are bereft of the use of reason, they are not bound by it in *actu secundo*.[12]

ARTICLE C.—VARIOUS CLASSES OF PERSONS WITH MENTAL DEFECTS AND THEIR OBLIGATION TO OBSERVE ECCLESIASTICAL LAWS

a) *Those Lacking the Use of Reason Totally*

Now it will be necessary to try to determine just who do not have a sufficient use of reason and therefore are not subject to purely ecclesiastical laws.

First of all, it is evident that all those who lack the use of reason totally are not subject to purely ecclesiastical laws.[13]

In this first class are included infants, i. e., those under the age of seven years,[14] whose mental and physical immaturity does not permit them to have intellectual cognition, and habitually insane persons (*amentes*) who on account of some defect, either organic or psychological, are unable to elicit that mental activity which is necessary to form a judgment. Such a condition may exist at birth and will never perhaps be remedied, or it may come about in adult life as the result of an accident or an affliction of the

[12] Maroto, *Institutiones Iuris Canonici*, I, p. 200, n. 194; p. 201, n. 195; Van Hove, *De Legibus Ecclesiasticis*, p. 203.

[13] Claeys-Bouuaert et Simenon, *Manuale Juris Canonici*, I, p. 92, n. 161.

[14] Canon 88, par. 3.

brain or the nerves.[15] It seems that in this class should also be included those who are known as *dementes* or monomaniacs, who are sane in regard to most things but are insane in regard to one or several factors.[16] They would be held to those laws that pertain to the objects about which they are in their right mind but not to laws which pertain to the factors about which they are insane. Also in this class would be included certain persons who are deaf, dumb, and blind from birth or early infancy. They may have the use of reason but because of these physical handicaps may have been prevented from acquiring a normal development of it and so are not endowed with a sufficient use of it.[17]

b) *Those without a Sufficient Use of Reason*

In a second class are those who lack a sufficient use of reason and whom canon 12 exempts from subjection to purely ecclesiastical laws. These persons may have a use of reason sufficient for placing some specific actions in a reasonable manner. For instance, they may be able to carry out simple directions for going from place to place; or they may be able to learn the names and uses of various ordinary objects of daily life; or they may even be able to receive some formal education of the most rudimentary character. But their reasoning powers are not sufficiently developed to enable them to perceive the morality of acts, either in the concrete or the abstract.[18] In this class are

[15] Cf. Michiels, *Normae Generales*, I, 291; Michiels, *De Delictis et Poenis* (Lubin [Polonia]: Universitas Catholica, 1934), p. 155.

[16] Sole, *De Delictis et Poenis* (Romae, 1920), n. 24: "...Amentia partialis seu dementia communiter dici solet monomania, quia uti vocabulum ipsum significat, demens non quoad omnia insanit, sed tantum quoad certum rerum genus..."

[17] Toso, *Ad Codicem Iuris Canonici Commentaria Minora*, II, pars I, p. 14, n. 5.

[18] Michiels, *Normae Generales*, I, 291.

those children who have passed the age of seven but who have not arrived at the mental maturity of normal children of their own age, or at least of the age of seven, the age at which ecclesiastical law presumes a person to have the use of reason,[19] and to be held to the observance of all the ecclesiastical laws accommodated to his age,[20] such as the law of abstinence from flesh meat,[21] but not the law of fasting.[22]

Also in this second class are adult idiots whose understanding and general mental development have remained in a primitive, immature stage because of various reasons, in many cases indeterminable.[23]

It should be noted, however, that, although such persons as are included in this second class are said not to be subject to purely ecclesiastical laws, the exemption really applies to preceptive, prohibitive and penal laws and does not extend to laws which grant rights.[24] This is so because the persons in this second class are capable of receiving rights even if they may have to exercise them through their parents or guardians.[25]

19 Canon 88, par. 3.

20 Cicognani, *Commentarium ad Librum I. Codicis,* p. 94.

21 Canon 1254, § 1.

22 Canon 1254, § 2.

23 Michiels, *Normae Generales,* I, 291.

24 Michiels, *Principia Generalia de Personis in Ecclesia* (Lublin [Polonia]: Universitas Catholica, 1932), pp. 38, 52: "... carentia usus rationis non extinguit personalitatem per baptismum acquisitam nec ipsam reddit incompletam; non impedit acquisitionem jurium quae ab infantibus acquiri possunt quaeque per alios sunt exercibilia, nec ullatenus tollit jura ante amentiam legitime acquisita; haec tamen, si mere personalia sunt et per alium exerceri nequeunt, durante amentia suspenduntur; si vero ab aliis exerceri possunt, a parentibus, tutoribus, curatoribus sunt exercenda ..."

25 Canon 1648, § 1; Ojetti, *Commentarium in Codicem Iuris Canonici,* I, 103.

c) *The Habitually Insane Who Have Lucid Intervals*

1. In regard to Non-Penal Laws

A third class of mental deficients is composed of those habitually insane persons who have lucid intervals. There is a difference of opinion as to whether or not these are bound by purely ecclesiastical laws during such intervals.

Genicot [26] states unreservedly that such persons in their better moments are subject to ecclesiastical laws. And Maroto [27] perhaps holds the same opinion, although he does not use the phraseology that is usually employed in referring to such persons. He speaks of *amentes temporales qui lucide habent intervalla,* saying that they are bound to ecclesiastical laws. Hence it seems that he is speaking of a class of temporarily insane persons who have lucid intervals, although he may mean that they are temporarily insane simply because they have the lucid intervals. If this is his meaning, then he holds the same opinion as Genicot, that is, that by lucid intervals they are prevented from being classed as perpetually insane, and as being temporarily insane merely, they are subject to ecclesiastical laws in their better moments.

Michiels,[28] basing his opinion on canon 88, § 3, which likens to infants those who habitually lack the use of reason, holds that, at least from the positive will of the legislator, the habitually insane most probably ought to be said never to be bound by ecclesiastical laws, not even in those moments when exceptionally they enjoy the use of reason. He does, however, cite the more rigorous ruling of canon 2201, which states in § 1 that those only are capable of committing a delict who lack the use of reason at the very

[26] *Institutiones Theologiae Moralis*, I, p. 86, n. 111, 6°.

[27] *Institutiones Iuris Canonici*, I, p. 202, n. 195-B.

[28] *Normae Generales*, I, 292.

moment of performing the action, and which furthermore states in § 2 that the habitually insane, although they sometimes have lucid intervals, are only presumed to be incapable of a delict.[29] Michiels[30] with Vermeersch[31] holds that the rule of canon 2201, §§ 1 and 2, is an exception to the rule of canon 88, § 3 and that therefore those who have lucid intervals are bound only to ecclesiastical penal laws when they have lucid intervals, inasmuch as such laws safeguard the public order more directly than non-penal laws. Toso[32] also seems to hold that those who have lucid intervals are not bound by non-penal laws the while they enjoy the use of reason during such intervals.

Claeys-Bouuaert et Simenon,[33] stating that the matter should be treated *moraliter*, take a middle course by distinguishing between short lucid intervals and protracted ones, in the latter of which it is possible for the person to cooperate morally in the purpose that the legislator intended when he made the law. For the cases in which there are short lucid intervals these two authors hold that such persons are exempt from ecclesiastical laws, but for the cases in which the lucid intervals are of longer duration these same authors hold that the persons who enjoy such intervals are during the time for which they possess them obliged to the observance of ecclesiastical laws.

Van Hove[34] holds that the habitually insane who have lucid intervals are bound by purely ecclesiastical laws at

[29] The discussion of this canon and canon 88, § 3, in their relation to canon 12 will be treated later.

[30] *Normae Generales*, I, 292.

[31] *Epitome*, I, p. 62, n. 80.

[32] *Ad Codicem Juris Canonici Commentaria Minora*, II, pars 1, p. 14, nn. 4, 5.

[33] *Manuale Juris Canonici*, I, p. 92, n. 161.

[34] *De Legibus Ecclesiasticis*, pp. 203, 204, 205.

least in *actu primo,* but that even when they have lucid intervals they are presumed, by a *praesumptio iuris tantum,* not to have the use of reason and, therefore, in *actu secundo,* not to be subject to purely ecclesiastical laws. He reaches this conclusion by a comparison of canons 12; 88, § 3; and 2201, § 2.

The first part of the conclusion is readily admitted, but not for the reason that is given. Van Hove states that he arrives at the first part of his conclusion from canon 12, which exempts from purely ecclesiastical laws only those who do not have a sufficient use of reason, for he says that during lucid intervals the habitually insane have the use of reason. He seems to be mistaken in saying that the reason these insane persons are bound to ecclesiastical laws in *actu primo* is the fact that they have the use of reason during lucid intervals. The real reason for their subjection in *actu primo* to ecclesiastical laws is the very fact of their valid baptism.

The second part of his opinion, namely, that the habitually insane, even when they have lucid intervals, are not bound in *actu secundo* by purely ecclesiastical laws, seems to leave too much uncertainty in practice since it is based on a presumption. He explains the second part of his opinion thus: Canon 88, § 3 does not contradict his doctrine when it likens to infants those who are habitually insane, because those habitually insane persons are likened to infants inasfar as infants are presumed, by a *praesumptio iuris tantum,* not to have the use of reason. And, therefore, the habitually insane even during lucid intervals are presumed, by a *praesumptio iuris tantum,* not to be *sui compos.*

It seems that it is better to hold that, as a general rule, the habitually insane who have lucid intervals are *not* bound to purely ecclesiastical laws, for in the category of those who are habitually insane and not subject to purely ecclesiastical laws there should be included also those who are insane but have intermittent lucid intervals,[35] at least because it is very difficult to determine externally when such lucid intervals actually occur. Chelodi-Bertagnolli[36] state that lucid intervals are not presumed nor ought they to be easily admitted since they can scarcely be proved. It is also difficult to determine whether the insane person actually has, during a lucid interval, a sufficient use of reason to subject him to purely ecclesiastical laws.[37]

At first glance it may seem that the habitually insane who have lucid intervals are bound by purely ecclesiastical laws if during these lucid intervals they have a sufficient use of reason.[38] This seems to follow from the clause of canon 12 which, if adapted by way of positive statement, indicates that those who have a sufficient use of reason are bound to ecclesiastical laws.

But canon 88, § 3 may be brought into the discussion to strengthen the conclusion as to the exemption of the habitually insane who have lucid intervals. That canon

[35] Michiels, *De Delictis et Poenis*, I, 155: "...Illi qui quacumque ex causa de facto laborant amentia ex se perpetua, in jure nostro dicuntur "*usu rationis habitus destituti*" (can. 88, § 3) vel "*habitualiter amentes*" (can. 2201, § 2), *etiamsi aliquando lucida habeant intervalla*...;" cf. also *ibid*., p. 171, and Noval, "De Semi-Amentibus et Semi-Imputabilitati Obnoxiis Utrum Revera Exsistant Aut in Iure Poenali Ecclesiae Agnoscantur,"—*Jus Pontificium*, IV (1924), p. 82, n. 13.

[36] *Ius De Personis*, p. 163, n. 91-b.

[37] Noval, *art. cit., ibid*., p. 83, where he quotes from an article by E. Ugarte de Ercilla: "...Difficile erit describere lineam separationis inter unum statum et alium, cum fere impossibile sit abstrahere ab influxu alicuius notionis vel ideae non rationalis, aut ruinae etiam partialis illius implexae machinae quae intellectui inservit."

[38] Cf. Michiels, *Principia Generalia De Personis in Ecclesia*, p. 54, where he states: "...amentes et dementes *exceptionaliter*, durante lucido intervallo morali cum certitudine probato et in sphaera in qua ratiocinare et sani esse indubie demonstrantur, non modo actus juridicos, puta contractum matrimonialem, valide et licite ponere possunt, sed et vera committere delicta, quae sunt iis moraliter et criminaliter, etsi minore sane gradu, imputabilia..."

states that those who habitually lack the use of reason are likened to infants. (Above it was concluded that those who have lucid intervals should be included in this general category of the habitually insane persons). But infants by a *praesumptio iuris tantum,*[39] noted in the same paragraph 3 of canon 88, are considered as not having the use of reason. Hence, the habitually insane who have lucid intervals are presumed not to have the use of reason. As a result they are presumed not to be subject to purely ecclesiastical laws.[40] From canon 12, however, it seems that they should be absolutely exempted from purely ecclesiastical laws; and this conclusion appears true even if the presumption of their not having the use of reason would give way to fact, e. g., if it were proved that the habitually insane person who enjoys temporary lucid intervals actually had the use of reason during such a lucid interval. The reason is that the habitually insane, including those who have lucid intervals, are likened to infants.[41] But infants by canon 88, § 3 are those who have not reached the age of seven[42] and by canon 12 those who have not reached the age of seven are not bound by purely ecclesiastical laws even if they have the use of reason, unless the law expressly states otherwise. Therefore, the habitually insane, including those who have lucid intervals, are no tbound by purely ecclesiastical laws even if during a lucid interval they have the use of reason, unless the law expressly states otherwise.

[39] Van Hove, *De Legibus Ecclesiasticis,* p. 204.

[40] Creusen (Vermeersch-Creusen, *Epitome,* III, p. 189, n. 389) says that canon 88, § 3 treats of persons in regard to their capacity for rights rather than in regard to their subjection to laws. He bases his contention on the context. But it seems that this contention should be rejected, for § 3 of Canon 88 makes no express reference to either rights or obligations, and, therefore, the words should be taken as they are.

[41] Cf. Canon 88, § 3.

[42] Canon 88, § 3.

This is a general conclusion referring to all purely ecclesiastical laws. And, since in the second and the third clauses of canon 12 the question is one regarding non-subjection in *actu secundo,* this general conclusion about insane persons who have lucid intervals has reference only to non-subjection in *actu secundo.* This is true because all those who have received valid baptism are by that very fact at all times subject to all ecclesiastical laws in *actu primo.*

2. In regard to Penal Laws

In the light of what has just been noted canon 2201 offers some difficulty. This canon in paragraph 2 explicitly notes that habitually insane persons who have lucid intervals are presumed to be incapable of committing a delict. That is only a *praesumptio iuris* and gives implicit acknowledgment that such persons are bound to penal laws not only in *actu primo* but also in *actu secundo* if the presumption in a given case is proved false. In regard to delicts there would be no need to speak of these insane persons who have lucid intervals if they were not subject to the laws in some way.

In paragraph 1, canon 2201 states a general norm which governs all those who are subject to ecclesiastical laws when it says that only those who at the very moment of placing an act are without the use of reason are incapable of committing a delict. Then in the next paragraph canon 2201 states that the habitually insane, even if they sometimes enjoy lucid intervals, are presumed to be incapable of a delict. As just noted, this is a *praesumptio iuris tantum.*[43] Hence, if it can be proved with moral certainty that an habitually insane person who has lucid intervals actually

[43] Augustine, *A Commentary on the New Code of Canon Law,* VIII, 28, 29; Van Hove, *De Legibus Ecclesiasticis,* p. 204; Ayrinhac-Lydon, *Penal Legislation in the New Code of Canon Law,* p. 8, n. 10-b; Michiels, *De Delictis et Poenis,* I, 172, and footnote 3; Vermeersch-Creusen, *Epitome,* III, p. 189, n. 389.

had the use of reason during one of his lucid intervals, and while in that condition performed an act that would be a delict in a sane person, then the presumption gives place to the truth and such an habitually insane person would be capable of a delict during such a lucid interval, according to canon 2201, § 1, because he had the use of reason at the moment of committing the forbidden act.[44] And, since he is capable of committing a delict, he must be acknowledged as subject not only in *actu primo,* but also in *actu secundo* to even ecclesiastical penal laws when he has the lucid interval, since it is impossible to commit a delict unless one is subject to the penal law by the violation of which the delict is committed.

Canon 2201, § 2, therefore, is an exception to the conclusion that habitually insane persons who have lucid intervals are not bound in *actu secundo* to purely ecclesiastical laws. But it is an exception only on those occasions when the insane person has a lucid interval in which he is capable of committing a true delict. And the reason for this interpretation derives from the fact that, notwithstanding the rule of strict interpretation in all penal legislation, penal laws are designed, more directly than non-penal laws, to safeguard the public order and social discipline in society.[45]

In regard to canon 2201, § 2, Van Hove states that the habitually insane who have lucid intervals are subject to penal laws but are presumed by a *praesumptio iuris tantum* to be incapable of a delict. This agrees with the opinion that has just been stated regarding canon 2201, § 2, but it does not admit that this canon is an exception to the general rule. This follows from the fact that Van Hove's general rule about the subjection of these insane persons to ecclesiastical laws is based only upon a presumption.

[44] Michiels, *De Delictis et Poenis,* I, 172 and footnote 3.

[45] Vermeersch-Creusen, *Epitome,* I, p. 62, n. 80; Michiels, *Normae Generales,* I, 292.

Other authors [46] hold that the presumption in canon 2201, § 2 is a *praesumptio iuris et de iure.* In such a case it would be necessary to prove not only that the insane person was sane when he performed the act, but that he was fully recovered from his insanity before he could be guilty of a delict. This, according to some authors [47] does not seem to be warranted by the words of the canon; and the Code itself expressly mentions only one *praesumptio iuris et de iure* which is found in canon 1904, § 1. But, although the compiler of the analytical index of the Code has canon 1972 listed as another such presumption, there is a difference of opinion on this point. Some [48] hold that canon 1972 does contain a *praesumptio iuris et de iure* while others [49] deny that such a presumption is in this canon.

Notwithstanding the discussion about whether the presumption in canon 2201, § 2 is a *praesumptio iuris tantum* or *iuris et de iure,* it is concluded, since there is in canon 2201, § 2 some kind of a presumption that the habitually insane who have lucid intervals are incapable of a delict, that canon 2201, §§ 1 and 2 form an exception to the opinion that the habitually insane who have lucid intervals are not bound to ecclesiastical laws.[50]

[46] Coronata, *Institutiones Iuris Canonici,* IV, 31; Noval, "De Semi-Amentibus et Semi-Imputabilitati Obnoxiis Utrum Revera Exsistant Aut in Iure Poenali Ecclesiae Agnoscantur"—*Jus Pontificium,* IV (1924), 83.

[47] Vermeersch-Creusen, *Epitome,* III, p. 189, n. 389; Van Hove, *De Legibus Ecclesiasticis,* p. 204.

[48] Chelodi, *Ius Matrimoniale iuxta Codicem Iuris Canonici,* p. 192, n. 176; Cappello, *Tractatus Canonico-Moralis de Sacramentis,* III, n. 879 but not expressly.

[49] Vermeersch-Creusen, *Epitome,* III, p. 130, n. 287; Claeys-Bouuaert et Simenon, *Manuale Juris Canonici,* III, p. 283, n. 444.

[50] It should be noted, however, that, since such persons have been likened to infants they are excused from *latae sententiae* punishments. (Cf. canon 2230; Van Hove, *De Legibus Ecclesiasticis,* pp. 204-205.

ARTICLE D.—THOSE DEPRIVED OF THE USE OF REASON ACCIDENTALLY

A fourth class of persons that must here be considered is comprised of those who are deprived of the use of reason only temporarily. Among these are intoxicated persons, including those who are under the influence of narcotic drugs; persons who are sleeping, especially somnambulists; those who are delirious because of a very high fever. Such persons are *fundamentally* or *radicaliter* and in *actu primo* bound by ecclesiastical laws by reason of their valid baptism and because the law affects these subjects according to their common state and condition inasmuch as law is enacted in adaptation to those things which usually happen and in conformity to the common capacities of its subjects.[51]

Michiels [52] states that *actually* or in *actu secundo* such persons are excused from the obligation of observing the law to which they were subjected in *actu primo,* and that this excuse from obligation is based on ignorance or some other reason determined by the cause of their accidental loss of reasoning powers. This is corroborated in a measure by canon 2201, § 3, in regard to penal laws. It states that, if a law is violated when a person is involuntarily intoxicated with an intoxication that takes away the use of reason totally, then all imputability ceases. This likewise seems to hold for all such accidental defects in reasoning power that may occur involuntarily, as long as the use of reason is totally absent when the act is committed.

This rule would be in effect, of course, only in cases wherein the cause is involuntary and the use of reason is taken away completely. If reason is only partially impeded

51 Bouquillon, *Theologia Moralis Fundamentalis* (2. ed., Brugis, 1890), p. 332, n. 140.

52 *Normae Generales,* I, 292.

then the imputability is merely lessened [53] in regard to the sin or the delict. If, on the other hand, anyone voluntarily causes himself to become intoxicated or drugged in order that he may more easily break the law, then he still remains bound to the law.

From what has just been noted it is concluded that when the use of reason is accidentally taken away entirely or diminished, then the imputability for delicts is taken away entirely or diminished; and whenever in such cases there is not sufficient use of reason present baptized persons in that condition are not subject *in actu secundo* to purely ecclesiastical laws. This conclusion is based on canon 2201, § 3 and on canon 12. It does not hold, of course, when the accidental loss or diminution of the use of reason is brought about voluntarily in order that a law might be more easily broken or in order that one might be freed from an obligation.

[53] Van Hove, *De Legibus Ecclesiasticis*, p. 203.

CHAPTER VIII

Baptized Persons who have not yet Completed the Seventh Year of Age, Even Though They have Attained the Use of Reason, are not Bound by Purely Ecclesiastical Laws, Unless the Law Expressly Rules Otherwise

The Latin text of the third clause of canon 12 is: *Legibus mere ecclesiasticis non tenentur . . . baptizati qui, licet rationis usum assecuti, septimum aetatis annum nondum expleverunt, nisi aliud iure expresse caveatur.*

ARTICLE A.—INTRODUCTORY NOTES

As has been set down already in the historical portion of this dissertation, there have been many discussions of the question of just when a person attained the use of reason. It was noted that the very nature of the matter under discussion made it very difficult to set a norm that could be followed in every case—the attainment of the use of reason varied with each person. Some attain it sooner than others. But it was shown that canonical experts at length conceded that normally the use of reason was present at approximately seven years of age.

Once this had been admitted, the question arose as to whether or not those who had the use of reason before the age of seven were bound by ecclesiastical laws.

In the eighteenth century the more common opinion was that those who had attained the use of reason before they reached the age of seven were bound by the ecclesiastical laws which were accommodated to their age.[1]

[1] Schmalzgruber, *Ius Ecclesiasticum Universum*, lib. I, tit. II, n. 39: "...Quamprimum usum rationis adepti sunt (quod ordinarie fit post com-

The opposite opinion was considered probable by Saint Alphonsus Liguori,[2] and in the nineteenth century this became the more common opinion. The principal argument for it was that laws are made to regulate those things which happen most commonly and that extraordinary circumstances are usually not considered by the lawgiver. Since it was admitted that the usual age at which a child attained the use of reason was seven, that age was held to be the one that should be taken as a norm for fixing the time at which a baptized person became subject to ecclesiastical laws. If in an unusual case a person attained the use of reason before that time it was maintained that he should not be subjected to ecclesiastical laws.[3]

It should be noted here that Schmalzgrueber and Pichler, as just quoted, in speaking of the laws to which they refer, use the expressions: *legibus ecclesiasticis* and *legibus humanis* which include purely ecclesiastical laws, since no distinction is made.

The opponents of the opinion which maintained that children who have the use of reason before seven are not

pletum septennium) legibus non solum naturalibus, et divinis, sed etiam ecclesiasticis obstringuntur, si materia istarum aetati illorum conveniat. ...Ratio est, quia sicut usus rationis illos facit capaces culpae, ita et facit capaces debiti, et obligationis per legem, cum hoc necessario supponatur ad culpam..."

[2] *Theologia Moralis*, I, Tract. II, *De Legibus*, II, n. 155; Van Hove, *De Legibus Ecclesiasticis*, p. 205.

[3] Pichler, *Jus Canonicum*, lib. I, tit. II, n. 49: "...Pueri et puellae legibus humanis obligantur sub peccato post annum 7 aetatis completum, saltem regulariter; non vero ante. Ita communior...sed post completum 7 aetatis annum pueri et puellae fiunt et sunt ordinarie rationis compotes, et praesumuntur habere annos discretionis; ergo, quod autem ante completum septennium numquam obligentur etiamsi ob praecocitatem ingenii citius sapiant, inde suadetur quia leges humanae attendunt ad ea, quae communiter et ordinarie contingunt, neque praesumitur legislator humanus velle obligationem imponere nisi secundum communem Naturae cursum: sed ante septennium completum communiter et ordinario non adest sufficiens usus rationis, ergo..."

bound to ecclesiastical laws argued that the very nature of law demanded that those who had the use of reason should be subject to law. These opponents also said that there was no positive law exempting such intellectually precocious persons.[4]

De Schepper, however,[5] maintains that the opinion that was more in favor prior to the promulgation of the Code of Canon Law was the one which stated that children who had the use of reason before they reached the age of seven were not subject to ecclesiastical laws. The Code in canon 12 settled the question by adopting this latter opinion,[6] at least in regard to purely ecclesiastical laws, by making seven the age at which a baptized person becomes subject to such laws even if he has the use of reason prior to that time. In this way by a definite general provision of law the Code has made it easier to determine when children are not actually bound to purely ecclesiastical laws.

ARTICLE B.—EXPLANATION OF TERMS

The phrase *rationis usus* has been sufficiently explained in the preceding chapter in dealing with the problem of those not having sufficient use of reason. It means simply the employing of the intellect and free will in positing actions that will in some way carry out the purpose intended by the legislator when he drafted the law.

Septimum aetatis annum expleverunt—means that the seventh year of a person's physical life must be completed

[4] Bouquillon, *Theologia Moralis Fundamentalis*, p. 332: "... nulla aetas positive determinata est pro generali legum obligatione. Cum igitur exemptio in favorem puerorum non demonstretur, merito theologi communius pronuntiant, ipsos, statim ac usum rationis adepti sunt, teneri legibus eorum aetati convenientibus ..."

[5] "De Exemptione a Legibus Ecclesiasticis Ratione Aetatis"—*Collationes Brugensis*, XXIV (1924), 296.

[6] Blat, *Commentarium*, I, 86; Van Hove, *De Legibus Ecclesiasticis*, p. 206.

according to canon 34, § 3, 3°,[7] and practically computed that means that the seventh year is completed at the end of the day of the same number as that on which the child was born.[8] This is the only section of canon 34 that some authors[9] note as being necessary to determine the completion of the age of seven; and it seems that as a general rule the use of that section alone will answer the purpose because it even gives as an example an age, corresponding to the age of seven (*decimus quartus aetatis annus*), that may be determined by the use of this section 3 of canon 34, § 3. There are, however, other authors who note other sections of this canon that should be used also, e. g., canon 34, § 3, 1°, 3°[10] and canon 34, § 3, 1°, 3° and 4°.[11] These other authors seem to note sections 1 and 4 along with 3 in order to provide for cases where unusual circumstances are present.

The phrase *physical life* was stressed particularly, because at seven a child's psychological age may or may not correspond to his physical age. Its psychological or mental age may be precociously developed or unnaturally retarded when it is physically seven years of age.

Another notation that must be made here is that the phrase *nisi aliud iure expresse caveatur* has been appended only to this clause of the canon. This is in accord with what seems to be the usual view among authors, even if

[7] "If the time consists of one or several months or years, one or several weeks, or several days, and the starting point does not coincide with the beginning of the day (e. g., the fourteenth year of age), the first day is not to be counted and the time expires with the end of the last day of the same number."—Woywod, *A Practical Commentary on the Code of Canon Law*, I, p. 20, n. 24.

[8] Van Hove, *De Legibus Ecclesiasticis*, p. 206.

[9] Beste, *Introductio in Codicem*, p. 69; Van Hove, *op. cit.*, p. 206.

[10] Blat, *Commentarium*, I, 86.

[11] Berutti, *Institutiones Iuris Canonici*, I, 77.

the wording and punctuation of the canon do not seem to warrant this. A discussion of the phrase will be noted on p. 202.

ARTICLE C.—CONSIDERATION OF THE THIRD CLAUSE OF CANON 12

The first point that should be noted about this third clause of canon 12 is that the legal principles underlying it are found in canon 88, § 3.

First of all, canon 88, § 3 gives the meaning of the terms *infans, puer* and *parvulus* when they are used in the Code. It indicates that all these terms are used for a child who has not completed his seventh year of age, and it adds that he is considered as not being capable of performing human acts.[12] Then the canon continues by noting that when the seventh year of age is completed the law presumes that such an *infans* has the use of reason.[13]

If these parts of canon 88, § 3 are considered in conjunction with the third clause of canon 12 it can be seen that this clause of canon 12 is based on two presumptions of the former canon (both *praesumptiones iuris tantum*). If, therefore, a child actually had the use of reason before he was seven years of age, usually he would have juridic capacity, since in such circumstances the *praesumptio iuris tantum* of canon 88, § 3 would yield to the truth. But the third clause of canon 12 provides for such a case: It states that even if a child has the use of reason before the age of seven he is still not bound to purely ecclesiastical laws. It should be noted, however, that this clause of canon 12 treats only of exemption from obligations, so that a child

12 This is a *presumptio iuris tantum*—Van Hove, *De Legibus Ecclesiasticis*, p. 204.

13 Also a *praesumptio iuris tantum*—Michiels, *Principia Generalia De Personis in Ecclesia*, p. 32.

who had the use of reason before seven would have the juridic capacity of acting in regard to his rights.[14]

This is true because a child by means of baptism receives all the rights and obligations that accompany membership in the Catholic Church, even though the use of some of these rights may be restricted and the fulfillment of some of the obligations may be impossible. For example, children under the age of puberty cannot use the right to choose any church for their funeral or the cemetery for their burial; this right is exercised for them by their parents or guardians.[15] But since they are validly baptized, they have the right to Christian burial which is given to all validly baptized persons.[16] These children by the reception of baptism receive also the right to receive all the other Sacraments when the conditions necessary for their reception have been fulfilled.[17] In an ecclesiastical trial, however, concerning either spiritual matters or such affairs as are connected with spiritual matters, minors who have the use of reason but who are not past the age of 14 may be plaintiffs or defendants without the consent of their fathers or guardians but they must act as plaintiff or defendant through a procurator given by the Ordinary.[18]

The other *praesumptio iuris tantum* which is mentioned in canon 88, § 3, namely, that a child who has completed his seventh year of age is presumed to have the use of reason, will also yield to proof that such a child does not possess the use of reason. But here again canon 12 has taken care of such a case in its second clause where, in

[14] Michiels, *Principia Generalia De Personis in Ecclesia*, p. 33 and footnote 1.

[15] Canon 1224, 1°.

[16] Canon 1239, § 3.

[17] Cf. Canon 737, § 1.

[18] Canon 1648, § 3.

following a principle of the natural law, it states that those who do not have a sufficient use of reason are not bound by purely ecclesiastical laws. And for the second time it may be concluded that canon 12 applies only to obligations, since those who do not have a sufficient use of reason nevertheless possess the legal rights which they received at baptism, even if they are incapable of exercising them personally. For example, their parents or guardians are bound to carry out in an ecclesiastical trial all that may be required of minors or of those who do not have the use of reason.[19]

Hence, it can be seen that, even if the legislation of the third clause of canon 12 derives from two presumptions of law, it is still very definite and stable, because the natural weakness of such presumptions has been provided for.

The third clause of canon 12 treats of an exemption from purely ecclesiastical laws by reason of age. The exemption in the first clause of the canon is based on the divine law; that in the second, on the natural law; but the exemption in the third clause is purely an ecclesiastical enactment.[20] In its positive sense it gives the minimum age at which a baptized person having sufficient use of reason becomes subject to purely ecclesiastical laws.

In order to understand this clause it is to be remembered that it is limited by the second clause, for if a child reaches the age of seven and does not have a sufficient use of reason he is not bound by purely ecclesiastical laws. This follows from canon 88, § 3, which states that a child is only presumed to have the use of his reason when he has completed his seventh year. This is a *praesumptio iuris tantum* which is based on a fact.[21] Hence, if a child *de facto* does not

[19] Canon 1648, § 1. Michiels, however (*Principia Generalia de Personis in Ecclesia*, p. 33, and footnote 2) states that such persons are always incapable of acting juridically both in regard to rights and duties.

[20] Cicognani, *Commentarium ad Librum I. Codicis*, p. 94.

[21] Michiels, *Principia Generalia De Personis in Ecclesia*, p. 32.

have the use of reason when he reaches the age of seven he is not subject to purely ecclesiastical laws.[22] After the consideration of these two further requisites for the subjection of baptized persons to ecclesiastical laws (age and the sufficient use of reason) the obligation of children as delineated in the Code may be described thus: After they have completed their seventh year and it is certain that they have the use of reason, they are bound by all the laws that do not require a more advanced age.

In the external forum, when a child has completed his seventh year he is presumed to have the use of reason by a *praesumptio iuris tantum*.[23] De Schepper [24] seems to indicate that in the external forum, if there is a positive and probable doubt whether a child who has completed his seventh year has the use of reason then that child is not subject even to those purely ecclesiastical laws which are accommodated to his age. This opinion, however, cannot be countenanced since it is against the strict principles that govern presumptions. These principles require definite proof to the contrary to remove a presumption of law.[26]

ARTICLE D.—EXCEPTIONS TO THE THIRD CLAUSE OF CANON 12

a) *Consideration of the Phrase " Nisi Aliud Iure Expresse Caveatur "*

From the third clause of canon 12 it is learned that those who certainly have the use of reason before they reached the age of seven are not subject to purely ecclesiastical laws

22 De Schepper, " De Exemptione a Legibus Ecclesiasticis Ratione Aetatis "—*Collationes Brugensis*, XXIV (1924), 298.

23 Canon 88, § 3.

24 " De Exemptione a Legibus Ecclesiasticis Ratione Aetatis "—*Collationes Brugensis*, XXIV (1924), 298.

26 Cf. Canon 1826.

unless the law expressly states otherwise. It will be necessary, therefore, to determine just which laws of the Code do expressly state otherwise. Before this is to be accomplished, however, the significance of the phrase *nisi aliud iure expresse caveatur* must be considered.

This phrase appears at the end of canon 12 and might be regarded as qualifying all three clauses of the canon, or only the last clause. Many of the authors[27] who treat of canon 12 regard it as qualifying only the last clause. This may be due to the fact that the exceptions which they record refer in every instance to the third clause. Their view seems to be justified, however, by an investigation of the other two clauses of canon 12, inasmuch as these clauses show that the phrase "*nisi aliud iure expresse caveatur*" does not refer to either of them.

It does not refer to the first clause because those who are mentioned there cannot be bound directly by any purely ecclesiastical laws. Such persons have never been brought under the jurisdiction of the Church by baptism.[28] They are not bound, either fundamentally or actually, by the purely ecclesiastical laws.[29]

This conclusion is based on the concepts of subjection to a lawgiver and of the jurisdiction of a lawgiver over his subjects. Canon 12 treats only of laws that are made by the Church—laws which it can enact only for those who have become its subjects by means of baptism. It is the reception of baptism, therefore, which begets the real, true

[27] Vermeersch-Creusen, *Epitome*, I, p. 62, n. 80; Leroux, "Le Sujet Des Lois Ecclésiastiques,"—*Revue Ecclésiastique de Liège*, XVI (1924-1925), 334; Blat, *Commentarium*, I, p. 86, n. 68; Bargilliat, *Praelectiones Juris Canonici*, I, 62; Prümmer, *Manuale Theologiae Moralis* (8. ed., 3 vols., ed. E. Münch, Friburgi Brisgoviae: Herder & Co., 1935-1936), I, p. 127, n. 189.

[28] Leroux, "Le Sujet Des Lois Ecclésiastiques"—*Revue Ecclésiastique de Liège*, XVI (1924-1925), 330.

[29] Ojetti, *Commentarium in Codicem Iuris Canonici*, I, 103, footnote 11.

subjection which thereafter is always present. The unbaptized have never become subjects of the Church, hence they are not under its jurisdiction and cannot be directly bound by its laws. Whenever an unbaptized person is indirectly influenced by an ecclesiastical law[30] it is not in virtue of the fact that he himself is truly subject to the ecclesiastical law but only in virtue of his association with a baptized person who is truly subject to the law.

In reference to the second clause of canon 12 and to those who do not possess sufficient use of reason, it must be noted that every law is strictly an ordinance of reason enacted by the legislator to foster the common good and to help to attain it by directing the human acts of the subjects of his society toward their proper end. It is true that those who have not yet attained sufficient use of reason have become subjects of the society which is the Church through the reception of Baptism but, simply because they have not sufficient use of reason they are not capable of performing any human acts. Moreover, the legislator cannot reasonably include them in his directive measures or laws since, by lacking the use of reason, they are and will, as long as they lack the use of reason, always remain incapable of any human acts. So it must also be concluded that the phrase *nisi aliud iure expresse caveatur* does not refer to the second clause of canon 12. Since, therefore, it does not refer either to the first or the second clause of this canon it must refer only to the last clause.

b) *Exceptions in relation to Baptism and Extreme Unction*

There are some laws in the Code which do expressly state that persons who have the use of reason, no matter what their age, are subject to them:

In relation to baptism, those who have the use of reason are to be considered as adults and are to be baptized only

[30] Cf. Canon 1036, § 3.

after they seek baptism of their own volition and usually have been given sufficient instruction.[31] In this category are the children who have the use of reason even before they reach the age of seven, for canon 745 simply mentions those who have the use of reason and makes no distinctions. Such children may also receive the Sacrament of Extreme Unction which may be administered to those who have attained the use of reason.[32] Since they may receive it there is an obligation to administer it to them. Some diocesan statutes mention this expressly.[33]

c) *Exceptions in relation to Holy Viaticum, Paschal Communion and Annual Confession*

When children who are not yet seven years of age, but who have already attained the use of reason, are in danger of death they are bound by the precept of receiving Holy Viaticum.[34] As they have the use of reason it seems logical to suppose that they can fulfill the conditions stipulated in canon 854, § 2, for the reception of Holy Viaticum, namely, that they be able to distinguish the Body of Christ from ordinary bread and that they be able to adore it reverently. That they are to be permitted to receive Holy Communion, even when not in danger of death, as soon as they have some use of reason, even if it is not the full use of it, is noted specifically by the Sacred Congregation of the Sacraments in its decree *Quam singulare* of August 8, 1910,[35]

[31] Canons 745, § 2, 2°; 752, §§ 1, 2; Van Hove, *De Legibus Ecclesiasticis*, p. 206; Michiels, *Normae Generales*, I, 294.

[32] Canon 940, § 1; Claeys-Bouuaert et Simenon, *Manuale Juris Canonici*, I, p. 92, n. 162; Cicognani, *Canon Law*, p. 564.

[33] Canon 944: cf. also statute # 315 of the First Synod of Fargo—*Synodus Dioecesana Fargensis Prima Diebus XXIX et XXX Septembris A.D. MCMXLI Habita* (Milwauchiae: Ex typographia Bruce, 1941), p. 61.

[34] Cf. Canon 864, § 1.

[35] *AAS*, II (1910), 577-583; *Fontes*, n. 2103.

wherein this Congregation treats of the time when children should receive their first Holy Communion. Some of the words of this decree are incorporated into the second paragraph of canon 854. Besides there are other canons in which these children are mentioned as becoming subject to the observance of the precept of Paschal Communion when they have attained the use of reason.[36] They must also receive the sacrament of penance because they are bound by the precept of annual confession [37] when, upon having attained the use of reason, they must render themselves worthy for the reception of Holy Communion.

The cited decree of the Sacred Congregation of the Sacraments makes the following statement about the age of reason and the obligation of children to observe the precepts of annual confession and Paschal Communion: ". . . Aetas discretionis tum ad confessionem tum ad S. Communionem ea est, in qua puer incipit ratiocinari, hoc est circa septimum annum, sive supra, sive etiam infra. Ex hoc tempore incipit obligatio satisfaciendi utrique praecepto confessionis et Communionis." Besides, there is a response issued on the 3rd of January, 1918,[38] by Cardinal Gasparri, the Prefect of the Commission for the Interpretation of the Code, in answer to the question: Whether children who, although they have not yet completed their seventh year of age, but who, on account of their having reached the age of discretion or the use of reason, have already been admitted to First Holy Communion, are bound by the double precept of confession at least once in a year and of Communion once in a year, at least in Paschal time? The answer was affirmative.

[36] Canons 859, § 1; 860.

[37] Canon 906.

[38] Sartori, *Enchiridion Canonicum*, pp. 19, 20; Bouscaren, *The Canon Law Digest*, I, 53, 54.

This response was never officially published in the *Acta Apostolicae Sedis.* But since it contains a simple declarative interpretation it did not need to be promulgated.[39]

The conclusion reached in the response may be reached by the following course of argument: These two precepts of annual confession and Paschal Communion arise from divine law, but the time at which they should be fulfilled is determined by ecclesiastical law. The obligation under the divine precept arises as soon as a validly baptized person attains the use of reason. The obligation under the ecclesiastical law depends upon the lawgiver, and once the ecclesiastical authorities decide that a child has a sufficient use of reason to admit him to First Communion then the ecclesiastical precept begins to bind. And that is the reason that children under seven who have been admitted to First Communion are bound by the two precepts just mentioned.[40]

The whole matter of children's obligation to go to confession and to receive Holy Communion seems to be conditioned, outside of the danger of death, on the judgment of those mentioned in canon 860,[41] since it is the obligation of such persons to determine when children are capable of fulfilling these obligations. Canon 860 treats directly only of the obligation of the reception of Holy Communion, but indirectly also of the obligation of making one's confession if one must render himself worthy for the reception of Holy Communion.

d) *Reason for Exceptions to the Third Clause of Canon 12*

It should be noted that the canons just cited as exceptions to the general rule of the third clause of canon 12 are not really exceptions, for they do not contain purely ecclesi-

[39] Cf. Canon 17, § 2.

[40] Cf. Cicognani, *Canon Law,* p. 571.

[41] "The obligation of the precept of receiving Communion, which binds *impuberes,* falls primarily on all those who have the care of them, namely, on the parents, guardians, confessor, instructors and the pastor."

astical laws. They may not, therefore, be classed strictly as examples of exceptions to the general principle of this third clause of canon 12.[42]

Since, however, these exceptions are noted by almost every author who treats of canon 12, the reason for their inclusion as exceptions to ecclesiastical law may be asked. The answer lies in the fact that there is an element of ecclesiastical law in every one of these precepts, though fundamentally they proceed from the divine law.

Are there, then, any real exceptions to the third clause of canon 12? De Schepper[43] indicates indirectly that there are none when he says that nothing would prevent the Church from constituting exceptions in purely ecclesiastical matters if it wished to do so. And many other authors quoted in this section note the so-called exceptions already indicated which are based on divine law and they give no indication that there are any exceptions relative to purely ecclesiastical laws.

Prümmer[44] notes that the law very rarely obliges *infantes,* and then indicates two canons[45] as if he meant that they were the rare exceptions. It is true that mention is made of persons " of any age " whatsoever in these canons, but the canons seem to bind only those who may admit such persons to the cloister. This is evident from the use of the words *admittantur* and *admittatur* which are taken in the sense of *to receive.*[46] It is also evident from the position of these canons in the title " *de obligationibus et privilegiis religiosorum.*"

[42] Cicognani, *Canon Law*, p. 564; Claeys-Bouuaert et Simenon, *Manuale Juris Canonici*, I, p. 92, n. 162; De Schepper, " De Exemptione a Legibus Ecclesiasticis Ratione Aetatis "—*Collationes Brugenses*, XXIV (1924), 299.

[43] *Art. cit., ibid.*, p. 299.

[44] *Manuale Theologiae Moralis*, I, 127, footnote 61.

[45] 598, § 1; 600.

[46] Coronata, *Institutiones Iuris Canonici*, I, p. 797, n. 612.

Scholion I.—THE EUCHARISTIC FAST—ITS OBLIGATION ON CHILDREN UNDER SEVEN WHO HAVE THE USE OF REASON AND HAVE BEEN ADMITTED TO FIRST HOLY COMMUNION

In regard to the reception of the Holy Eucharist a question arises concerning those who have been admitted to First Holy Communion when they enjoy the use of reason but have not reached the age of seven years. Are they bound to observe the law requiring the Eucharistic Fast,[47] i. e., the natural fast from midnight?[48] In order to answer this question the law of the Eucharistic Fast itself must be considered.

It is admitted by canonists[49] and moral theologians[50] that the law requiring the Eucharistic Fast is an ecclesiastical law. The authors quoted do not state expressly that it is a purely ecclesiastical law. Cappello, however,[51] states definitely that this is a merely ecclesiastical law with its proximate foundation in the divine-natural law which demands the greatest reverence towards the Sacrament of the Eucharist both in regard to purity of soul and the proper disposition of the body. Sartori[52] also mentions that it is purely ecclesiastical.

The fact that the Church grants dispensations from the Eucharistic Fast,[53] and also the fact that this regulation did

47 Canon 858, § 1.

48 Cf. Anglin, *The Eucharistic Fast*, The Catholic University of America Canon Law Studies, n. 124 (Washington, D. C.: The Catholic University of America Press, 1941), pp. 116, 117.

49 Cf. Claeys-Bouuaert et Simenon, *Manuale Juris Canonici*, II, 99, Cicognani, *Canon Law*, p. 571.

50 Cf. Genicot-Salsmans, *Institutiones Thelogiae Moralis*, II, p. 172, n. 199; Noldin-Schmitt, *Summa Theologiae Moralis*, III, p. 149, n. 146.

51 *De Sacramentis*, I, p. 451, n. 498.

52 *Enchiridion Canonicum*, p. 20.

53 Cf. Noldin-Schmitt, *Summa Theologiae Moralis*, III, p. 157, n. 159; Aertnys-Damen, *Theologia Moralis* (13. ed., 2 vols., Taurini: Marietti, 1939), II, p. 119, n. 163.

not exist in the very early days of the Church, are indications that it is a purely ecclesiastical law.[54]

With this point established, the next step is to apply to canon 858, § 1 the general principle of canon 12 which indicates that children under seven who have the use of reason are not bound to the observance of purely ecclesiastical laws. Such children, therefore, even though they have been admitted to First Holy Communion, are not bound, according to the strict principles of law, by the purely ecclesiastical law of the Eucharistic Fast. This is true because there is no special phrase in canon 858, § 1, which includes the children in question within its scope. Canonists conclude, therefore, that such children are not bound to observe the Eucharistic Fast.[55] One author,[56] though he was writing *ex professo* from the point of view of moral theology, gave the canonical conclusion to this discussion: ". . . infans . . . in rigore iuris non tenetur servare ieiunii eucharistici praeceptum, quippe quod sit mere ecclesiasticum."

Moralists, on the other hand, hold that such children are bound to observe the Eucharistic Fast once they have been admitted to First Communion.[57] The reasons they give are: [58] Even though the law is strictly eccelsiastical, it is opportune and equitable that such children be required to do everything that is necessarily required of others who receive Holy Communion. And, if such children did not observe the Eucharistic Fast, they might be a source of

[54] Cf. "Questions des Sciences Ecclesiastiques," *L'Ami du Clergé*, XLVI (1929), 89.

[55] Cf. Cicognani, *Canon Law*, p. 571.

[56] Prümmer, *Manuale Theologiae Moralis*, I, p. 127, n. 189.

[57] Cf. *Cicognani, Canon Law*, p. 571.

[58] Cf. Anglin, *The Eucharistic Fast*, p. 116; *tit., cit., L'Ami du Clergé*, XLVI (1929), 89.

scandal to other children who might begin to regard the Eucharistic Fast lightly. Even the children who would be excused from it might come to think of the Eucharistic Fast as something that was not entirely necessary and might thus lose their respect for the law when they actually become old enough to be subject to it. Then again, reverence for the Holy Eucharist seems to demand that the proper respect be shown to it by abstaining from food for a few hours for such a practice constitutes an excellent way of showing this reverence. There is also a spiritual significance by which those who observe the fast are reminded that Christ in the Eucharist should be their first and primary food.[59] And, finally, all children from a tender age should be taught to obey the laws of the Church.[60]

As is evident, the view of the moral theologians that such children are subject to the regulation of the Eucharistic Fast has no foundation in law. And the reasons on which the view is based do not seem to be strong enough to warrant that this law should be imposed on them. It seems, therefore, that they should be urged to observe the Eucharistic Fast, but should not be held to it as an obligation.

Some of the dangers that are foreseen as coming from their not observing the Eucharistic Fast could easily be forestalled by a clear explanation of the reason for the exemption. At least the danger of scandal would be prevented and others would then know why these children were not fasting. Then again those who are exempt could very easily be impressed with the fact that it is only their tender age that permits them to do something that is forbidden to older persons, and that as soon as they reach the age of seven they too will be required, under pain of sin to observe the Eucharistic Fast.

59 Aertnys-Damen, *Theologia Moralis*, II, p. 112, n. 154.

60 Van Hove, *De Legibus Ecclesiasticis*, p. 206.

The argument which draws upon the concept of reverence which is due to the Holy Eucharist is readily admitted, but this does not seem to be the only basis for the establishment of the law on the Eucharistic Fast, and seem to be of necessity disregarded to a certain extent whenever dispensations from the observance of this Fast are granted. It must be remembered that another and very important reason for the establishment of this Fast seems to have been to overcome abuses caused by the intemperate use of food and drink just prior to the reception of the Sacred Species.[61] And it does not seem at all likely that the same abuse would come into existence again in the case of children who would be excused from this Fast, inasmuch as in their tender years they are usually under the close watch of parents and others who would prevent such an abuse. It seems, therefore, that the argument which is inspired by the concept of reverence cannot be insisted upon very strongly in this regard.

It is also readily admitted that children from an early age should be taught to obey ecclesiastical laws, but teaching can be given in other ways then by imposing upon them a law to which they are not strictly subject. The practice, however, seems to be to follow the opinion of the moral theologians, for the few children under seven who are admitted to First Communion in this country are customarily required to observe the Eucharistic Fast.

Scholion II.—THE EXEMPTION OF CHILDREN UNDER SEVEN FROM ECCLESIASTICAL PENAL LAWS

In a discussion of the subjection to or exemption from penal laws the matter of delictual capacity must be treated. For those children who do not have the use of reason and who are under seven years of age this delictual capacity is not present. This is evident from the pre-Code opinion

[61] Cf. Anglin, *The Eucharistic Fast*, p. 3.

that a child is considered *capax doli,* i. e., capable of committing a sin or other action that is punishable, only when it has attained the use of reason, which, as this opinion held, usually occurred around the seventh year. And the Code takes this into consideration in canon 12.

Since such children do not have a sufficient use of reason, they are included not only under the exemption in the third but also under that of the second clause of canon 12 which states that those who do not have a sufficient use of reason are not held to the observance of purely ecclesiastical laws. This is based on the natural law. What has been said about those not having a sufficient use of reason would *a fortiori* apply to children not having the use of reason at all.

The discussion, therefore, will be restricted to the case of children who are under the age of seven, but who already have the use of reason and are considered *capax doli.* And since they are *capax doli,* it seems to follow that they have delictual capacity for at least some delicts that are sanctioned by punishments in the Code.

The first point that must be noted is that all who have been validly baptized are, at least *in actu primo,* subject to ecclesiastical laws, including the purely ecclesiastical laws.[62] Hence, every validly baptized person is subject to ecclesiastical penal laws *in actu primo.* Among such persons are all baptized children who are under seven years of age.

[62] Ojetti, *Commentarium in Codicem Iuris Canonici,* I, 103, footnote 11: "Nota, hic illud, quod in canone dicitur de exclusione non baptizatorum et baptizatorum quidem, sed nondum usu rationis fruentium, aut etsi fruentium, qui tamen nondum ad septimum aetatis annum pervenerunt, probe esse intelligendum. Nam non baptizati legibus non ligantur, quia ecclesiae non subduntur; alii vero, baptizati, quicumque, quum auctoritati ecclesiae subdantur, in actu primo ligantur, sed in actu secundo et obligatione perfecta a lege non attinguntur. Quare optimo iure Codex quum de utrisque simul loquatur, dicit eos non teneri, id est non obligari, illos quidem tum in actu primo tum in actu secundo, hos in actu secundo tantum."

The next question is: Are children under seven years of age who already have the use of reason subject *in actu secundo* to ecclesiastical penal laws? In answer the initial consideration will be given to the canon which treats of those who are subject to ecclesiastical punishments. Canon 2226, § 1, states that one is subject to the punishment attached to a law or a precept if one is bound by a law or precept, unless one is expressly exempted. In this rule two things are noted: A person must be bound by the penal law before he can incur the punishment attached to it; and he must not be expressly exempted.

Now, children under seven, even if they have the use of reason, are not bound by purely ecclesiastical laws unless the law expressly states otherwise.[63] Since no distinction is made in canon 12 when it mentions ecclesiastical laws all purely ecclesiastical laws are included in that mention. Further it seems that all the penal laws of the Code are purely ecclesiastical, since all of them were constituted by the Church. Even though some of them attach sanctions to divine laws, the penal laws themselves are ecclesiastical because they are enacted by the Church. There seems to be no point, therefore, to making a distinction between penal laws that safeguard divine laws and penal laws that add sanctions to purely ecclesiastical enactments.

This distinction seems to have been made by a certain writer[64] who stated that penal laws in which the sanctions safeguard divine laws are not purely ecclesiastical laws. He gave as examples canons 2314 (an *ipso-facto*-incurred excommunication imposed on apostates, heretics and schismatics) and 2320 (an *ipso-facto*-incurred excommunication imposed on those who treat the Sacred Species in various

[63] Canon 12.

[64] Baumer, "De Iure Poenali pro Delinquentibus Minoris Aetatis in Codice Iuris Canonici et Novissimo Schemate Codicis Poenalis Helvetici,"—*Apollinaris*, VI (1933), 453-495, esp. 458-461.

unlawful and unbecoming ways). Hence he seemed to hold that there are two classes of penal laws: 1) ecclesiastical penal laws; 2) purely ecclesiastical penal laws.

This may be a valid distinction based on the origin of the law to which the Church has added its sanction. It is readily seen that it is possible to make a distinction between a penal law that adds a sanction to a divine law and a penal law that adds a sanction to an ecclesiastical law, e. g., the penal law which punishes the violation of the cloister.[65] But such a distinction seems to have no legal significance, since the Church is the primary and only authority that establishes the sanctions.

Furthermore, it seems that the only legal distinction that could be made in regard to the origin of penal laws is a distinction between lawgivers, e. g., between God as a lawgiver and the Church as a lawgiver. By means of such a distinction one may speak of a divine penal law (one enacted by God); a purely ecclesiastical penal law (one enacted by the Church); an ecclesiastical penal law based on a divine penal law (when the Church establishes greater definiteness for a divine sanction already extant). These distinctions would have some legal significance in regard to penal laws for the sanctions would come from different sources. But neither the first nor the last is known in the canonical system.

In regard to laws which are other than penal laws a legal distinction may indeed be properly made between purely ecclesiastical laws, e. g., the canon on the form of marriage [66] and ecclesiastical laws that are based on divine laws, e. g., the precept of Paschal Communion.[67] For example, Christ actually commanded His followers to receive the Holy

[65] Canon 2342, 1°, 2°.

[66] Canon 1099.

[67] Canon 859, § 1.

Eucharist [68] and the Church merely makes this command more definite in the conditions which attend its fulfillment. In the case of penal laws that safeguard the divine law, however, Christ did not declare a sanction which was later made more definite by the Church, or simply recorded by the Church in its penal code. Any penal law in the Code is of purely ecclesiastical origin and does not depend upon a general sanction already invoked by Christ.

Hence it seems that it must be held that all the penal laws of the Code are of ecclesiastical origin. Because of this the third clause of canon 12 excuses from all penal laws children under seven years of age, even though they have the use of reason. This is the general rule.

Canon 2201, § 1, however, appears to be an implicit exception to this clause of canon 12, because in its positive sense it seems to imply that those who actually have the use of reason are capable of committing a delict.[69] Hence a child under seven, who has the use of reason, would seem to be capable of committing a delict and, therefore, be subject to the punishment decreed for that delict whatever it is. The very fact that such children are bound by the law of annual confession [70] indicates that they are *capax doli,* and *capacitas doli* is the basis for subjection to the penal law.[71] Nevertheless, canon 12 requires an express provision if a child under seven, even one who has the use of reason, is subjected to an ecclesiastical law. But since children under seven who have the use of reason are not mentioned expressly in this canon 2201, § 1, it seems that this cannot be considered as an exception to canon 12.

[68] John VI: 54, 55.

[69] Canon 2201, § 1 is: "Delicti sunt incapaces qui actu carent usu rationis." In its positive sense this would read: "Delicti sunt capaces qui actu habent usum rationis."

[70] Canon 906.

[71] Canons 2195, 2199, 2200, § 1.

Another canon that may offer some difficulty is canon 2230, which expressly exempts *impuberes* from *latae sententiae* punishments and states that they should be given educative punishments instead. It thereby implies that such *impuberes* may be subject to *ferendae sententiae* punishments. Now, if in the category of the *impuberes* are included children under seven years of age who have the use of reason, then it would seem that such children too are subject to *ferendae sententiae* penalties if they ever commit a delict that is punishable by such a penalty. This, of course, is impossible for children who do not have the use of reason inasmuch as they are without delictual capacity, but it might be possible for those who have the use of reason. Still it seems that they too should be ruled out of inclusion under canon 2230, for in the penal matter under discussion the word *impuberes* should be given a strict interpretation, which is that the category of the *impuberes* is constituted solely by those who are between the age of seven and the age of legal puberty.[72]

Indeed, as far as can be determined, there are no express exemptions mentioned in the penal section of the Code as benefitting children under seven years of age. None were necessary. The reason is obvious, inasmuch as all the penal laws are purely ecclesiastical and a general exemption from all purely ecclesiastical laws is given to children under seven in the third clause of canon 12. On the other hand, such children are not expressly mentioned as being bound by any penal laws. It appears, therefore, that children under seven, even if they have the use of reason, are not subject actually to any of the penal laws of the Church.

[72] Cf. canon 88, §§ 2, 3; Prümmer, *Manuale Theologiae Moralis*, I, p. 127, n. 188.

CONCLUSIONS

As a summary of the important points in the foregoing historical and canonical treatment of canon 12 the following conclusions are set down:

(1) As far as could be ascertained the Church as a spiritual ruler throughout the centuries prior to the Code always adhered to the principle that the unbaptized are not subject to its jurisdiction.

(2) When the Church did seem to deviate from this principle, as in the case of the Jews prior to the Code, it did so not primarily and much less exclusively by reason of its spiritual jurisdiction, but either with ecclesiastico-civil power, as a temporal ruler, or as exercising its right of self-defense, or as fulfilling its divine commission to teach all nations.

(3) The words of canon 12 do not of themselves lead to the inference that all validly baptized persons, even though some of them were never affiliated with the Catholic Church, if they have the sufficient use of reason and are seven years of age, are *actually* bound by strictly ecclesiastical laws. But this inference may be deduced when canon 12 is considered along with canons 87 and 88, § 3, and particularly in view of the explicit exemptions made in canons 1070, § 1, and 1099, § 2.

(4) Heretics and schismatics when validly baptized outside of the Catholic Church, even though they are still in good faith, are *fundamentally* (*per se seu radicaliter*) and *actually* (*actualiter*) subject to all purely ecclesiastical laws even those providing merely for personal sanctification, unless they are expressly exempted by the Church. The

opposite opinion concerning laws providing merely for personal sanctification, according to certain authors, has no actual foundation in law but in view of its extrinsic authority it may be considered as probable and hence may be followed in practice.

(5) If one follows the opinion that an intention of freeing themselves from the obligations of a law, an intention of abolishing the law, is necessary in those who establish a custom contrary to law, then heretics in good faith who do not know of their obligation to the purely ecclesiastical laws enacted for their personal sanctification cannot have the intention of freeing themselves from those laws by acting contrary to them and, therefore these heretics cannot establish a custom contrary to an ecclesiastical law.

(6) In regard to doubtful baptism among Catholics, schismatic Orientals and non-Catholics of sects which usually confer valid baptism:

In a doubt of fact in the external forum such doubtfully baptized persons are theoretically free from any obligation to strictly ecclesiastical laws.

In a doubt of law in the external forum such persons are subject to purely ecclesiastical laws, for the presumption of their valid baptism militates necessarily for the presumption of their subjection to the law.

In the internal forum in a doubt of fact or of law such doubtfully baptized persons are considered as exempt from the purely ecclesiastical laws.

(7) When the case involves members of denominations in which the conferred baptism always remains a doubtful issue, it seems that the doubtfully baptized persons should be presumed not to be subject in either forum to purely ecclesiastical laws when the evidence appears stronger both on the side of invalidity relative to the factually conferred baptism and also on the side of the non-reception of the sacrament of baptism.

(8) The habitually insane who have lucid intervals are actually subject to ecclesiastical penal laws only during the time when they are enjoying definite certified lucid intervals, i. e., they are subject to them in *actu secundo* during such intervals. This manifestly is implied by the norms of canon 2201, §§ 1-2. Since, however, they are presumptively likened to infants they are also presumptively excused by canon 2230 from the incurring of *latae sententiae* punishments.

(9) The third clause of canon 12 seems to be based on two *praesumptiones iuris tantum,* as found in canon 88, § 3, but this third clause and the second clause of canon 12 are so worded as to rise above these mere presumptions and to imply and establish a definite, exact norm for children under seven years of age.

(10) The phrase *nisi aliud iure expresse caveatur* of canon 12 applies only to the third clause of this canon, and not to the first or second clauses.

(11) Children under the age of seven, even though they have the use of reason, are not *actually* bound by purely ecclesiastical laws, and thus by necessary consequence they also are not actually bound by the Church's penal laws.

BIBLIOGRAPHY

Sources

Acta Apostolicae Sedis, Commentarium Officiale, Romae, 1909—

Acta et Decreta Sacrorum Conciliorum Recentiorum, Collectio Lacensis, 7 vols., Friburgi Brisgoviae, 1870-1890.

Acta Sanctae Sedis, 41 vols., Romae, 1865-1908.

Berger, Elie, *Les Registres D'Innocent IV*, 4 vols., Paris, 1884-1897.

Bullarium Benedicti XIV, 3 vols. in 4, Prati, 1845-1847.

Bullarum Diplomatum et Privilegiorum Sanctorum Romanorum Pontificum Taurinensis Editio, 25 vols., Augustae Taurinorum, 1857-1872.

Codex Iuris Canonici Pii X Pontificis Maximi iussu digestus Benedicti Papae XV auctoritate promulgatus, Romae: Typis Polyglottis Vaticanis, 1917.

Codicis Iuris Canonici Fontes cura Emi. Petri Card. Gasparri Editi, 9 vols., Romae (postea Civitate Vaticana): Typis Polyglottis Vaticanis, 1923-1939. (Vols. VII, VIII et IX ed. cura et studio Emi. Iustiniani Card. Serédi).

Collectanea S. Congregationis de Propaganda Fide, 2. ed., 2 vols., Romae, 1907.

Concilii Plenarii Baltimorensis II., in Ecclesia Metropolitana Baltimorensi, a die VII. ad diem XXI. Octobris, A. D. MDCCCLXVI., Habiti, et a Sede Apostolica Recogniti, Acta et Decreta, Baltimorae: John Murphy, 1868.

Corpus Iuris Canonici, ed. Lipsiensis 2., post Aemilium L. Richter instruxit Aemilius Friedberg, 2 vols., Lipsiae, 1879-1881.

Denzinger, Henr., et Bannwart, Clem., *Enchiridion Symbolorum, Definitionum, et Declarationum de Rebus Fidei et Morum*, 16. et 17. ed., Friburgi Brisgoviae: Herder, 1928.

Hardouin, Jean, *Acta Conciliorum et Epistolae Decretales ac Constitutiones Summorum Pontificum*, 12 vols., Parisiis, 1714-1715.

Jaffé, Philippus, *Regesta Pontificum Romanorum ab condita Ecclesia ad annum post Christum natur MCXCVIII*, 2 vols. in 1, Lipsiae, 1885-1888.

Mansi, Joannes D., *Sacrorum Conciliorum Nova et Amplissima Collectio*, 53 vols. in 59, edition adited & printed at Paris, Leipzig, & Arnhem, 1901-1927.

Migne, Jacques Paul, *Patrologiae Cursus Completus, Series Graeca*, 161 vols., Parisiis, 1856-1866.

——, *Patrologiae Curus Completus, Series Latina*, 221 vols., Parisiis, 1844-1864.

Monumenta Germaniae Historica, 188 vols. et *Epistolae*, Tom. VIII, Karolini Aevi VI, Fasc. I et *Poetae Latini Medii Aevi*, Tom. V., Fasc. II, Hannoverae, Lipsiae, Berolini, 1877 —

——, *Leges*, 5 vols., ed. G. Pertz, J. Merkel, Fr. Blume, K. de Richthofen, K. F. de Richthofen, A. Boretius, G. Haenel, R. Sohm, K. Zeumer, 1835-1889.

——, *Gregorii I Papae Registrum Epistolarum*, 4 vols., ed. L. M. Hartmann et P. Ewald, 1887-1899.

——, *Epistolae Karolini Aevi*, 5 vols. in 8, ed. E. Duemmler, K. Hampe, A. de Hirsch-Gereuth, E. Perels, E. Caspar, 1892-1928.

Potthast, Augustus, *Regesta Pontificum Romanorum inde ab a. post Christum natum MCXCVIII ad a. MCCCIV*, 2 vols., Berolini, 1874-1875.

Synodus Dioecesana Fargensis Prima Diebus XXIX et XXX Septembris A. D. MCMXLI Habita Milwauchiae: Ex typographia Bruce, 1941.

Thesaurus Resolutionum Sacrae Congregationis Concilii, 167 vols., Romae, 1718-1908.

Reference Works

Aertnys, J.—Damen, C. A., *Theologia Moralis*, 13. ed., 2 vols., Taurini: Marietti, 1939.

Alphonsus Liguori, St., *Theologia Moralis*, ed. M. Sanchez, 2 vols. in 1, Matriti, 1876.

Anglin, Thomas F., *The Eucharistic Fast*, The Catholic University of America Canon Law Studies, n. 124, Washington, D. C.: The Catholic University of America Press, 1941.

Augustine, Charles, *A Commentary on the New Code of Canon Law*, 8 vols., St. Louis: Herder, 1918-1922.

Ayrinhac, H. A.—Lydon, P. J., *Marrirage Legislation in the New Code of Canon Law*, new revised ed., New York: Benziger Brothers, 1936.

——, *Penal Legislation in the New Code of Cnanon Law*, N. Y.: Benziger Bros., 1936.

Ballerini, A.—Palmieri, D., *Opus Theologicum Morale in Busenbaum Medullam*, 3. ed., 7 vols., Prati, 1898-1901.

Barbosa, Augustinus, *Collectanea Doctorum tam Veterum quam Recentiorum in Ius Pontificium Universum*, 5 vols. in 4, Lugduni, 1656.

Bargilliat, M., *Praelectiones Juris Canonici*, 37. ed., 2 vols., Parisiis: Apud Baston, Berche et Pagis, 1923.

Bellarminus, Robertus, St., *Opera Omnia*, Nova Editio iuxta Venetam Anni 1721 dicata Xisto R. Sforza, 8 vols., Neapoli, 1872.

Berutti, Christophorus, Institutiones Iuris Canonici, 4 vols., Taurini-Romae: Marietti, 1936-1940. (Vols. I et III, 1936; vol. IV, 1940; vol. VI, 1938).

Beste, Udalricus, *Introductio in Codicem*, Collegeville, Minn.: St. John's Abbey Press, 1938.

Blat, Albertus, *Commentarium Textus Codicis Iuris Canonici*, 6 vols., 1921-1927.

Bouquillon, Thomas, J., *Theologia Moralis Fundamentalis*, 2. ed., Brugis, 1890.

Bouscaren, T. L., *The Canon Law Digest*, 2 vols. and 2 supplements, Milwaukee: Bruce Publishing Company, 1934-1938; supplements, 1938, 1941.

Cance, Adrien, *Le Code de Droit Canonique*, 16. ed., 3 vols., Paris: J. Cabalda et Fils, 1930.

Cappello, Felix, M., *Summa Iuris Canonici*, 3 vols., Romae: Apud Aedes Universitatis Gregorianae, 1936-1939. (Vols. I et II, 3. ed.; vol. III, 1. ed.).

——, *Summa Iuris Publici Ecclesiastici*, 3. ed., Romae: Apud Aedes Universitatis Gregorianae, 1932.

——, *Tractatus Canonico-Moralis de Censuris iuxta Codicem Iuris Canonici*, 2. ed., Taurinorum Augustae: Marietti, 1925.

——, *Tractatus Canonico-Moralis de Sacramentis*, 3 vols. in 6, Taurinorum Augustae: Marietti, 1932-1939. (Vol. I et vol. II, Pars I, 3. ed.; vol. II, Partes II et III, 1. ed.; vol. III, Partes I et II, 4. ed.).

Carberry, John J., *The Juridical Form of Marriages*, The Catholic University of America Canon Law Studies, n. 84, Washington, D. C.: The Catholic University of America, 1934.

Carlyle, R. W. and Carlyle, A. J., *A History of Mediaeval Political Theory in the West*, 6 vols., New York: G. P. Putnam's Sons, 1903-1928. (Vol. V., *The Political Theory of the Thirteenth Century*).

Cathrein, V., *Philosophia Moralis*, 16. ed., Friburgi Brisgoviae: Herder & Co., 1932.

Cavagnis, Felix, *Institutiones Iuris Publici Ecclesiastici*, 4. ed., 3 vols., Romae, 1906.

Chelodi, Ioannes, *Ius Matrimoniale iuxta Codicem Iuris Canonici*, 3. ed., Tridenti: Libr. Edit. Tridentum, 1921.

——, *Ius Poenale et Ordo Procedendi in Iudiciis Criminalibus iuxta Codicem Iuris Canonici*, 4. ed., Tridenti: Libraria Moderna Editrice A. Ardesi, 1935.

Chelodi, I.—Bertagnolli, E., *Ius de Personis iuxta Codicem Iuris Canonici*, 2. ed., Tridenti: Libr. Edit. Tridentum, 1927.

Cicognani, Amleto, *Canon Law*, Authorized English Version by J. O'Hara and F. Brennan, 2. ed., Philadelphia: Dolphin Press, 1935.

——, *Commentarium ad Librum I. Codicis*, Romae: Ex Schola Typographica Pio X, 1925.

Claeys-Bouuaert, F., et Simenon, G., *Manuale Juris Canonici*, 3 vols., Gandae et Leodii: Prostat apud Auctores in Seminariis Gandavensi et Leodiensi, 1930-1931. (Vols. I and III, 3. ed., vol. II, 1. ed.).

Cocchi, Guidus, *Commentarium in Codicem Iuris Canonici ad Usum Scholarum,* 5 vols. in 8, Taurinorum Augustae: Marietti, 1931-1938. (Vols. III-VII, 3. ed., vols. II et VIII, 4. ed., vol. I, 5. ed.).

Coronata, Matthaeus Conte a, *Institutiones Iuris Canonici,* 5 vols., Taurini: Marietti, 1928-1936.

De Angelis, Phillipus, *Praelectiones Juris Canonici ad Methodum Decretalium Gregorii IX Exactae,* 4 vols. in 8, Romae, 1877-1887.

De Lugo, J., *Disputationes Scholasticae et Morales,* nova ed., 8 vols., Parisiis, 1868-1869.

De Smet, Al., *Tractatus Theologico-Canonicus de Sponsalibus et Matrimonio,* 4. ed., Brugis: Car. Beyaert, 1927.

Feije (also Feye), Henricus, Joannes, *Dissertatio Canonica de Matrimoniis Mixtis,* Lovanii, 1847.

Ferraris, F. Lucius, *Bibliotheca—Canonica, Juridica, Moralis, Theologica, necnon Ascetica, Polemica, Rubricistica, Historica,* 9 vols., Romae, 1885-1899. (Vol. 9—Supplement—ed. I. Bucceroni, Romae, 1899).

Funk, Francis X., *A Manual of Church History* (Translated by P. Perciballi; edited by W. H. Kent, O.S.C.), 2 vols., London: Burns, Oates & Washbourne, Ltd., 1931.

Gasparri, Petrus, *Tractatus Canonicus de Matrimonio,* ed. nova ad mentem Codicis I. C., 2 vols., Civitate Vaticana: Typis Polyglottis Vaticanis, 1932.

——, *Tractatus Canonicus de Sacra Ordinatione,* 2 vols., Parisiis, 1893-1894.

Genicot, E.—Salsmans, I., *Institutiones Theologiae Moralis,* 12 ed., 2 vols., Louvain: Museum Lessianum, 1931.

Gibalini, Josephus, *Scientia Canonica et Hieropolitica,* 2 vols., Lugduni, 1670.

Gregory, Donald, *The Pauline Privilege,* The Catholic University of America Canon Law Studies, n. 68, Washington, D. C.: The Catholic University of America, 1931.

Guilfoyle, Merlin, J., *Custom,* The Catholic University of America Canon Law Studies, n. 105, Washington, D. C.: The Catholic University of America, 1937.

Hefele, Carolus, et Leclercq, Henricus, *Histoire des Conciles,* 8 vols. in 16, Paris, 1907-1921.

Hetzenauer, Michael, *Biblia Sacra, Vulgati Editionis Sixti V. Pont. Max. iussu recognita et Clementis VIII. auctoritate edita,* Ratisbonae, 1914.

Hickey, John J., *Irregularities and Simple Impediments in the New Code of Canon Law,* The Catholic University of America Canon Law Studies, n. 7, Washington, D. C.: The Catholic University of America, 1920.

Hostiensis, Cardinalis (Henricus de Segusio), *Commentaria in Quinque Decretalium Libros,* 5 vols. in 3, Venetiis, 1581.

Hyland, Francis E., *Excommunication—Its Nature, Historical Development, and Effects,* The Catholic University of America Canon Law Studies, n. 49, Washington, D. C.: The Catholic University of America, 1928.

Kerin, Charles A., *The Privation of Christian Burial,* The Catholic University of America Canon Law Studies, n. 136, Washington, D. C.: The Catholic University of America Press, 1941.

Kuttner, Stephan, *Kanonistische Schuldlehre von Gratian bis auf die Dekretalen Gregors IX,* Studi e Testi, n. 64, Citta del Vaticano: Bibliotheca Apostolica Vaticana, 1935.

Lehmkuhl, Augustinus, *Theologia Moralis,* 9. ed., 2 vols., Friburgi Brisgoviae, 1898.

MacKenzie, Eric, *The Delict of Heresy in Its Commission, Penalization, Absolution,* The Catholic University of America Canon Law Studies, n. 77, Washington, D. C.: The Catholic University of America, 1932.

Mannajoli, D., *De Obligationibus Christianorum Propriis Quibus in Genere Dubie Baptizati Obstringuntur,* Romae, 1913.

——, *Supplementum Editioni Quintae Summulae Theologiae Moralis Josephi Card. D'Annibale,* Romae, 1909.

Maritain, Jacques, *The Things That Are Not Caesar's,* Unicorn Series, n. 10, translation by J. F. Scanlan, London: Sheed & Ward, 1939.

Maroto, Philippus, *Institutiones Iuris Canonici ad Normam Novi Codicis,* 2 vols., Matriti, 1919.

——, *Institutiones Iuris Canonici ad Normam Novi Codicis,* 3. ed., 1 vol., Romae: Apud Commentarium pro Religiosis, 1921.

Michiels, Gommarus, *Normae Generales Juris Canonici,* 2 vols., Lublin: Universitas Catholica, 1929.

——, *De Delictis et Poenis,* 1 vol., Lublin: Universitas Catholica, 1934.

——, *Principia Generalia de Personis in Ecclesia,* Lublin: Universitas Catholica, 1932.

Noldin, H. — Schmitt, A., *Summa Theologiae Moralis iuxta Codicem Iuris Canonici,* 22. ed., 3 vols., Oeniponte: Typis et Sumptibus Fel. Rauch, 1934.

Noldin, H.—Schönegger, A., *De Censuris,* 26. ed., Oeniponte: Typis et Sumptibus Fel. Rauch, 1933. (In Noldin, H.—Schmitt, A., *Summa Theologiae Moralis iuxta Codicem Iuris Canonici,* Vol. I of edition just cited).

Ojetti, B., *Commentarium in Codicem Iuris Canonici,* 4 vols., Romae: Univ. Greg., 1927-1931.

Onclin, Gulielmus, *De Territoriali vel Personali Legis Indole,* Universitas Catholica Lovaniensis Dissertationes ad Gradum Magistri in Facultate Theologica vel in Facultate Iuris Canonici Consequendum Conscriptae, Series II, t. 31, Gambloci: J. Duculot, 1938.

Ottaviani, Alaphridus, *Institutiones Iuris Publici Ecclesiastici,* 2. ed., 2 vols., Civitate Vaticana: Typis Polyglottis Vaticanis, 1935-1936.

Panormitanus, Abbas (Nicolaus de Tudeschis), *Commentaria in Quinque Libros Decretalium,* 5 vols. in 7, Venetiis, 1588.

Payen, G., *De Matrimonio in Missionibus ac Potissimum in Sinis Tractatus Practicus et Casus*, 2. ed., 3 vols., Zi-ka-wei: In Typographia T'ou-sé-wé, 1935-1936.

Pelella, Josephus, *Canones et Decreta Concilii Tridentini ex Editione Romana a. MDCCCXXXIV Repetiti*, Neapoli, 1859.

Petrovits, Joseph, *The New Church Law on Matrimony*, Philadelphia, 1919.

Pichler, Vitus, *Jus Canonicum secundum Quinque Decretalium Titulos Gregorii Papae IX Explicatum*, 2 vols., Ravennae, 1741.

Prümmer, Dominicus, M., *Manuale Theologiae Moralis*, 8. ed., 3 vols., ed. E. Münch, Friburgi Brisgoviae: Herder & Co., 1935-1936.

Reiffenstuel, Anacletus, *Ius Canonicum Universum*, 5 vols. in 7, Parisiis, 1864-1882.

Roberti, Franciscus, *De Delictis et Poenis*, 1 vol. in 2, Romae: Apud Custodiam Librariam Pontificii Instituti Utriusque Iuris, 1938.

Roskovány, A. de, *Matrimonium in Ecclesia Catholica Potestati Ecclesiasticae Subjectum, cum Amplissima Collectione Monumentorum et Literatura*, 4 vols., Pestini, 1870-1882.

Sägmüller, I. B., *Lehrbuch des katholischen Kirchenrechts*, Freiburg im Breisgau, 1900.

Sanchez, Thomas, *Disputationum de Sancto Matrimonii Sacramento Libri Tres*, Antverpiae, 1626.

Sanguineti, Sebastiano, *Iuris Ecclesiastici Privati Institutiones*, Romae, 1884.

Santi, Franciscus, *Praelectiones Juris Canonici*, 2 vols., Ratisbonae, 1886.

Sartori, P. Cosmas, *Enchiridion Canonicum*, 6. ed., Vicetiae: Ex Typographia Commerciali, 1938.

Schenk, Francis J., *The Matrimonial Impediments of Mixed Religion and Disparity of Cult*, The Catholic University of America Canon Law Studies, n. 51, Washington, D. C.: The Catholic University of America, 1929.

Schmalzgrueber, Franciscus, *Ius Ecclesiasticum Universum*, 5 vols. in 12, Romae, 1843-1845.

Schroeder, H. J., *Canons and Decrees of the Council of Trent*, St. Louis: Herder, 1941.

Sohm, Rudolph, *The Institutes, A Textbook of the History and System of Roman Private Law* (translated by J. C. Ledlie), 3. ed., Oxford, 1926.

Sole, Iacobus, *De Delictis et Poenis*, Romae, 1920.

Suarez, Franciscus, *Opera Omnia*, 26 vols., Parisiis, 1856-1866. (Two Indices, 1878).

Tanquerey, Ad., *Synopsis Theologiae Dogmaticae ad Usum Seminariorum*, 3 vols., Vols. I et III, 23. ed., vol. II, 24. ed., Parisiis: Desclée et Socii, 1933-1934.

Tarquini, Camille, *Iuris Ecclesiastici Publici Institutiones*, Romae, 1862.

Thomas Aquinas, St., *Summa Theologica, Editio Altera Romana*, 6 vols., Romae, 1894.

Toso, Albertus, *Ad Codicem Iuris Canonici Commentaria Minora*, 2. ed., 5 vols., Romae: Marietti, 1920-1934.

Van Hove, A., *Commentarium Lovaniense in Codicem Iuris Canonici*, 1 vol. in 5 tomes, Mechliniae-Romae: H. Dessain 1928-1939. (Tom. II, *De Legibus Ecclesiasticis*, 1930).

Vermeersch, A., *Theologia Moralis*, 3. ed., 4 vols. in 3, Romae: Università Gregoriana, 1933-1937.

Vermeersch, Arthurus—Creusen, Iosephus, *Epitome Iuris Canonici*, 2. ed., 3 vols., Mechliniae-Romae: H. Dessain, 1924-1925.

Vlaming, Th. M., *Praelectiones Iuris Matrimonii*, 3. ed., 2 vols., Bussum in Hollandia, 1919.

Wahl, Francis X., *The Matrimonial Impediments of Consanguinity and Affinity*, The Catholic University of America Canon Law Studies, n. 90, Washington, D. C.: The Catholic University of America, 1934.

Wernz, Franciscus X., *Ius Decretalium*, 6 vols. in 8, Prati, 1908-1915.

Wernz, F.—Vidal, P., *Ius Canonicum*, 7 tom. in 8 vols., Romae: Apud Aedes Universitatis Gregorianae, 1923-1938.

Woywod, S., *A Practical Commentary on The Code of Canon Law*, 5. ed., 2 vols., New York: Joseph F. Wagner, Inc., 1939.

Ziegler, Aloysius K., *Church and State in Visigothic Spain*, Washington, D. C.: The Catholic University of America, 1930.

Articles

Baumer, A., " De Iure Poenali pro Delinquentibus Minoris Aetatis in Codice Iuris Canonici et Novissimo Schemate Codicis Poenalis Helvetici,"—*Apollinaris*, VI (1933), 453-495.

Castillon, P., " Le Baptême de Valeur Douteuse et Les Obligations Qu'il Produit,"—*Nouvelle Revue Théologique*, XLVI (1914-1919), 581-598.

De Schepper, R., " De Haereticis relate ad Leges Ecclesiasticas,"—*Collationes Brugenses*, XXIV (1924), 209-213.

——, " De Exemptione a Legibus Ecclesiasticis Ratione Aetatis,"—*Collationes Brugenses*, XXIV (1924), 296-299.

Gillmann, Franz, " Die '*anni discretionis*' im Kanon *Omnis utriusque sexus*,"—*Archiv für katholisches Kirchenrecht*, CVIII (1928), 556-617.

Leroux, E., " Le Sujet Des Lois Ecclésiastiques,"—*Revue Ecclesiastique de Liège*, XVI (1924-1925), 329-334.

——, " Les Baptêmes D'Adultes,"—*Revue Ecclésiastique de Liège*, XVII (1925-1926), 341-352.

Michiels, G., " De Vera Impedimenti Affinitatis Natura,"—*Jus Pontificium*, V (1925), 142-159.

Noval, J., " De Semi-Amentibus et Semi-Imputabilitate Obnoxiis Utrum Revera Exsistant aut in Iure Poenali Ecclesiae Agnoscantur,"—*Jus Pontificium*, IV (1924), 76-86.

Wasner, Francis, " De Authenticitate 'Libelli Responsionum' Beati Gregorii Magni Papae ad S. Augustinum Angliae Apostolum Animadversiones,"— *Jus Pontificium*, XVIII (1938), 174-185; 293-299.

PERIODICALS

Analecta Ecclesiastica, Romae, 1893-1911.

Apollinaris, Romae, 1928 —

Archiv für katholisches Kirchenrecht, Vols. I-VI, Innsbruck, 1857-1861; Vols. VII —, Mainz, 1862 —

Collationes Brugenses, Brugis Flandrorum, 1895 —

Jus Pontificium, Romae, 1921 —

L'Ami du Clergé, Paris, 1878 —

Nouvelle Revue Théologique, Paris, 1869 —

Periodica de Re Canonica et Morali utili praesertim Religiosis et Missionariis, Brugis, 1905 —; ab anno 1927: *Periodica de Re Morali, Canonica, Liturgica.*

Revue Ecclésiastique de Liège, Leodii. 1908—

ABBREVIATIONS

AAS—*Acta Apostolicae Sedis.*

AKKR—*Archiv für katholisches Kirchenrecht.*

ASS—*Acta Sanctae Sedis.*

Bullarum Taur.—*Bullarum Diplomatum et Privilegiorum Sanctorum Romanorum Pontificum Taurinensis Editio.*

Collect. S.C. de Prop. Fide—*Collectanea Sacrae Congregationis de Propaganda Fide.*

Fontes—*Codicis Iuris Canonici Fontes cura ... Gasparri editi.*

Hardouin—*Acta Conciliorum, etc.*

J E—Jaffé, *Regesta Pontificum Romanorum, etc.*—Section edited by Ewald.

J K—Jaffé, *Regesta Pontificum Romanorum, etc.*—Section edited by Kaltenbrunner.

J L—Jaffé, *Regesta Pontificum Romanorum, etc.*—Section edited by Loewenfeld.

Mansi—*Sacrorum Conciliorum Nova et Amplissima Collectio.*

MGH—*Monumenta Germaniae Historica.*

MPG—Migne, *Patrologia Graeca.*

MPL—Migne, *Patrologia Latina.*

Potthast—*Regesta Pontificum Romanorum.*

S.C.C.—*Sacra Congregatio Concilii.*

S.C. de Prop. Fide—Sacra Congregatio de Propaganda Fide.

S.C.S. Off.—Sacra Congregatio Sancti Officii.

S.R.R.—Sacra Romana Rota.

BIOGRAPHICAL NOTE

JOSEPH ALOYSIUS MCCLOSKEY was born on July 26, 1908, at Philadelphia, Pennsylvania. He attended Our Lady of Mount Carmel parochial school of that city and was graduated from it. He made his high school studies at the Roman Catholic High School, Philadelphia. In 1930 he entered the Theological Seminary of Saint Charles Borromeo, Overbrook, Philadelphia, Pennsylvania, where he received the degree of Bachelor of Arts in June, 1935. He was ordained to the Sacred Priesthood on June 3, 1939. In September of that year he entered the Catholic University of America, Washington, D. C., to pursue graduate studies in the School of Canon Law. In June, 1940, he received the Baccalaureate in Canon Law, and in June, 1941, the Licentiate in Canon Law.

ANALYTICAL INDEX

CANON LAW STUDIES

1. Freriks, Rev. Celestine A., C.PP.S., J.C.D., Religious Congregations in Their External Relations, 121 pp., 1916.
2. Galliher, Rev. Daniel M., O.P., J.C.D., Canonical Elections, 117 pp., 1917.
3. Borkowski, Rev. Aurelius L., O.F.M., J.C.D., De Confraternitatibus Ecclesiasticis, 136 pp., 1918.
4. Castillo, Rev. Cayo, J.C.D., Disertación Historico-Canonica sobre la Potestad del Cabildo en Sede Vacante o Impedida del Vicario Capitular, 99 pp., 1919 (1918).
5. Kubelbeck, Rev. William J., S.T.B., J.C.D., The Sacred Penitentiaria and its Relations to Faculties of Ordinaries and Priests, 129 pp., 1918.
6. Petrovits, Rev. Joseph, J.C., S.T.D., J.C.D., The New Church Law On Matrimony, X-461 pp., 1919.
7. Hickey, Rev. John J., S.T.B., J.C.D., Irregularities and Simple Impediments in the New Code of Canon Law, 100 pp., 1920.
8. Klekotka, Rev. Peter J., S.T.B., J.C.D., Diocesan Consultors, 179 pp., 1920.
9. Wanenmacher, Rev. Francis, J.C.D., The Evidence in Ecclesiastical Procedure Affecting the Marriage Bond, 1920 (Printed 1935).
10. Golden, Rev. Henry Francis, J.C.D., Parochial Benefices in the New Code, IV-119 pp., 1921 (Printed 1925).
11. Koudelka, Rev. Charles J., J.C.D., Pastors, Their Rights and Duties According to the New Code of Canon Law, 211 pp., 1921.
12. Melo, Rev. Antonius, O.F.M., J.C.D., De Exemptione Regularium, X-188 pp., 1921.
13. Schaaf, Rev. Valentine Theodore, O.F.M., S.T.B., J.C.D., The Cloister, X-180 pp., 1921.
14. Burke, Rev. Thomas Joseph, S.T.D., J.C.D., Competence in Ecclesiastical Tribunals, IV-117 pp., 1922.
15. Leech, Rev. George Leo, J.C.D., A Comparative Study of the Constitution, "Apostolicae Sedis" and the "Codex Juris Canonici," 179 pp., 1922.
16. Motry, Rev. Hubert Louis, S.T.D., J.C.D., Diocesan Faculties According to the Code of Canon Law, II-167 pp., 1922.
17. Murphy, Rev. George Lawrence, J.C.D., Delinquencies and Penalties in the Administration and Reception of the Sacraments, IV-121 pp., 1923.
18. O'Reilly, Rev. John Anthony, S.T.B., J.C.D., Ecclesiastical Sepulture in the New Code of Canon Law, II-129 pp., 1923.
19. Michalicka, Rev. Wenceslas Cyrill, O.S.B., J.C.D., Judicial Procedure in Dismissal of Clerical Exempt Religious, 107 pp., 1923.

20. Dargin, Rev. Edward Vincent, S.T.B., J.C.D., Reserved Cases According to the Code of Canon Law, IV-103, pp. 1924.
21. Godfrey, Rev. John A., S.T.B., J.C.D., The Right of Patronage According to the Code of Canon Law, 153 pp., 1924.
22. Hagedorn, Rev. Francis Edward, J.C.D., General Legislation on Indulgences, II-154 pp., 1924.
23. King, Rev. James Ignatius, J.C.D., The Administration of the Sacraments to Dying Non-Catholics, V-141 pp., 1924.
24. Winslow, Rev. Francis Joseph, O.F.M., J.C.D., Vicars and Prefects Apostolic, IV-149 pp., 1924.
25. Correa, Rev. Jose Servelion, S.T.L., J.C.D., La Potestad Legislativa de la Iglesia Catolica, IV-127 pp., 1925.
26. Dugan, Rev. Henry Francis, A.M., J.C.D., The Judiciary Department of the Diocesan Curia, 87 pp., 1925.
27. Keller, Rev. Charles Frederick, S.T.B., J.C.D., Mass Stipends, 167 pp., 1925.
28. Paschang, Rev. John Linus, J.C.D., The Sacramentals According to the Code of Canon Law, 129 pp., 1925.
29. Piontek, Rev. Cyrillus, O.F.M., S.T.B., J.C.D., De Indulto Exclaustrationis necnon Saecularizationis, XIII-289 pp., 1925.
30. Kearney, Rev. Richard Joseph, S.T.B., J.C.D., Sponsors at Baptism According to the Code of Canon Law, IV-127 pp., 1925.
31. Bartlett, Rev. Chester Joseph, A.M., LL.B., J.C.D., The Tenure of Parochial Property in the United States of America, V-108 pp., 1926.
32. Kilker, Rev. Adrian Jerome, J.C.D., Extreme Unction, V-425 pp., 1926.
33. McCormick, Rev. Robert Emmett, J.C.D., Confessors of Religious, VIII-266 pp., 1926.
34. Miller, Rev. Newton Thomas, J.C.D., Founded Masses According to the Code of Canon Law, VII-93 pp., 1926.
35. Roelker, Rev. Edward G., S.T.D., J.C.D., Principles of Privilege According to the Code of Canon Law, XI-166 pp., 1926.
36. Bakalarczyk, Rev. Richardus, M.I.C., J.U.D., De Novitiatu, VIII-208 pp., 1927.
37. Pizzuti, Rev. Lawrence, O.F.M., J.U.L., De Parochis Religiosis, 1927 (Not printed).
38. Bliley, Rev. Nicholas Martin, O.S.B., J.C.D., Altars According to the Code of Canon Law, XIX-132 pp., 1927.
39. Brown, Mr. Brendan Francis, A.B., LL.M., J.U.D., The Canonical Juristic Personality with Special Reference to Its Status in the United States of America, V-212 pp., 1927.
40. Cavanaugh, Rev. William Thomas, C.P., J.U.D., The Reservation of the Blessed Sacrament, VIII-101 pp., 1927.
41. Doheny, Rev. William J., C.S.C., A.B., J.U.D., Church Property: Modes of Acquisition, X-118 pp., 1927.
42. Feldhaus, Rev. Aloysius H., C.PP.S., J.C.D., Oratories, IX-141 pp., 1927.

43. Kelly, Rev. James Patrick, A.B., J.C.D., The Jurisdiction of the Simple Confessor, X-208 pp., 1927.
44. Neuberger, Rev. Nicholas J., J.C.D., Canon 6 or the Relation of the Codex Juris Canonici to the Preceding Legislation, V-95 pp., 1927.
45. O'Keefe, Rev. Gerald Michael, J.C.D., Matrimonial Dispensations, Powers of Bishops, Priests and Confessors, VIII-232 pp., 1927.
46. Quigley, Rev. Joseph, A.B., A.M., J.C.D., Condemned Societies, 139 pp., 1927.
47. Zaplotnik, Rev. Johannes Leo, J.C.D., De Vicariis Foraneis, X-142 pp., 1927.
48. Duskie, Rev. John Aloysius, A.B., J.C.D., The Canonical Status of the Orientals in the United States, VIII-196 pp., 1928.
49. Hyland, Rev. Francis Edward, J.C.D., Excommunication, Its Nature, Historical Development and Effects, VIII-181 pp., 1928.
50. Reinmann, Rev. Gerald Joseph, O.M.C., J.C.D., The Third Order Secular of Saint Francis, 201 pp., 1928.
51. Schenk, Rev. Francis J., J.C.D., The Matrimonial Impediments of Mixed Religion and Disparity of Cult, XVI-318 pp., 1929.
52. Coady, Rev. John Joseph, S.T.D., J.U.D., A.M., The Appointment of Pastors, VIII-150 pp., 1929.
53. Kay, Rev. Thomas Henry, J.C.D., Competence in Matrimonial Procedure, VIII-164 pp., 1929.
54. Turner, Rev. Sidney Joseph, C.P., J.U.D., The Vow of Poverty, XLIX-217 pp., 1929.
55. Kearney, Rev. Raymond A., A.B., S.T.D., J.C.D., The Principles of Delegation, VII-149 pp., 1929.
56. Conran, Rev. Edward James, A.B., J.C.D., The Interdict, V-163 pp., 1930.
57. O'Neil, Rev. William H., J.C.D., Papal Rescripts of Favor, VII-218 pp., 1930.
58. Bastnagel, Rev. Clement Vincent, J.U.D., The Appointment of Parochial Adjutants and Assistants, XV-257 pp., 1930.
59. Ferry, Rev. William A., A.B., J.C.D., Stole Fees, V-135 pp., 1930.
60. Costello, Rev. John Michael, A.B., J.C.D., Domicile and Quasi-Domicile, VII-201 pp., 1930.
61. Kremer, Rev. Michael Nicholas, A.B., S.T.B., J.C.D., Church Support in the United States, VI-136 pp., 1930.
62. Angulo, Rev. Luis, C.M., J.C.D., Legislación de la Iglesia sobre la intención en la aplicación de la Santa Misa, VII-104 pp., 1931.
63. Frey, Rev. Wolfgang Norbert, O.S.B., A.B., J.C.D., The Act of Religious Profession, VIII-174 pp., 1931.
64. Roberts, Rev. James Brendan, A.B., J.C.D., The Banns of Marriage, XIV-140 pp., 1931.
65. Ryder, Rev. Raymond Aloysius, A.B., J.C.D., Simony, IX-151 pp., 1931.
66. Campagna, Rev. Angelo, Ph.D., J.U.D., Il Vicario Generale del Vescovo, VII-205 pp., 1931.

67. Cox, Rev. Joseph Godfrey, A.B., J.C.D., The Administration of Seminaries, VI-124 pp., 1931.
68. Gregory, Rev. Donald J., J.U.D., The Pauline Privilege, XV-165 pp., 1931.
69. Donohue, Rev. John F., J.C.D., The Impediment of Crime, VII-110 pp., 1931.
70. Dooley, Rev. Eugene A., O.M.I., J.C.D., Church Law On Sacred Relics, IX-143 pp., 1931.
71. Orth, Rev. Raymond Clement, O.M.C., J.C.D., The Approbation of Religious Institutes, 171 pp., 1931.
72. Pernicone, Rev. Joseph M., A.B., J.C.D., The Ecclesiastical Prohibition of Books, XII-267 pp., 1932.
73. Clinton, Rev. Connell, A.B., J.C.D., The Paschal Precept, IX-108 pp., 1932.
74. Donnelly, Rev. Francis B., A.M., S.T.L., J.C.D., The Diocesan Synod, VIII-125 pp., 1932.
75 Torrente, Rev. Camilo, C.M.F., J.C.D., Las Processiones Sagradas, V-145 pp., 1932.
76. Murphy, Rev. Edwin J., C.PP.S., J.C.D., Suspension Ex Informata Conscientia, XI-122 pp., 1932.
77. Mackenzie, Rev. Eric F., A.M., S.T.L., J.C.D., The Delict of Heresy in its Commission, Penalization, Absolution, VII-124 pp., 1932.
78. Lyons, Rev. Avitus E., S.T.B., J.C.D., The Collegiate Tribunal of First Instance, XI-147 pp., 1932.
79. Connolly, Rev. Thomas A., J.C.D., Appeals, XI-195 pp., 1932.
80. Sangmeister, Rev. Joseph V., A.B., J.C.D., Force and Fear as Precluding Matrimonial Consent, V-211 pp., 1932.
81. Jaeger, Rev. Leo A., A.B., J.C.D., The Administration of Vacant and Quasi-Vacant Episcopal Sees in the United States, IX-229 pp., 1932.
82. Rimlinger, Rev. Herbert T., J.C.D., Error Invalidating Matrimonial Consent, VII-79 pp., 1932.
83. Barrett, Rev. John D. M., S.S., J.C.D., A Comparative Study of the Third Plenary Council of Baltimore and the Code, IX-221 pp., 1932.
84. Carberry, Rev. John J., Ph.D., S.T.D., J.C.D., The Juridical Form of Marriage, X-177 pp., 1934.
85. Dolan, Rev. John L., A.B., J.C.D., The Defensor Vinculi, XII-157 pp., 1934.
86. Hannan, Rev. Jerome D., A.M., S.T.D., LL.B., J.C.D., The Canon Law of Wills, IX-517 pp., 1934.
87. Lemieux, Rev. Delisle A., A.M., J.C.D., The Sentence in Ecclesiastical Procedure, IX-131 pp., 1934.
88. O'Rourke, Rev. James J., A.B., J.C.D., Parish Registers, VII-109 pp., 1934.
89. Timlin, Rev. Bartholomew, O.F.M., A.M., J.C.D., Conditional Matrimonial Consent, X-381 pp., 1934.

90. Wahl, Rev. Francis X., A.B., J.C.D., The Matrimonial Impediments of Consanguinity and Affinity, VI-125 pp., 1934.
91. White, Rev. Robert J., A.B., LL.B., S.T.B., J.C.D., Canonical Ante-Nuptial Promises and the Civil Law, VI-152 pp., 1934.
92. Herrera, Rev. Antonio Parra, O.C.D., J.C.D., Legislación Ecclesiástica sobre el Ayuno y la Abstinencia, XI-191 pp., 1935.
93. Kennedy, Rev. Edwin J., J.C.D., The Special Matrimonial Process in Cases of Evident Nullity, X-165 pp., 1935.
94. Manning, Rev. John J., A.B., J.C.D., Presumption of Law in Matrimonial Procedure, XI-111 pp., 1935.
95. Moeder, Rev. John M., J.C.D., The Proper Bishop for Ordination and Dimissorial Letters, VII-135 pp., 1935.
96. O'Mara, Rev. William A., A.B., J.C.D., Canonical Causes for Matrimonial Dispensations, IX-155 pp., 1935.
97. Reilly, Rev. Peter, J.C.D., Residence of Pastors, IX-81 pp., 1935.
98. Smith, Rev. Mariner T., O.P., S.T.L., J.C.D., The Penal Law for Religious, VII-169 pp., 1935.
99. Whalen, Rev. Donald W., A.M., J.C.D., The Value of Testimonial Evidence in Matrimonial Procedure, XIII-297 pp., 1935.
100. Cleary, Rev. Joseph F., J.C.D., Canonical Limitations on the Alienation of Church Property, VIII-141 pp., 1936.
101. Glynn, Rev. John C., J.C.D., The Promoter of Justice, XX-337 pp., 1936.
102. Brennan, Rev. James H., S.S., A.M., S.T.B., J.C.D., The Simple Convalidation of Marriage, VI-135 pp., 1937.
103. Brunini, Rev. Joseph Bernard, J.C.D., The Clerical Obligations of Canons 139 and 142, X-121 pp., 1937.
104. Connor, Rev. Maurice, A.B., J.C.D., The Administrative Removal of Pastors, VIII-159 pp., 1937.
105. Guilfoyle, Rev. Merlin Joseph, J.C.D., Custom, XI-144 pp., 1937.
106. Hughes, Rev. James Austin, A.B., A.M., J.C.D., Witnesses in Criminal Trials of Clerics, IX-140 pp., 1937.
107. Jansen, Rev. Raymond J., A.B., S.T.L., J.C.D., Canonical Provisions for Catechetical Instruction, VII-153 pp., 1937.
108. Kealy, Rev. John James, A.B., J.C.D., The Introductory Libellus in Church Court Procedure, XI-121 pp., 1937.
109. McManus, Rev. James Edward, C.SS.R., J.C.D., The Administration of Temporal Goods in Religious Institutes, XVI-196 pp., 1937.
110. Moriarity, Rev. Eugene James, J.C.D., Oaths in Ecclesiastical Courts, X-115 pp., 1937.
111. Rainer, Rev. Eligius George, C.SS.R., J.C.D., Suspension of Clerics, XVII-249 pp., 1937.
112. Reilly, Rev. Thomas F., C.SS.R., J.C.D., Visitation of Religious, VI-195 pp., 1938.
113. Moriarty, Rev. Francis E., C.SS.R., J.C.D., The Extraordinary Absolution from Censures, XV-334 pp., 1938.

114. Connolly, Rev. Nicholas P., J.C.D., The Canonical Erection of Parishes, X-132 pp., 1938.
115. Donovan, Rev. James Joseph, J.C.D., The Pastor's Obligation in Prenuptial Investigation, XII-322 pp., 1938.
116. Harrigan, Rev. Robert J., M.A., S.T.B., J.C.D., The Radical Sanation of Invalid Marriages, VIII-208 pp., 1938.
117. Boffa, Rev. Conrad Humbert, J.C.D., Canonical Provisions for Catholic Schools, X-211 pp., 1939.
118. Parsons, Rev. Anscar John, O.F.M. Cap., J.C.D., Canonical Elections, XII-236 pp., 1939.
119. Reilly, Rev. Edward Michael, A.B., J.C.D., The General Norms of Dispensation, X-156 pp., 1939.
120. Ryan, Rev. Gerald Aloysius, A.B., J.C.D., Principles of Episcopal Jurisdiction, XII-172 pp., 1939.
121. Burton, Rev. Francis James, C.S.C., A.B., J.C.D., A Commentary on Canon 1125, X-222 pp., 1940.
122. Miaskiewicz, Rev. Francis Sigismund, J.C.D., Supplied Jurisdiction According to Canon 209, XII-340 pp., 1940.
123. Rice, Rev. Patrick William, A.B., J.C.D., Proof of Death in Prenuptial Investigation, VIII-156 pp., 1940.
124. Anglin, Rev. Thomas Francis, M.S., J.C.D., The Eucharistic Fast, VIII-183 pp., 1941.
125. Coleman, Rev. John Jerome, J.C.D., The Minister of Confirmation, VI-153 pp., 1941.
126. Downs, Rev. John Emmanuel, A.B., J.C.D., The Concept of Clerical Immunity, XI-163 pp., 1941.
127. Esswein, Rev. Anthony Albert, J.C.D., Extrajudicial Penal Powers of Ecclesiastical Superiors, X-144 pp., 1941.
128. Farrell, Rev. Benjamin Francis, M.A., S.T.L., J.C.D., The Rights and Duties of the Local Ordinary Regarding Congregations of Women Religious of Pontifical Approval, V-195 pp., 1941.
129. Feeney, Rev. Thomas John, A.B., S.T.L., J.C.D., Restitutio in Integrum, VI-169 pp., 1941.
130. Findlay, Rev. Stephen William, O.S.B., A.B., J.C.D., Canonical Norms Governing the Deposition and Degradation of Clerics, XVII-279 pp., 1941.
131. Goodwine, Rev. John, A.B., S.T.L., J.C.D., The Right of the Church to Acquire Property, VIII-119 pp., 1941.
132. Heston, Rev. Edward Louis, C.S.C., Ph.D., S.T.D., J.C.D., The Alienation of Church Property in the United States, XII-222 pp., 1941.
133. Hogan, Rev. James John, A.B., S.T.L., J.C.D., Judicial Advocates and Procurators, VIII-200 pp., 1941.
134. Kealy, Rev. Thomas M., A.B., Litt.B., J.C.D., Dowry of Women Religious, IX-152 pp., 1941.
135. Keene, Rev. Michael James, O.S.B., J.C.D., Religious Ordinaries and Canon 198.

136. Kerin, Rev. Charles A., S.S., M.A., S.T.B., J.C.D., The Privation of Christian Burial, XVI-279 pp., 1941.
137. Louis, Rev. William Francis, M.A., J.C.D., Diocesan Archives, X-101 pp., 1941.
138. McDevitt, Rev. Gilbert Joseph, A.B., J.C.D., Legitimacy and Legitimation, X-247 pp., 1941.
139. McDonough, Rev. Thomas Joseph, A.B., J.C.D., Apostolic Administrators, X-217 pp., 1941.
140. Meier, Rev. Carl Anthony, A.B., J.C.D., Penal Administrative Procedure Against Negligent Pastors, XI-240 pp., 1941.
141. Schmidt, Rev. John Rogg, A.B., J.C.D., The Principles of Authentic Interpretation in Canon 17 of the Code of Canon Law, XII-331 pp., 1941.
142. Slafkosky, Rev. Andrew Leonard, A.B., J.C.D., The Canonical Episcopal Visitation of the Diocese, X-197 pp., 1941.
143. Swoboda, Rev. Innocent Robert, O.F.M., J.C.D., Ignorance in Relation to the Imputability of Delicts, IX-271 pp., 1941.
144. Dubé, Rev. Arthur Joseph, A.B., J.C.D., The General Principles for the Reckoning of Time in Canon Law, VIII-299 pp., 1941.
145. McBride, Rev. James T., A.B., J.C.D., Incardination and Excardination of Seculars, XX-585 pp., 1941.
146. Król, Rev. John J., J.C.L., The Defendant in Contentious Trials.
147. Comyns, Rev. Joseph J., C.SS.R., J.C.L., The Papal and Episcopal Administration of Church Property.
148. Barry, Rev. Garrett Francis, O.M.I., J.C.L., Violation of the Cloister.
149. Bolduc, Rev. Gatien, C.S.V., A.B., S.T.L., J.C.L., Les études dans les religions cléricales.
150. Boyle, Rev. David John, M.A., J.C.L., The Juridic Effects of Moral Certitude on Pre-Nuptial Guarantees.
151. Canavan, Rev. Walter Joseph, M.A., Litt.D., J.C.L., The Profession of Faith.
152. Desrochers, Rev. Bruno, A.B., Ph.L., S.T.B., J.C.L., Le Premier Concile Plénier de Québec et le Code de Droit Canonique.
153. Dillon, Rev. Robert Edward, A.B., J.C.L., Common Law Marriage.
154. Dodwell, Rev. Edward John, Ph.D., S.T.B., J.C.L., The Time and Place for the Celebration of Marriage.
155. Donnellan, Rev. Thomas Andrew, A.B., J.C.L., The Obligation of the Missa pro Populo.
156. Eltz, Rev. Louis Anthony, A.B., J.C.L., Cooperation in Crime.
157. Gass, Rev. Sylvester, Francis, M.A., J.C.L., Ecclesiastical Pensions.
158. Guiniven, Rev. John Joseph, C.SS.R., J.C.L., The Precept of Hearing Mass on Sundays and Holy Days of Obligation.
159. Gulczynski, Rev. John Theophilus, J.C.L., The Desecration and Violation of Churches.
160. Hammill, Rev. John Leo, M.A., J.C.L., The Obligations of the Traveler according to Canon 14.

161. Haydt, Rev. John Joseph, A.B., J.C.L., Reserved Benefices.
162. Huser, Rev. Roger John, O.F.M., A.B., J.C.L., The Crime of Abortion in Canon Law.
163. Kearney, Rev. Francis Patrick, A.B., S.T.L., J.C.L., The Principles of Canon 1127.
164. Linahen, Rev. Leo James, S.T.L., J.C.L., De Absolutione Complicis In Peccato Turpi.
165. McCloskey, Rev. Joseph Aloysius, A.B., J.C.L., The Subject of Ecclesiastical Law according to Canon 12.
166. O'Neill, Rev. Francis Joseph, C.SS.R., J.C.L., The Dismissal of Religious in Temporary Vows.
167. Prince, Rev. John Edward, A.B., S.T.B., J.C.L., The Diocesan Chancellor.
168. Riesner, Rev. Albert Joseph, C.SS.R., J.C.L., Apostates and Fugitives from Religious Institutes.
169. Stenger, Rev. Joseph Bernard, J.C.L., The Mortgaging of Church Property.
170. Waldron, Rev. Joseph Francis, A.B., J.C.L., The Minister of Baptism.
171. Willett, Rev. Robert Albert, J.C.L., The Probative Value of Documents in Ecclesiastical Trials.
172. Woeber, Rev. Edward Martin, M.A., J.C.L., The Interpellations.

www.ingramcontent.com/pod-product-compliance
Lightning Source LLC
LaVergne TN
LVHW050252080826
844660LV00012B/625

* 9 7 8 0 8 1 3 2 2 3 5 4 4 *